BRAM STOKER: CENTENARY ESSAYS

BRAM STOKER
Centenery essays

Jarlath Killeen
EDITOR

FOUR COURTS PRESS

Set in 10.5 on 13 point AGaramond for
FOUR COURTS PRESS LTD
7 Malpas Street, Dublin 8, Ireland
www.fourcourtspress.ie
and in North America by
FOUR COURTS PRESS
c/o ISBS, 920 N.E. 58th Avenue, Suite 300, Portland, OR 97213.

© The various authors and Four Courts Press 2014

ISBN 978-1-84682-407-4

A catalogue record for this title
is available from the British Library.

All rights reserved. No part of this publication may be reproduced, stored in or introduced into a retrieval system, or transmitted, in any form or by any means (electronic, mechanical, photocopying, recording or otherwise), without the prior written permission of both the copyright owner and the publisher of this book.

Printed in England
by Antony Rowe Ltd, Chippenham, Wilts.

Contents

LIST OF ILLUSTRATIONS	7
LIST OF CONTRIBUTORS	9
ACKNOWLEDGMENTS	13
Introduction: remembering Bram Stoker Jarlath Killeen	15
1 Bram Stoker: the child that went with the fairies David J. Skal	37
2 Bram Stoker: the facts and the fictions Paul Murray	56
3 Bram Stoker: a man of notes Elizabeth Miller	73
4 Bram Stoker: Ireland and beyond Carol A. Senf	87
5 *The shoulder of Shasta*: Bram Stoker's California romance Andrew J. Garavel, SJ	103
6 'Rumours of the Great Plague': medicine, mythology and the memory of the Sligo cholera in Bram Stoker's *Under the sunset* William Hughes	114
7 'The sport of opposite forces': Bram Stoker's generational anxiety David Floyd	131

CONTENTS

8 'See how the bog can preserve': bogs, snakes and Irish stereotypes in
   The snake's pass   147
   Valeria Cavalli

9 *The lair of the white worm*; or, what became of Bram Stoker?   163
   Darryl Jones

10 Mr Stoker's holiday   179
   Christopher Frayling

INDEX   201

Illustrations

WILLIAM HUGHES

1 W.V. Cockburn's illustration to 'The invisible giant' — 121

2 Robert Seymour, 'Cholera tramples the victors and the vanquish'd both' (1832) — 123

3 Robert Seymour, 'The cholera morbus' (1832) — 124

4 F. Fritz Graetz, 'Cholera on the bowsprit' (1883) — 125

5 Charles Kendrick, 'Is this a time for sleep?' (1883) — 126

6 Unsigned plate for 'The invisible giant' — 130

VALERIA CAVALLI

7 William H. Boucher, 'At last' (*Judy*, 26 October 1881) — 152

8 William H. Boucher, 'Another triumph for Jonathan – biggest reptile in the universe' (*Judy*, 17 May 1882) — 153

DARRYL JONES

9 'They could follow the tall white shaft' — 172

10 'Lady Arabella was dancing in a fantastic sort of way' — 173

11 Colman Smith, 'The World' (1909) — 175

12 Colman Smith, 'The Tower' (1909) — 176

Contributors

VALERIA CAVALLI studied English and French at the Università Cattolica del Sacro Cuore, Milan, where she specialized in information and mass communication sciences (2004). In 2006 she completed an MPhil in Popular Literature at Trinity College Dublin. Her dissertation focused on the representation of Ireland in Bram Stoker's fiction. She is currently a doctoral candidate in the School of English, Trinity College Dublin. Her research concentrates on the treatment of insanity in the fiction of Joseph Sheridan Le Fanu.

DAVID FLOYD is assistant professor of English at Charleston Southern University, with a PhD from the University of Stirling. He is the author of *Street urchins, degenerates and sociopaths: orphans of late-Victorian and Edwardian fiction* (forthcoming, University of Wales Press) and has delivered papers on Gothic, Victorian and medieval literature in the US, England and Scotland. More recently, his research has focused on nineteenth-century imperial discourse and the construction of identities, the development of nineteenth-century psychological theory, changing perspectives of the family in Victorian culture and African history.

CHRISTOPHER FRAYLING was until recently rector of the Royal College of Art and chair of Arts Council England. An historian, a critic and an award-winning broadcaster on radio and television ('The art of persuasion', 'The face of Tutankhamun', 'Nightmare – the birth of horror'), he has written nineteen books on art, design and popular culture – the latest being *Ken Adam – the art of production design*, *On Craftsmanship* and the Bfi Classics volume on *The innocents* – the film adaptation of Henry James' *The turn of the screw*. His pioneering study of *The vampyre – Lord Byron to Count Dracula*, first published in 1977 and updated since, helped to inspire the recent and current academic interest in the subject. Christopher's next book, an analysis of *The yellow peril – the rise of cultural anxieties about China*, will be published by Thames and Hudson in summer 2014. He is currently professor emeritus of cultural history at the Royal College of Art, visiting professor at the University of Lancaster and a fellow of Churchill College Cambridge.

ANDREW J. GARAVEL, SJ is an assistant professor of English at Santa Clara University in California. He holds master's degrees from the Universities of Chicago and Toronto and received his doctorate from New York University. He has had essays published on Lewis Carroll, John Wilson Croker, Flannery O'Connor and Somerville and Ross.

WILLIAM HUGHES is professor of Gothic studies at Bath Spa University, and the editor of *Gothic Studies*, the refereed journal of the International Gothic Association. He has published widely on the works of Bram Stoker, and his books include *Beyond* Dracula*: Bram Stoker's fiction and its cultural context* (London, 2000), Dracula*: a reader's guide* (London, 2009), *Bram Stoker:* Dracula (London, 2009), student editions of *Dracula* (Artswork, 2007) and *The lady of the shroud* (Dublin, 2001) and *The historical dictionary of Gothic literature* (Landham, MD, 2013). With Andrew Smith he has also co-edited a number of essay collections, including *Bram Stoker: history, psychoanalysis and the Gothic* (Palgrave, 1998), *Empire and the Gothic* (London, 2003), *Queering the Gothic* (Manchester, 2009), *The Victorian Gothic* (Edinburgh, 2012) and *EcoGothic* (Manchester, 2013). He has also co-edited, with Andrew Smith and David Punter, the definitive two-volume *Encyclopædia of the Gothic* for Blackwell (2013), and is at present writing a monograph on phrenology.

DARRYL JONES is professor of English at Trinity College Dublin, and a fellow of the College. He teaches nineteenth-century fiction and popular literature. He is the author or editor of nine books, including most recently the Oxford edition of *The collected ghost stories of M.R. James* (2011). He is currently editing an anthology of Victorian and Edwardian horror stories, and editions of H.G. Wells' *The war of the worlds* and *The island of Doctor Moreau*, also for OUP, and working on a monograph entitled *Dead London: representing the shadow city in the nineteenth century*.

JARLATH KILLEEN is a lecturer in Victorian literature in English in Trinity College Dublin. He is the editor of *Oscar Wilde: Irish writers in their time* (Dublin, 2011), and author of *Gothic Ireland* (2005), *The faiths of Oscar Wilde* (London, 2005), *The fairy tales of Oscar Wilde* (Faversham, 2007), *Gothic literature, 1825–1914* (Cardiff, 2009), and most recently *The emergence of Irish Gothic fiction* (Edinburgh, 2013).

ELIZABETH MILLER is recognized internationally as a leading Stoker/*Dracula* scholar. Her many publications include Dracula*: sense and nonsense* (Southend-on-Sea, Essex, 2006), *Bram Stoker's notes for* Dracula*: a facsimile edition* (2008, with Robert Eighteen-Bisang), *Bram Stoker's* Dracula*: a documentary journey* (Berkeley, 2009) and *The lost journal of Bram Stoker* (2012, with Dacre Stoker).

PAUL MURRAY is a writer and former diplomat. His biography, *From the shadow of Dracula: a life of Bram Stoker*, was published (Jonathan Cape: London) in 2004. His previous biography, *A fantastic journey: the life and literature of Lafcadio Hearn* (UK, 1993; US, 1997; Japan (translation, 2000)) won the 1995 Koizumi Yakumo Literary Prize in Japan and was awarded the Lord Mayor of Dublin's Prize the same year. He was the recipient of the Gold Medal of the Ireland Japan Association in 1999 for services to Ireland–Japan relations. His selection of the horror writings of Lafcadio Hearn was published as *Nightmare-touch* (London, 2010). Murray was Ambassador of Ireland to South Korea (1999–2004) and, concurrently, North Korea (2004). He was Ambassador to the OECD and UNESCO in Paris (2006–12).

CAROL A. SENF is professor and associate chair of the School of Literature, Media and Communication at the Georgia Institute of Technology. She has written three books on Stoker – *Bram Stoker* (Cardiff, 2010), *Science and social science in Bram Stoker's fiction* (Greenwood, 2002), *Dracula: between tradition and modernism* (Twayne, 1998) – as well as introductions to *Bram Stoker's other Gothics* (Dublin, 2010) and *The critical response to Bram Stoker* (Greenwood, 1994), and annotated two of Stoker's novels – *The mystery of the sea* (Valancourt, 2007) and *Lady Athlyne* (Southend-on-Sea, Essex, 2007). Her goal is to have people talking about Stoker's other novels.

DAVID J. SKAL is a writer, lecturer, and filmmaker whose books include *Hollywood Gothic: the tangled web of* Dracula *from novel to stage to screen* (, 1990)and *The monster show: a cultural history of horror* (, 1993). He has produced, written and directed a dozen DVD and Blu-ray documentaries on classic horror and science fiction films, as well as a behind-the-scenes chronicle of the Academy Award-winning film *Gods and monsters*. He has lectured on the subject of horror and monsters at dozens of colleges, universities, and cultural institutions, including the Musée de Louvre, and has taught courses based on his books at the University of Victoria and Trinity College Dublin, where he was also a 2010 recipient of a Long Room Hub Visiting Research Fellowship in support of his forthcoming cultural biography, *Bram Stoker: the final curtain*.

Acknowledgments

Thanks must first go to the contributors to this collection who were also participants in a conference on 'Bram Stoker: Life and Writing' held in the Long Room Hub, Trinity College Dublin, in July 2012. As anyone who has found themselves editing a collection like this knows, the process requires a certain amount of coordination, cooperation and fortitude at each of its many stages, and I am very grateful to all the contributors for being so willing to work with, and more importantly put up with, me. My thanks also to Jürgen Barkhoff and Eva Muhlhause of the Long Room Hub who facilitated the event, the Trinity Foundation, the Arts and Social Sciences Benefaction Fund and the School of English, Trinity College Dublin, for financing the conference, and to Professor Roy Foster who delivered the keynote lecture. Paul Murray first approached me with the idea for the conference, and has been an invaluable source of information and support since that initial meeting. I would particularly like to acknowledge the encouragement of many members of the extended Stoker family over a number of years, and also their attendance and active involvement in the conference discussions. Thanks especially to Noel Dobbs, Robin McCaw, Dacre Stoker and Douglas Appleyard. The broader community of Stoker enthusiasts and scholars has also been supportive, especially Brian Showers and Professor Luke Gibbons. On a personal level I would like to mention Darryl Jones, Margaret Robson, Diane Sadler, Tina Morin, Meghanne Flynn, Fionnuala Barrett, Bernice Murphy and Elizabeth McCarthy (especially for the poster): they were all both helpful and amusing throughout the process. The staff at Four Courts Press was enthusiastic from the start and guided me through the editing process carefully.

And, as always, I am most grateful to Mary Lawlor and our daughter Eilís for their love and also their patience when my mind was elsewhere.

Introduction: remembering Bram Stoker

JARLATH KILLEEN

That Bram Stoker is remembered at all, one hundred years after his death, would have surprised most of his contemporaries, and that he is remembered for his creation of an aristocratic vampire would almost certainly have shocked the author himself. When he died in April 1912, obituaries highlighted his 'business management' of and 'intimate friendship' with Henry Irving, the greatest ham of the late Victorian stage. The *New York Times* claimed that *Personal reminiscences of Henry Irving* (1908) was Stoker's 'best-known publication', and just included *Dracula* (1897) in a long list of 'his other works'.[1] For the London *Times*, Stoker's loyalty to Irving was the most important fact about him, although it also noted that he was 'master of a particularly lurid and creepy kind of fiction, represented by "Dracula"', and in an aside mentioned 'other novels'.[2] Together, Irving and Dracula have continued to edge Stoker out of the picture and have attracted more attention than him in the subsequent century, even when the author himself has been the ostensible subject under discussion. Often yoked together (so that Dracula is Irving is Dracula), they have obscured attention to the Irish writer, who often appears apprentice-like to two much more interesting masters.[3]

Part of the problem in trying to get to Stoker is that, set alongside such great performers as his boss and his best character, he seems rather boring. Terry Eagleton has joked that in literary history the bad guys get all the best lines: 'Milton's God sounds like a bureaucratic bore or constipated civil servant, while his Satan shimmers with mutinous life'.[4] Stoker, of course, was at one time a civil servant, and spent most of his working life as a bureaucrat or administrator of one kind or another, so it is no wonder that critics find it easy to get distracted away from him. Both Irving and Dracula, even if they are not essentially the same person, seem on an initial impression to be much better company than the former

---

[1] 'Bram Stoker dead at 64', *New York Times*, 23 April 1912. [2] 'Mr Bram Stoker', *Times*, 22 April 1912. [3] This tendency is perhaps most obvious in Barbara Belford's biography, *Bram Stoker and the man who was Dracula* (Cambridge, MA, 2002). [4] Terry Eagleton, 'The nature of evil', *Tikkun*, 26:80 (Winter 2011). http://www.tikkun.org/nextgen/the-nature-of-evil. Accessed 2 May 2013.

Inspector of Courts of Petty Sessions who had the good fortune to become associated with them both. Dracula, like a few other literary characters, has grown completely independent of his creator, and almost seems self-generated. Stoker's friend Arthur Conan Doyle was bemused and a bit irritated by the tendency of many readers and 'fans' to refer to Sherlock Holmes as if he was a real person, and to the writer as if he was simply Dr Watson's literary agent;[5] Stoker too was destined to become a mere hanger-on, a side-line figure to the Count, and even of the other characters populating his great novel. Indeed, even in the official sequel, *Dracula: the un-dead* (2009) by Dacre Stoker and Ian Holt, where he makes a brief appearance, Stoker is only a failed author, obsessed with Irving, to whom a crazed Dr Van Helsing revealed the original story to keep in circulation the knowledge of how to destroy the vampire. At one point a frustrated Mina Harker complains, '*Damn it!* Who the hell was this Bram Stoker?'[6] Likewise, in Elizabeth Kostova's *The historian* (2005), Stoker's novel is represented as a derivative and melodramatic treatment of a real life and extraordinarily charismatic vampire. In both cases, Stoker's association with Dracula is accidental, or fortuitous – for Stoker, that is, an otherwise boring man who was lucky to have bumped into a figure of such monumental and charismatic power.

There is actually a good deal of truth about such characterizations. Where, after all, would Stoker be without Dracula? His friend, Hall Caine, to whom he dedicated his Gothic masterpiece, was a major figure in late-Victorian and Edwardian publishing, whose work far out-sold that of Stoker, but he is now almost completely forgotten except by literary historians. No one, except a maniac, would claim that Stoker was a particularly great writer, although he is better than his reputation would have you believe. Admittedly, his novels are often tedious, over or under plotted, sometimes nonsensical, confusing, confused, and *Dracula*, in as much as it is a Gothic masterpiece, is clearly a kind of fluke. Even with *Dracula*, we are dealing with a very uneven novel. Long parts of it are monotonous (there is at least one blood transfusion too many, and the middle section drags), and with the creation of his vampire-hunter-in-chief, the barmy Dutch scientist with an MLitt from Oxford, Dr Abraham Van Helsing, Stoker made a literary mistake. However, there are sections of the novel – especially the opening scenes where Jonathan Harker meets Dracula in his castle – which are claustrophobic, feverish and brilliant. For those who want a genuinely good read, I would also recommend *The jewel of seven stars* (1903), one of the great 'mummy craze' novels, sadly neglected now, and *The lair of the white worm* (1911), one of the most absurd novels ever written, a novel of which it is virtually impossible to make sense, but which remains compelling and haunting, and which has stayed in at

---

5 Harold Orel (ed.), *Sir Arthur Conan Doyle: interviews and recollections* (London, 1991), p. 81. **6** Dacre Stoker and Ian Holt, *Dracula: the un-dead* (London, 2009), p. 171.

least some kind of print since it was first published. Many of Stoker's short stories are great examples of the form, and there are some wonderful moments in his other novels. Even though on a closer examination *Dracula* remains the key text, Stoker turns out to be noteworthy in many ways. Not only are the various versions of his best novel significant in tracing popular opinion through the twentieth and now into the twenty-first centuries, but Stoker's life and work can serve as portals into late-Victorian and Edwardian Britain. Literary analysis has long seen *Dracula* as a compendium of the many 'anxieties' (a perhaps over-used and over-cooked term) of the late Victorians (sexual, racial, imperial, gender-related, financial, whatever-you-are-having-yourself). However, to a reader of Stoker's entire oeuvre his experiments in the genres of romance, adventure, horror, the occult, realism, memoir, empire fiction, children's literature, and his life as an immigrant and member of a theatrical set, who also had strong connections to the worlds of politics, art, writing, medicine, sport, administration, turn out to be enormously insightful in terms of understanding that *fin de siècle* world.

Many are coming to the view that Stoker is an important figure in understanding British culture at the turn of the twentieth century. This publication, which comes out of a conference on 'Bram Stoker: life and works', held in Trinity College Dublin in July 2012, marks another instalment of what could be called a 'Stoker renaissance'. Academic interest in *Dracula* has, of course, been steady since the 'Gothic turn' of the 1970s and 1980s, but until recently few Gothicists had been tempted to look at Stoker's career in the round (David Glover, Carol Senf and William Hughes are honourable exceptions here).[7] However, the last decade has witnessed the publication by Penguin of *Dracula's guest and other weird tales* (which included *The lair of the white worm*) and *The jewel of seven stars* (1903), both with brilliant introductions and notes by Kate Hebblethwaite.[8] More quietly, Desert Island Books has been keeping faith with Stoker for years, under the guidance of Dracula enthusiast Clive Leatherdale. The press has reissued a number of minor Stoker texts, including *The shoulder of Shasta* (1895), *Lady Athlyne* (1908), and *The lady of the shroud* (1909), all three annotated with a substantial introduction by a Stoker scholar.[9] Meanwhile Valancourt has also released editions of *The snake's pass* (1890), *The mystery of the sea* (1902), *The watter's mou'* (1895) and *The lady of the shroud*.[10] The 'Dracula Notes', stored in the Rosenbach Library have been transcribed and annotated by Robert

---

[7] David Glover, *Vampires, mummies and liberals: Bram Stoker and the politics of popular fiction* (Durham, NC, 1996); Carol A. Senf, *Science and society in Bram Stoker's fiction* (Westport, CT, 2002); William Hughes, *Beyond* Dracula: *Bram Stoker's fiction and its cultural context* (New York, 2000). [8] Bram Stoker, *Dracula's guest and other weird stories*, ed. Kate Hebblethwaite (London, 2006); idem, *The jewel of seven stars*, ed. Kate Hebblethwaite (London, 2008). [9] Bram Stoker, *Lady Athlyne*, ed. Carol Senf (Southend-on-Sea, Essex, 2007); idem, *The primrose path*, ed. Richard Dalby (Southend-on-Sea, Essex, 1999); idem, *The shoulder of Shasta*, ed. Alan Johnson (Southend-on-Sea, Essex, 2000); idem, *The lady of the shroud*, ed. William Hughes (Southend-on-Sea, Essex, 2000). [10] Arthur Conan Doyle and Bram Stoker, *The parasite and The watter's mou'*, ed. Catherine Wynne (Kansas, 2009); Bram Stoker, *The snake's pass* (Kansas, 2006); idem,

Eighteen-Bisang and Elizabeth Miller, who has also, with Dacre Stoker, annotated Stoker's Dublin journal.¹¹ Finally, Stoker's 'forgotten writings' have also been gathered together, and his dramatic reviews collected.¹² With these publications – and one hopes, future reprints – the reassessment of Stoker can really start to take off, and perhaps, as his biographer Paul Murray has suggested, we can finally begin to get Stoker out from under the 'shadow of Dracula'.¹³

For academics, the shadow cast on Stoker is not simply the monumental one of *Dracula* and the hundreds of cinematic and televisual adaptations that the novel has inspired, but is also the critical shadow of the thousands of scholarly (and not-so-scholarly) studies that have focused on this one novel, and I think it is important in a collection like this to acknowledge the dominance of *Dracula* in assessments of Stoker. A student recently asked me: 'Is *Dracula* the *Hamlet* of the Gothic canon?' She had been enthusiastically planning an essay on *Dracula* but after I sent her away to do some preliminary reading, came back disheartened and anxious, having encountered what is now a veritable library of criticism, including (that ultimate critical endorsement) the single-text monograph.¹⁴ Indeed, so voluminous has the criticism of *Dracula* grown, that newcomers to the novel are in need of guidance through the morass, thankfully provided by Stoker expert William Hughes.¹⁵ In his *Guide* (2009), Hughes places the novel squarely in the context of Stoker's entire body of writing and encourages students to use the neglected Stoker as a way into understanding *Dracula*. He also identifies serious problems in the existing criticism on the novel: not only have critics ignored Stoker's other writings, but they have tended to focus – almost exclusively – on a small number of scenes and characters to the exclusion of other, perhaps equally important, moments and characters. Hughes particularly emphasizes how psychoanalysis has effectively set the agenda for critical study of *Dracula* so that even when critics have attempted to utilize other critical methodologies, the assumptions of psychoanalysis have leached in to their studies. Hughes is careful not to argue that psychoanalysis should now be dumped, but instead raises important questions about what the future of *Dracula* criticism might look like and the proper position of psychoanalysis in this future.

The mystery of the sea, ed. Carol A. Senf (Kansas, 2007); idem, *The lady of the shroud*, ed. Sarah E. Maier (Kansas, 2012). **11** *Bram Stoker's notes for* Dracula: *a facsimile edition*, annotated and transcribed by Robert Eighteen-Bisang and Elizabeth Miller (Jefferson, NC and London, 2008); Elizabeth Miller and Dacre Stoker (eds), *The lost journal of Bram Stoker* (London, 2012). **12** John Edgar Browning (ed.), *The forgotten writings of Bram Stoker* (New York, 2012); Catherine Wynne (ed.), *Bram Stoker and the stage: reviews, reminiscences, essays and fiction* (London, 2012). **13** Paul Murray, *From the shadow of Dracula: a life of Bram Stoker* (London, 2004). **14** Noel Montague-Etienne Rarignac, *The theology of* Dracula: *reading the book of Stoker as sacred text* (London, 2011); Matthew Gibson, Dracula *and the Eastern question* (London, 2006); Carol A. Senf, *Bram Stoker's* Dracula: *between tradition and modernity* (New York, 1998); Clive Leatherdale, Dracula – *the novel and the legend: a study of Bram Stoker's masterpiece* (Southend-on-Sea, Essex, 1985); Catherine Wynne, *Bram Stoker,* Dracula *and the Victorian Gothic stage* (London, 2013). **15** William Hughes, *Bram Stoker's* Dracula: *a reader's guide* (London, 2009).

Indeed, considering how dominant psychoanalysis has been in studies of the vampire novel, my student's question comparing *Dracula* to *Hamlet* is very appropriate. Where Sigmund Freud found in *Hamlet* positive proof of his psychoanalytical hypotheses,[16] *Dracula* has also been an exemplary test case for the psychosexual scholar, and, via *Dracula*, Stoker too has been put on the doctor's couch retrospectively. So central has psychoanalysis been to understanding the novel and its author that an earlier collection of academic essays devoted to Stoker came with the subtitle, 'History, Psychoanalysis and the Gothic', its editors carefully explaining the role psychoanalysis played in the academic rehabilitation of Stoker: 'Stoker's life, documented as it is by oblique references in his own biographical writings and supported by the on-going research (and at times speculation) of biographers presents a classic opportunity for Freudian analysis under the assumption that the text expresses the neurosis of the writer'.[17] Poor Stoker has come out rather badly from all this retrospective analysis, and if everything that psychobiographers have said about him is true, he could have made a lucky analyst very rich indeed. Repressed homosexuality, oedipal desires, childhood sexual trauma, deep-seated misogyny, castration anxieties, sibling rivalry, incest, and a sexless marriage (with either Henry Irving or Oscar Wilde as a silent third party) have all appeared as biographical 'explanations' for *Dracula* itself. Speculation about Stoker's psychological health have understandably left a bad taste in the mouths of some, with Elizabeth Miller being up front in designating such conjecture 'nonsense'.[18]

Sex has been central to this psychoanalytic criticism, and thus sex has hijacked discussion of Stoker and *Dracula*. The sexual angle was, of course, something that the novel's Victorian readers apparently completely overlooked about it – because, as we all know, they were so sexually repressed themselves.[19] The early reviews for *Dracula* were generally positive, but say little about its erotic content. The *Manchester Guardian*, for example, considered it a novel 'more grotesque than terrifying', explaining that while 'it says no little for the author's powers that in spite of its absurdities the reader can follow the story with interest to the end', it was still 'a mistake to fill a whole volume with horrors'.[20] The *Athenaeum* concluded that '"Dracula" is highly sensational, but it is wanting in the constructive art as well as in the higher

---

16 Sigmund Freud, *The interpretation of dreams*, trans. James Strachey (Avon, NY, 1965), p. 299. **17** William Hughes and Andrew Smith, 'Introduction: Bram Stoker, the Gothic and the development of cultural studies' in *Bram Stoker: history, psychoanalysis and the Gothic* (London, 1998), p. 3. **18** See especially Daniel Farson, *The man who wrote* Dracula: *a biography of Bram Stoker* (London, 1975), pp 212–16; Joseph S. Bierman, '*Dracula*: prolonged childhood illness and the oral triad', *American Imago*, 29 (1972), 186–98. For Miller's undermining of the claims of Farson and Bierman, see *Sense and nonsense* (Southend-on-Sea, Essex, 2006) pp 50–3, 80–1. **19** Here we have a good example of one of the difficulties psychoanalytic readings can get into – the acceptance of what Michel Foucault calls the 'repression hypothesis' about the Victorians allows the critic to easily explain how something we now consider so obvious (that *Dracula* is a novel about sex) passed by the contemporary readers so easily. *The history of sexuality*, 1 (London, 1990). **20** *Manchester Guardian*, 15 June 1897, cited in *Bram Stoker's* Dracula: *the critical feast*, compiled and anno-

literary sense. It reads at times like a mere series of grotesquely incredible events'.[21] Others were more enthusiastic, the *Bookman* warning: 'Keep "Dracula" out of the way of nervous children',[22] and the *Pall Mall Gazette* insisted that:

> Mr Bram Stoker should have labelled his book 'For Strong Men Only,' or words to that effect. Left lying carelessly around, it might get into the hands of your maiden aunt who believes devoutly in the man under the bed, or of the new parlourmaid with unsuspected hysterical tendencies. 'Dracula' to such would be manslaughter. It is for the man with a sound conscience and digestion, who can turn out the gas and go to bed without having to look over his shoulder more than half a dozen times as he goes upstairs, or more than mildly wishing that he had a crucifix and some garlic handy to keep the vampires from getting at him.[23]

For these reviewers the issue was whether or not *Dracula* was frightening; should you let your maiden aunt, or your parlour maid read it? Nowadays, we appear certain that being 'frightening' is not what the dark Count is about at all. Indeed, we might think that should our maiden aunt happen to meet Count Dracula on the stairs she is more likely to invite him into her bedroom than run terrified from the house, and the screams he generates would probably be more of pleasure than terror. For a reading public which thinks the sadistic and unhinged Christian Grey of E.L. James' phenomenal *Fifty shades of grey* (2011) is the dreamiest man alive, with his Red Room of Pain, and his instruments of torture which seem to be taken straight from the dungeons of the Spanish Inquisition, what is a bit of harmless blood sucking between friends and lovers?[24] We're not really afraid of Dracula anymore – in fact, we kind of like him. He's the kind of man that men want to be, and women want to be with. Dracula has gone from being a terrifying emissary of the devil, to a sexy but probably unavailable heartthrob. He was once played by Max Shrek, in the 1922 classic *Nosferatu* (dir. F.W. Murnau), hardly anyone's idea of the sexiest man on the planet; since then Dracula has been attempted by the likes of Bela Lugosi (1931), Christopher Lee (1958), Frank Langella (1979), Richard Roxburgh (2004), and Jonathan Rhys Meyers (2013), and it might seem churlish to turn such mesmerically attractive men away from your bedroom in the middle of the night. If Tom Cruise or Brad Pitt can play vampires, most are not going to complain if they take a love bite a bit further than is usual.

tated by John Edgar Browning (Berkley, CA, 2011), p. 44. **21** *Athenaeum*, 26 June 1897, cited in *Critical feast*, pp 55–6. **22** *Bookman*, August 1897, cited in *Critical feast*, pp 70–1. **23** *Pall Mall Gazette*, 1 June 1897, cited in *Critical feast*, pp 29–31. **24** It should be remembered that Christian Grey was originally a character in 'Master of the Universe', a Twilight fanfiction published online under E.L. James' pseudonym Snowqueen's Icedragon. In that story, Grey was Edward Cullen, a version of the vampire in the Twilight series.

Indeed, while earlier cinema audiences screamed with terror when Dracula appeared, audiences now scream with delight, anticipating thrills of a less psychological and more psychosexual nature.

For today's pop culture audience *Dracula* reads more like something we might call 'Fifty shades of red'. All that sucking, all that blood-drinking, all that male-bonding ... we know what it all means now. The psychosexual readings probably reached their apotheosis in the claims of the great Maurice Richardson, for whom 'From a Freudian standpoint – and from no other does the story really make any sense – [the novel] is seen as a kind of incestuous, necrophilious, oral-anal-sadistic all-in wrestling match'.[25] In *Fifty shades of grey*, the contract that Anastasia Steele is asked to sign before she starts exploring her sensuality with the man she is expected to call 'Master' and 'Sir', specifically rules out the shedding of blood during BDSM sex play,[26] but Count Dracula knows that blood makes his kind of sex even kinkier. In her 1973 book *Fear of flying*, Erica Jong famously and controversially coined the term 'the zipless fuck' to describe sex in a contraceptive society as one without repercussion and responsibilities.[27] If we are to believe many critics, both Bram Stoker and the Count were there well before Jong, because Dracula practices the ultimate zipless fuck, sex from the neck up. Or, as the tagline to the 1987 vampire film *The lost boys* (dir. Joel Schumacher) puts it: 'Sleep all day. Party all night. Never grow old. Never die. It's fun to be a vampire. Being wild is in their Blood'.

In this version of the novel, *Dracula* is a coded narrative, and in reading it the deeply repressed Victorians imaginatively acted out all the carnal fantasies denied to them in their real lives, and then purged these desires by having Dracula killed at the end of the story. In other words, the novel provided a proxy erotic life for the poor sex-deprived Victorian reader, in which Dracula, the alpha male, swoops in to repressed England as a sexual adventurer and liberator, a kind of Indiana Jones of the bedroom, freeing women from the ideological bondage of the Victorian patriarchy. No more would they have to just lie back and think of England. Lucy says in an early part of the novel that she would like to be permitted to marry three men,[28] but she isn't allowed to because of the repressive rules of a conservative society. Dracula comes to the rescue, and having been bitten by him, Lucy is transformed into an extraordinarily sexy vamp wandering around Hampstead Heath looking, I suppose, for some meat to fulfil her lascivious desires. Jonathan Harker, too, clearly wants more from his sex life than the staid and respectable Mina. When confronted by three vampire brides, his libido goes into overdrive. He certainly describes the vampire brides in raunchy terms: 'All

[25] Maurice Richardson, 'The psychoanalysis of ghost stories', *Vampyres: Lord Byron to Count Dracula*, ed. Christopher Frayling (London, 1991), pp 418–19.   [26] E.L. James, *Fifty shades of grey* (London, 2011), p. 173.   [27] Erica Jong, *Fear of flying* (New York, 1973), p. 14.   [28] Bram Stoker, *Dracula*, ed. Maurice Hindle (London, 2003), pp 64–5.

three had brilliant white teeth, that shone like pearls against the ruby of their voluptuous lips. There was something about them that made me uneasy, some longing and at the same time some deadly fear. I felt in my heart a wicked, burning desire that they would kiss me with those red lips'.[29] Even Mina, the respectable angel-of-the-house, seems to enjoy it when Dracula secretly visits her at night to drink her blood. 'Strangely enough', she confesses, 'I did not want to hinder him'.[30] We don't think it is all that strange – better a varied love life, than the sexless hell that a marriage to the dreary Jonathan Harker would bring about.

In Dacre Stoker's *The un-dead*, the twentieth century's postulation of Dracula's sexual prowess is retrospectively confirmed. In the novel Jonathan Harker ends his life an alcoholic, haunted by the fact that he simply can't match up to Dracula in bed, driven wild by his wife Mina's dreams where she relives her former experiences with the vampire:

> While trying to make love to his wife, Jonathan discovered through a slip of his wife's tongue that it was Dracula who had taken Mina's virginity. Dracula, with centuries of experience, first introduced her to passion. He'd left such a profound impression on her that Jonathan, no matter how hard he tried, could never match it.[31]

What man could, though! Twenty-first-century audiences know that life as a vampire offers freedom from the sexual rules and regulations of normal society – or at least they have had countless film and television vampire stories tell them that it does – and therefore it is easier to see Dracula as a romantic hero than a devil. The other characters in Bram Stoker's novel, however, are stuck in the sexual Middle Ages, and having let the erotic secret out of Pandora's box, and having treated themselves to Lucy's irresistible body through numerous blood transfusions, they must – like all Victorian hypocrites – punish the sexually transgressive woman by thrusting an enormous phallic stake into her body, and then follow through by destroying her sexual liberator too. Through the novel, then, readers can act out the sexual fantasies that terrify them in their waking hours (but which they indulge during the dark hours of the night, in dreams), and then make themselves feel better by punishing the transgressors at the end. Thus decoded, *Dracula* sounds a bit like a very depressing pornographic novel in which, after the bored housewife has had her wicked way with the well-equipped functionaries, her husband arrives home to kill them all.

So normative and self-evident has this version of *Dracula* as crypto-pornography become that, in order to spice up the vampire mythology, some have resorted to imagining the blood-suckers as celibates. Readers got rather tired of the promis-

---

29 Ibid., p. 45. **30** Ibid., p. 306. **31** Stoker, *Un-dead*, p. 103.

cuous Count Dracula, and many now like their vampires chaste and pure. In Stephanie Meyer's Twilight series (2005–8), the teenage vampire Edward Cullen is tall, handsome and sexually desirable all right, but he heroically abstains from biting into the neck of his soulmate Bella Swan because he loves her so much, by which Meyer clearly means that Edward wants to refrain from sexual consummation until they get married. It is important to note that Edward is supposed to have been born in 1901, which would mean that he arrived just as the Victorian era was coming to an end, and just four years after the publication of *Dracula*. Whereas the Count is the opposite of what we think Victorian gentlemen were like, Edward is an embodiment of gentlemanly virtue. He is a fabulously wealthy relic from a nobler age, extraordinarily polite, very good at school, enterprising and virtuously motivated by Mormon values.

For us, then, the vampire is a sex symbol, biting is sexual penetration, and a stake is never just a stake … Understandably, this psychosexual approach to Stoker, where his work is read as an articulation of his personal or cultural pathologies, has provoked concerns (and in some cases, annoyance and frustration). When all kinds of pathologies are read back into the life of a dead writer, and his writings used as a kind of dreamwork, so that the psychoanalytic critic feels free to posit repressed memories of child sexual abuse, repressed sexual desires, repressed misogyny, repressed colonial guilt, and a variety of other traumas and neuroses, as explanatory guides to an adventure/horror novel, then some kind of interpretive decorum may have been breached. In Stoker's case such analyses can be found not simply on the margins of literary critical and author study but are in fact firmly at the centre of a small cottage industry. A certain frustration is perfectly understandable. When, in November 2012, I chaired a 'discussion' of *Dracula* by a panel including Stoker biographer Paul Murray, James Joyce specialist and Senator David Norris, and acclaimed author and historian Ruth Dudley Edwards, I was somewhat startled by the latter's provocative opening gambit that the critical history of the novel demonstrated that English Studies is a bankrupt discipline and constitutes evidence that Departments of English should be closed down. Edwards proceeded to read aloud some quotations from one of the most widely cited of all studies of the novel, Christopher Craft's '"Kiss me with those red lips"' (1984), as proof of just how crazy things had become. Craft's interpretation of *Dracula* is deeply indebted to a psychoanalytic explanation of vampirism as inherently sexual, and to the view that Stoker's novel explores the repressed and subversive desires of late Victorian culture.[32] Some of Edwards' annoyance was generated by the widely held belief that English Studies is a pointless discipline anyway, and that lecturers in English say the strangest things about great books for no apparent reason, and she was simply

[32] Christopher Craft, '"Kiss me with those red lips": gender and inversion in Bram Stoker's *Dracula*', *Representations*, 8 (1984), 107–33.

feeding into the kind of sensationalizing that used to track papers delivered at the MLA for the most eyebrow raising title. Famously, Eve Kosofsky Sedgwick's 1989 lecture 'Jane Austen and the Masturbatory Girl' was cited as proof that literary studies had gone down a Theoretically directed cul-de-sac. Edwards declared herself 'against shite', and being 'against bullshit' has become something of a trend in recent years, prompted in part by Harry G. Frankfurt's stimulating 2005 anatomy of empty rhetoric presented as analysis.[33] Given that the intellectual credibility of psychoanalysis has been seriously challenged by people in quite authoritative positions, from one perspective the study of both *Dracula* and Bram Stoker has been (mostly) bullshit. Over-influenced by Freud, and having watched too many bad but mildly erotic adaptations, the critics have been incapable of seeing the novel as in itself it really is.

That *Dracula* is a psychoanalyst's dream text is difficult to dispute, although the tendency to read it through psychoanalytic lens is probably due in part to its position as one of the masterpieces of the Gothic genre. Gothic, with its emphasis on the dark and shadowy depths running alongside the world of light and surface, did appear ready-made for a psychoanalytic analysis once that vocabulary came into existence. Given that Horace Walpole claimed that *The castle of Otranto* (1764), the 'origin text' of the Gothic, was derived from a private nightmare, the temptation to read the canon of Gothic fiction as a kind of dreamwork through the discourse of psychoanalysis has been difficult to resist.[34] Gothic was, we were told, the 'flipside' of the Enlightenment, an exploration of all that was hidden by a dedication to rationalist science.[35] The Freudian view that anxieties and fears that are too difficult to be faced by an individual or a culture are repressed and re-emerge in monstrous form has been particularly fruitful in terms of examining the genre, and 'the return of the repressed' has been a preoccupation of much of the best criticism.[36] As Noel Carroll perceptively argued, 'if psychoanalysis does not afford a comprehensive theory of horror it remains the case that psychoanalytic imagery often reflexively informs work within the genre which, of course, makes psychoanalysis germane to interpretations of the genre'.[37]

In the early twentieth century the causal influence of psychoanalysis on the emerging horror cinema in many ways conditioned critical responses. There is an obvious implication of psychoanalysis in the work of the German expressionist

---

33 Harry G. Frankfurt, *On bullshit* (Princeton, NJ, 2005); Gary L. Hardcastle and George A. Reisch (eds), *Bullshit and philosophy* (Chicago, 2006).   **34** As he wrote, 'I waked one morning in the beginning of last June, from a dream, of which, all I could ever recover was, that I had thought myself in an antient castle (a very natural dream for a head filled like mine with Gothic story), and that on the uppermost banister of a great staircase I saw a gigantic hand in armour'. Horace Walpole to Revd William Cole, 9 March 1765, *The letters of Horace Walpole*, ed. Helen Paget Toynbee (Oxford, 1903–25), vi, 194–5.   **35** Rosemary Jackson, *Fantasy: the literature of subversion* (London, 1981), pp 4, 95–7.   **36** Although the term is rather overused in Gothic criticism. Valdine Clemens, *The return of the repressed: Gothic horror from* The castle of Otranto *to* Alien (New York, 1999).

film-makers, particularly in the canonical *The cabinet of Dr Caligari* (1920; dir. Robert Wiene), and *Secrets of a soul* (1926; dir. Georg Wilhelm Pabst) (where psychoanalysis is both subject and context). Psychoanalytic theories are referenced in the Gothic work of Alfred Hitchcock such as *Spellbound* (1945 – repressed trauma) and *Psycho* (1960 – unresolved Oedipus complex), Michael Powell's *Peeping Tom* (1960 – scopophilia), and the films of Brian de Palma, especially *Dressed to kill* (1980 – castration anxieties). Lucio Fulci's out-of-control *The house by the cemetery* (1981), has as its villain the crazed Dr Freudstein, and M. Night Shyamalan's *The sixth sense* (1999) mines Freud's theories of mourning and melancholia. Given the pervasive influence of psychoanalysis on horror, it seemed almost natural to use Freud to decode the meanings of such films. If the 'masters of horror' were so attracted to the idiom of psychoanalysis, who were critics to demur? Indeed, the imprimatur of the most successful horror writer ever was given to psychoanalytic methodology when Stephen King explained, 'the dream of horror is in itself an out-letting and a lancing ... and it may well be that the mass-media dream of horror can sometimes become a nationwide analyst's couch'.[38]

For some influential theorists of Gothic, indeed, the genre had actually prefigured the 'discoveries' of the psychoanalytic method, and, as Anne Williams explained, psychoanalysis could be read as simply making explicit what had already been demonstrated by the Gothic.[39] For Maggie Kilgour, the Gothic anticipates psychoanalysis, so that 'psychoanalysis is itself a Gothic, necromantic form, that resurrects our psychic pasts'.[40] Indeed, according to William Patrick Day 'no discussion of the Gothic can avoid discussing Freud; one of the most obvious ways of thinking about the genre is to read it in terms of Freud's system. ... We cannot pretend that the striking parallels between Freud's thought and the Gothic fantasy do not exist'.[41]

So, when psychoanalysis became mainstream in literary criticism, the Gothic seemed like a ready-made genre for probing the unconscious of a supposedly rational culture. Indeed, it would probably be true to say that psychoanalysis has been the most influential approach to the Gothic, from Ernest Jones' reading of the vampire onwards.[42] Many of the most significant studies of Gothic have drawn heavily from psychoanalysis, including seminal work by David Punter, Rosemary Jackson, Robin Wood, Carol Clover, Barbara Creed, Andrew Smith and Steven J. Schneider.[43] As Nicholas Daly has emphasized, 'the linkage of Gothic to the

---

37 Noel Carroll, *The philosophy of horror, or, paradoxes of the heart* (London, 1990), p. 168. **38** Stephen King, *Danse macabre* (London, 2000), p. 27. **39** Anne Williams, *Art of darkness: a poetics of Gothic* (Chicago, 1995), p. 23. **40** Maggie Kilgour, *The rise of the Gothic novel* (London, 1995), p. 220. **41** William Patrick Day, *In the circles of fear and desire: a study of Gothic fantasy* (Chicago, 1985), p. 177. **42** Ernest Jones, *On the nightmare*. International Psycho-analytical Library Series, n. 20. 1931 (rpr., New York, 1951). **43** David Punter, *The literature of terror: a history of Gothic fictions from 1765 to the present day* (London–New York, 1996), two volumes; Jackson, *Fantasy*; Robin Wood, 'The American nightmare: horror in the 70s' in *Hollywood from Vietnam to Reagan ... and beyond* (New York, 2003), pp 63–84; Carol Clover, *Men,*

unconscious has entailed the assumption that the business of Gothic fiction is to explore the taboo areas of a particular culture and to express – and sometimes recontain – the anxieties and crises produced when the walls around these taboo areas begin to crumble'.⁴⁴

Probably because of this dominance, though, psychoanalysis has become an easy target for critics trying to re-conceptualize and re-theorize the Gothic and suggest new ways of looking at the phenomenon. It is difficult to pick up a book on Gothic these days without being told that psychoanalysis is old hat and that we need to break out of the psychoanalytic prison in which Gothic studies has found itself trapped. Moreover, given that the Gothic is now rather more persuasively read as a defence and promotion of Enlightenment liberal values, rather than as an attack on them, the view of it as the 'flip side' of realism is less tenable. For this reason Chris Baldick and Robert Mighall suggest that a turn to historicism and away from psychoanalysis is necessary in order to understand the genre.⁴⁵ Indeed, particularly for those critics who come from a more historicist background, the apparent universality of the claims of psychoanalysis in reading the Gothic appear very problematic.

Dracula has, once again, been a perfect text on which to test new theories for those intent on purging Gothic criticism of the psychoanalytic. Mighall's provocative reading of the staking of Lucy Westenra strongly rejects a psychosexual interpretation, insisting: '*Dracula* is a horror story about vampires; the scene in the crypt depicts a vampire-slaying; the stake is a stake; and Lucy is a vampire who is destroyed according to the method prescribed by folklore'.⁴⁶ Others have followed in his footsteps. Paul Murray in his biography has looked rather askance at the psychoanalytic understandings of the novel, and of its author.⁴⁷ Christopher Frayling, in this collection, produces a startlingly intense picking through the biographical facts, motored by what he calls a 'radical empiricism', rather than a reading expanded from a speculative theoretical base.⁴⁸ For others, psychoanalysis is a pseudoscience, best understood as a cheap and easy way for critics to posit a reading of a text (or a society, or an individual) that fits with what he wishes to endorse under the cover of either the personal, political or cultural unconscious. In one such harsh dismissal of all psychoanalytically-influenced studies, Richard Haslam, for example, complains that despite:

women and chainsaws: gender in the horror film (Princeton, 1992); Barbara Creed, *The monstrous-feminine: film, feminism, psychoanalysis* (London–New York, 1993); Andrew Smith, *Victorian demons: medicine, masculinity and the Gothic at the* fin de siécle (Manchester, 2004); Steven J. Schneider, 'Monsters as (uncanny) metaphors: Freud, Lakoff and the representation of monstrosity in cinematic horror', *Other Voices*, 1:3 (1999), http://www.othervoices.org/1.3/sschneider/monsters.php. Accessed 2 May 2013. **44** Nicholas Daly, *Modernism, romance and the* fin de siécle: *popular fiction and British culture, 1880–1914* (Cambridge, 1999), 15. The most important discussion is the collection edited by Steven J. Schneider, *Horror film and psychoanalysis – Freud's worst nightmare* (Cambridge, 2004). **45** Chris Baldick and Robert Mighall, 'Gothic criticism', *A companion to the Gothic*, ed. David Punter (Oxford, 2000), pp 209–28. **46** Robert Mighall, *A geography of Victorian Gothic fiction: mapping history's nightmares* (Oxford, 1999), p. 246. **47** Murray, *From the shadow*, pp 16, 191. **48** See Chapter 10 of this collection.

the growing number of historical, philosophical and scientific studies implacably establishing the fraudulent origins and flawed procedures of psychoanalysis, widespread recognition of its pseudoscientific status has been long delayed within European and American intellectual communities whose various schools from the post-structural to the post-colonial remain heavily indebted to the idiom of Freud and his epigones.[49]

Let me be as frank as I can here, and also as generous as possible. Critics (including myself) should be more hesitant when employing models from other disciplines to literary analysis, not least because these models often operate under such long shadows of suspicion – and perhaps the psychoanalytic critic has more to be wary of than others, because of the ideological baggage this intellectual tradition carries and the sheer amount of criticism it has attracted. It is now widely and perhaps too casually said that it is only the recalcitrant and the crazy who hang on to this outmoded, old fashioned and exploded way of thinking. However, it is also important to recognize that there is a concerted effort at trying to close down debate through the sheer rhetorical force of the invective launched against practitioners of psychoanalytic criticism, often despite a supposed commitment to dialogue and debate. Hence, Haslam urges that we submit 'psychoanalytical *methodologies* to the vampire-vanquishing stake of Ockham's Razor' (my emphasis), which simultaneously demonizes and banishes all psychoanalytical readings to the dustbin of history.[50] The rhetorical overplay Haslam employs here is something he has, unfortunately, acquired from his hero, the once-committed psychoanalytic critic turned scourge of the psychoanalytic establishment, Frederick Crews, for whom Freud was not simply wrong, but a kind of diabolical Joker in chief (and a drug-addicted, monomaniacal one at that).[51] The howl of the lapsed believer is always to be considered suspect, and the zeal with which Crews has pursued anyone who disagrees with him is rather unedifying at this stage.

My aim here is not to defend psychoanalysis itself against its critics. For some, it is clearly a pseudoscience. Freud himself was dedicated to what he mistook to be scientific rationality in his bid to consign religion to the infantile period of species history, and he misguidedly and repeatedly insisted that he was scientist rather than a mythographer. For most of us, psychoanalysis is an imaginative project, enormously telling when it comes to providing a deep, suggestive and coherent account of complex individual and supra-individual processes and activities. However, it is not a project necessarily capable of confirmation by scientific experiment (this

---

49 Richard Haslam, '"A race bashed in the face": imagining Ireland as a damaged child', *Jouvert: a Journal of Postcolonial Studies*, 4:1 (1999) http://english.chass.ncsu.edu/jouvert/v4i1/hasla.htm. Accessed 2 May 2013. **50** Richard Haslam, 'Irish Gothic' in *The Routledge companion to Gothic*, ed. Catherine Spooner and Emma McEvoy (London, 2007), p. 91. **51** See especially Frederick Crews, *Out of my system: psychoanalysis, ideology and critical method* (Oxford, 1975); idem, *The memory wars: Freud's legacy in dispute* (New York, 1995).

would be to make a category error, one which Freud himself made because of his anti-religious prejudice). Psychoanalysis is inductive rather than deductive, and at times amounts to the 'best possible explanation' the interpreter can provide given the flawed evidence. For the ideologues of certainty, like Crews, this means it should be banished to the outer darkness with other previously respected 'disciples' like astrology, but this is self-evidently an extreme position to take.

What motivates a great deal of the aggressive rejection of psychoanalysis as a legitimate means of enquiry is not (as some disciples of Freud would have it) that its critics are suffering from some deeply repressed Oedipal issues, but rather that a more general cultural attachment to an empirical and rationalist worldview has led to an increasing conviction that any form of analysis that seeks to expose things 'below' the surface, whether that be below the surface of the conscious mind, or below the surface of the literal text, are straightforwardly wrong. The notion that there are important, indeed crucial, meanings for us that are obscured and occluded seems to many to be an affront of some kind. However, declaring that psychoanalysis must be classified as a 'pseudoscience' because it makes claims that cannot be verified to the degree of certainty required by the hard sciences is not merely tendentious but borders on the ridiculous. Yet this is the kind of attack that psychoanalysis has had to endure for years now.[52] A large part of the difficulty for psychoanalysis lies in its attempt to get behind the apparent, to probe the hidden and sometimes repressed motivations for human actions, which means that there will always be a level of deniability when it comes to psychoanalytic interpretations (just as there is often the temptation to go too far beyond the evidence into the realm of pure unadulterated speculation for the psychoanalytic interpreter).

The attack on psychoanalysis is part of a broader struggle against all kinds of interpretation which suggest that the available evidence is often not all it's cracked up to be, and often not to be trusted at all because human beings are rather obscure and unreliable, motivated by a variety of different desires, some unknown even to themselves. Just when I think I am acting at my most rational, I may, in fact, be motivated by the most deeply bigoted of hatreds and fears, and the language of psychoanalysis may help to begin to reveal these hidden motivations, to make explicit the occluded. Texts, too, are rather less transparent than some would have it, and behind the attacks on the psychoanalytic critic and the renewed appeal to 'authorial intention', I can hear the (to my mind mistaken) insistence that we are to take things as they initially appear rather than ask intrusive questions about that which lies beneath. Caution is recommended before throwing the baby of psychoanalysis out with its dirty bathwater. Working with too-strict and hard-and-fast dichotomies (if historically determined then psychoanalytically impenetrable) when

---

52 See especially the work of Adolf Grünbaum, *Validation in the clinical theory of psychoanalysis: a study in the philosophy of psychoanalysis* (Madison, CN, 1993).

it comes to the Gothic does not work, because the Gothic is concerned with hesitation, qualification, is populated by liminal creatures and dramatizes liminal states of identity. Janus-faced, the Gothic both supports and undermines Enlightenment values, banishes and revels in darkness and perversity, and examines historically specific, culturally-bound anxieties and concerns, and also appeals to a more basic human sense of fear and terror common to all cultures.[53] As long as psychoanalysis is just one more tool in the critic's methodological box, there is a great deal of justification for its continued use in Gothic Studies.

This is not to say that I disagree with those – including contributors to this volume – who think that psychoanalytic readings of Stoker and his novel have gotten out of control. Indeed, some of the more ambitious readings seem rather Gothic in excess themselves, and some 'bullshit detection' is certainly called for at times. Students should be taught to read such criticism with a certain healthy (but not corrosive) scepticism. Before attempting a psychoanalytic reading of any of Stoker's novels, it is important to avoid making unqualified claims about repressed sexuality and Victorian culture's attitudes to the body – it is these claims that distort interpretation, I think, rather than the psychoanalytic paradigm itself. We certainly need to finally dispense with the view that the Victorians were so sexually repressed that they couldn't recognize a pornographic novel when they read it,[54] and claims that Stoker was little more than a collection of neuroses should be put in perspective. Readings of *Dracula* as a sex-novel should be contextualized in readings of Stoker's other novels. Far from repressing sexual desire, or being terrified by its power, Stoker's other novels prove that he celebrated it and wrote about it quite frankly. When in a letter to Prime Minister William Gladstone, Stoker explained that 'There is nothing base in [*Dracula*]',[55] he was probably including rather than ignoring (or overlooking) the sexual element in this description. As indicated by his article on censorship, Stoker certainly thought that sexual desire was sometimes dangerous,[56] but only the deluded would insist that all desire is positive. The notion that Stoker viewed sexual desire as something which needed repressing does not stand up to even a cursory reading of his fiction as a whole. He appears to have thought that healthy sex was necessary for social progression, and his fiction constantly celebrates this kind of forward-looking sexuality, while simultaneously warning against desire powered only by degenerate lust.

This can be illustrated by turning briefly to one of Stoker's novels that is very different from *Dracula* to get some sexual perspective. Stoker's largely unread,

---

[53] Moreover, it goes without saying that some of the replacements for psychoanalysis offered so far would not please many of the critics of the psychoanalytic approach. To be told that Freud and Lacan were being substituted by Deleuze and Guattari would produce a suitably horrified reaction in believers in the transparency of text like Robert Mighall.   [54] Ronald Pearsall, *The worm in the bud: the world of Victorian sexuality* (London, 2003).   [55] Bram Stoker, Letter to William Gladstone, 24 May 1897. *Journal of Dracula Studies*, 1 (1999), 48.   [56] Bram Stoker, 'The censorship of fiction', *The Nineteenth-Century and After*, 64 (September, 1908), 479–87; reprinted in *Dracula*, ed. Maurice Hindle (London, 2003), pp 419–30.

almost totally forgotten 1908 novel *Lady Athlyne* is sexually charged to an extraordinary degree, and reveals that rather than the sexually repressed neurotic of many critical studies, Stoker really resembles other popular culture figures who posit an intimate and positive connection between sexuality and technology. For example, *Lady Athlyne* has a great deal in common with later films like *Bullitt* (dir. Peter Yates; 1968), *The French connection* (dir. William Friedkin; 1971), *Smokey and the bandit* (dir. Hal Needham; 1977), *The blues brothers* (dir. John Landis; 1980), *The cannonball run* (dir. Hal Needham; 1981), *The Bourne identity* (dir. Doug Liman; 2002), *Death proof* (dir. Quentin Tarantino; 2007). Superficially, the only thing these texts share is a plot dependent on what has come to be known as the 'car chase/race', where automobiles speed dangerously over difficult terrain, either to get to a particular place by a particular time, or in pursuit of another technological propellant. In *Bullitt* the terrain is the famously bumpy streets of San Francisco; the Blues Brothers have to drive through a shopping mall; in *Lady Athlyne* the car race against time takes place on the (ostensibly) rather less treacherous stretch between Ambleside in the Lake District and Carsphairn in Scotland. The heroine, Joy Ogilvie, has been enjoying a rather dangerous liaison with Lord Athlyne without the permission of her father, and has only three hours to cover the hundred miles back to the hotel where her parents are expected. Should she fail to get there in time, her reputation could be in jeopardy, and her already enraged father will have another reason to hate her paramour. Joy has to make this journey alone because Lord Athlyne has unfortunately been arrested for speeding; under pressure for time, in an unknown country, and with a thick fog all around, Joy crashes and fails to make it back.

The presence of a car race is not, however, the most important link between this series of texts. A more critical connection is that they all fetishize, indeed, eroticize, the automobile and what the automobile represents: futurity, 'progress', modernity, the conquering of time and space. These are all texts deeply invested in the notion that technology, especially the technology of movement and speed, represents not simply a means but an end, and articulate what is in effect an epistemology of the car and celebrate the growth of what Neil Postman has called the Technopolis.[57] Stoker's evident delight in the motor car makes his novel at times sound like a prefiguring of the 1910 manifesto of the Futurist Filippo Tommaso Marinetti, which affirmed: 'the world's magnificence has been enriched by a new beauty: the beauty of speed ... We want to hymn the man at the wheel, who hurls the lance of his spirit across the Earth, along the circle of its orbit'.[58]

---

[57] Neil Postman, *Technopoly: the surrender of culture to technology* (New York, 1992). [58] Marinetti, 'The founding and manifesto of Futurism' in Umbro Apollonio (ed.), *Futurist manifestos* (London, 1973), p. 21. For more on the obsession with speed and movement in this period, see Andrew Thacker, 'E. M. Forster and the motor car', *Literature and History*, 9:2 (2000), 37–52.

This techno-fetishism pits Stoker's novel and its technophile fellow travellers against a rather different series of texts including Kenneth Grahame's *The wind in the willows* (1908), Richard Matheson's 'Duel' (1971) (adapted by Steven Spielberg in the same year), J.G. Ballard's *Crash* (1973) (and its 1996 adaptation, directed by David Cronenberg), *The hitcher* (dir. Robert Harmon; 1986), and *Crash* (dir. Paul Haggis; 2004), where the car is seen as representing not so much the utopian future, but a (often Gothic) threat to individual integrity and bucolic security. Moreover, the gendered implications of the love of the car is clear as, like its fellow automophilic narratives, *Lady Athlyne* is careful to connect the car with masculine prowess and is deeply suspicious of female attempts to 'master' this new technological future, which clearly belongs to men and their magnificent machines. This suspicion of women behind the wheel is generated not because the novel presents female *sexuality* as frightening or dangerous and in need of 'repression' or suppression, but because, drawing liberally on Otto Weininger's very illiberal theories of sexuality and gender, Stoker thinks femininity has a different function to masculinity. Whereas the hero, Lord Athlyne, has easily adapted to his shiny new car, and can speed up and down secondary roads with ease of spirit – until arrested by the dialect speaking and intellectually backward Scottish policemen, enforcing a speeding law that simply should not apply to men like Lord Athlyne – Joy is effectively a disaster when put behind the wheel. The kind of physical and psychological exertion required to keep control of this machine is too much for her and she crashes not once but twice in her journey, and must eventually run to another man for rescue.[59]

Technology here facilitates sexual intimacy. In fact, in driving her in his car, Athlyne effectively consummates his relationship with Joy, and they *both* thoroughly enjoy themselves:

> 'Joy won't you come with me for a ride. I have my motor here, and we can go alone. There is much I want to say to you – much to tell you, and the speed will help us. I want to rush along – to fly. Earth is too prosaic for me – now!' Joy looking softly up caught the lightning that flashed from his eyes, and his own fell. A tide of red swept her face; this passed in a moment, however, leaving a divine pink like summer sunset on snowy heights.[60]

Their journey certainly constitutes a marriage and, according to Scottish law, Athlyne and Joy find that they are legally wed the next day. The car serves as a

---

[59] Carol Senf is far more sympathetic to Stoker's treatment of women in their relationship to technology and the automobile than I have been above, and argues that the hero and heroine of the novel have an *equal* 'facility with modern technology … [and] ability to use it effectively … [B]oth are comfortable in world of the train, telegraph and automobile'. 'Introduction', Bram Stoker's *Lady Athlyne* (Southend-on-Sea, Essex, 2007), p. 10. [60] Bram Stoker, *Lady Athlyne*, ed. Carol A. Senf (Southend-on-Sea, 2007), p. 140.

space in which sexual energy can pass between Athlyne and Joy, although in a completely open and public way, and both confirms their love for each other *and* their sexual passion. For Stoker it is clear that technology is an aid to human contact and creativity – especially sexual creativity (facilitating the relationship between Athlyne and Joy and powering it), and here Stoker's vision is very unlike that of D.H. Lawrence, for whom technology was a kind of sexual inhibitor. In *Lady Chatterley's lover* (1928), a post-coital Mellors complains vociferously about the way in which mechanization has interfered in the 'natural' relationships between 'natural' men and women: 'Tha's got a proper, woman's arse, proud of itself. It's none ashamed of itself, this isna … An' if I only lived ten minutes, an' stroked thy arse an' got to know it, I should reckon I'd lived one life, see ter! Industrial system or not!'.[61] Far from coming between lovers, in Stoker's novels mechanization often seems to enable a more authentic bodily communion.

Stoker's focus on the car as a phallic motor towards a techno-topia should be seen as part of his intellectual devotion (with some reservations) to the project of modernity which can be detected throughout his oeuvre, from his homage to modern bureaucracy, *The duties of clerks of petty sessions in Ireland* (1879), and new agricultural techniques in *The snake's pass* (1890) at the start of his career, to the valorizing of research into radiation and electricity in his final works. The critical emphasis on *Dracula* has tended to obscure this larger project because his most famous novel tends towards ambiguity and opens up interpretive possibilities, even in the area of technological progress, and given that most readers (including academic readers) of *Dracula* will never go on to encounter anything else by Stoker, it has provided a distorted sense of the novelist's loyalties. Where *Dracula* appears from one reading to be highly critical of the 'nineteenth century up-to-date' as producing a critical myopia in its inhabitants,[62] when placed with the rest of Stoker's writings, the crucial weapons against the vampire are revealed to be not the crucifix and the Communion wafer, but the typewriter and the phonograph. Of course, relics of the medieval past can use these things too, and Dracula has memorized the English train timetable, but the point is that these relics use the instruments of the modern future rather badly and end up being thwarted by them and having to retreat into their medieval bunkers once professional late-Victorian men catch on to what is really happening.

Joy's father, Colonel Ogilvie is the atavistic, backward character in *Lady Athlyne*, and Stoker consistently associates him with the past and the outmoded, and at times depicts him as possibly deranged in his obsession with a bizarre and unwritten series of rules and regulations to which all must adhere or face a duel with him (we are told in the opening chapters that he has killed many in duels over questions of honour and reputation). Indeed, towards the end of the novel,

61 D.H. Lawrence, *Lady Chatterley's lover* (London, 1960), pp 232–3. **62** Stoker, *Dracula*, p. 43.

after he has discovered his daughter and Lord Athlyne in apparent *flagrante delicto* he announces his intention to murder Athlyne and works himself into a state of inappropriate insanity: 'Realizing that he could rely implicitly on the dignity of the man before him, he allowed himself a further latitude. He could afford, he felt, to be unrestrained in such a presence; and so proceeded to behave as though he was stark, staring raving mad', in a scene reminiscent of Van Helsing's 'King Laugh' breakdown after Lucy's death in *Dracula*.⁶³ That this relic from the American South cannot drive particularly well whereas his daughter can at least get by on the roads, indicates that she represents the future, and he the best-left-behind past. Joy *can* drive, but she probably *shouldn't*, and would herself like to leave such matters in the future to her husband.

The perfect woman has a great deal of technological ability in Stoker's vision, but she knows better than to exercise it because when she does so, it always ends in disaster. This is particularly the case when it comes to women tackling the instruments of modernity, whether shorthand or car driving: Mina Harker has astonishing powers when it comes using the equipment and techniques suitable to the modern office, but happily gives them up to become a wife and mother. Indeed, there is a suggestion that the mental strain her use of these technologies has caused may have left her vulnerable to the attack of Dracula himself. Likewise, Joy comes to realize that while being driven by Lord Athlyne resembles a fairy tale, trying to drive herself is a nightmare best avoided in the future. Stoker not only anticipates but celebrates and promotes the masculinist version of the technological future found in the films and texts to which I have already referred. His interest in the phonograph, the Kodak camera, the typewriter and stenography in *Dracula*, and the automobile in *Lady Athlyne*, resonates with his celebration of new weapons of war in *The lady of the shroud*, where armaments are described and detailed in an extraordinarily fetishistic manner, the warship with which the hero is possessed loaded with 'electric guns and the latest Massillion water-guns, and Reinhardt electro-pneumatic "deliverers" for pyroxiline shells. She is even equipped with war-balloons easy of expansion, and with compressible Kitson aeroplanes'.⁶⁴

At this point, I would suggest two contexts in which Stoker's technofetishism could be placed. It is not insignificant that it was a Co. Clare inventor and Irish nationalist, John Philip Holland, who developed the submarine and the torpedo for the US navy, thus bringing together Stoker's own nationality and technological innovation. Indeed, given the new histories of the Irish Revival of the late nineteenth century being written, and the position of science and technology within these histories,⁶⁵ Irish Studies can provide a very useful starting point for under-

---

63 Stoker, *Lady Athlyne*, p. 192. 64 Stoker, *Lady of the shroud* (Kansas, 2012), p. 170. For more on Stoker and future fiction, see Luke Gibbons, 'It's not all about *Dracula*: Stoker's 17 other books', *Irish Times*, 18 April 2012. 65 P.J. Mathews, *Revival: the Abbey Theatre, Sinn Féin, the Gaelic league and the Co-operative Movement* (Cork, 2003).

standing the link between Stoker the Gothic writer and Stoker the technophile. Stoker is just one of a large number of late nineteenth-century Irish nationalists interested in reconstructing Ireland as a crucible of technology and modernity – hence his interest in the Irish Industrial Revolution in his articles on the Donnybrook Fair and the Harland and Wolff's shipbuilding industry in 1907.[66] As they lost control of Irish politics, many Irish Protestants reinvested energies in techno-futurity – and also wrote Gothic novels, which suggests that there may be a correlation between these two enterprises.[67] This reassessment should help to reassert Stoker's position in Irish Studies and in the more complicated versions of the late nineteenth-century 'Revival' that are now emerging. Given P.J. Mathews' connection of the literary revival with 'self-help' schemes including Horace Plunkett's co-operatives and the Irish Agricultural Organization Society, Stoker's dedication to the power of technology and professionalism can be partly understood in relation to his background in middle-class Protestant enterprise and entrepreneurial skill. I should say here that I think this a rather more convincing connection between Ireland and Stoker than some being offered, with the bizarre but apparently attractive notion that 'Dracula' derives from '*droch fhola*' – bad blood – being unwisely repeated *ad nauseum* in some circles.[68]

The second context is the psychoanalytic one, which can then be brought to bear on the centrality of technology to Stoker's Gothic vision.[69] Shifting the psychoanalytic focus away from Stoker-the-neurotic and *Dracula*-as-coded-pornography would help allay concerns about the narrow range and sex-obsessed interpretations of the past. This application of psychoanalysis has to remain tentative here, but Sigmund Freud's description of the 'death drive' can help the critic see past the apparently life-affirming celebration of technological innovation so central to Stoker's work, to the darkness underpinning this devotion.[70] To the psychoanalytic critic, it is no surprise that so much energy in technological development goes into the expansion of instruments of death and warfare, because lurking behind Eros is Thanatos, which would also help us understand why both the living dead (vampires, mummies, the comatose lady in the shroud, the white worm) as well as state-of-the-art technology are constant presences in Stoker's work. For Freud, humans are devoted to death as well as to love, and indeed the two are inextricably intertwined. Rupert St Leger's love of both planes of war and a woman who spends much of her existence in a coma and wrapped in a shroud,

---

66 Bram Stoker, 'The great white fair in Dublin' and 'The world's greatest shipbuilding yard', *A glimpse of America, and other lectures, interviews and essays*, ed. Richard Dalby (Southend-on-Sea, Essex, 2002), pp 145–53. **67** For Irish Gothic and the loss of Irish Protestant political power see R.F. Foster, 'Protestant Magic', *Paddy and Mr Punch: connections in Irish and English history* (London, 1995), pp 212–32. **68** Peter Haining and Peter Tremayne, *The un-dead: the legend of Bram Stoker and Dracula* (London, 1997), p. 71. **69** For Stoker as best understood as a Gothic writer, even in his ostensibly non-Gothic work, see Senf, *Bram Stoker*, p. 1. **70** Sigmund Freud, *Beyond the pleasure principle* in *The standard edition of the complete psychological works*, xviii, trans. James Strachey (London, 1999).

is a good example of such a dangerous intersection. As Terry Eagleton emphasizes: 'This, then, is the true scandal of psychoanalysis – not infant sexuality, which had been recognized for a long time (not least by infants), but the proposal that human beings unconsciously desire their own destruction. At the core of the self is a drive to absolute nothingness'.[71]

Moreover, given that writing Gothic fiction and intellectually investing in technological development was not specific to Stoker, but characteristic of *fin de siècle* Irish Anglicanism, psychoanalysis may genuinely have something to tell us about cultural rather than just personal pathologies. Erich Fromm has argued that some cultures are 'necrophilious', or characterized by an intense investment in the discourses of death and horror, and also mechanization and technology.[72] Eagleton, for example, dubs Protestant Gothic the 'political unconscious of Anglo-Irish society, the place where its fears and fantasies most definitively emerge',[73] and for an enclave whose power was dwindling, and which invested energy in Gothic and technological fantasies, a necrophilious discourse may have represented one way to escape the psychological challenges thrown up by political change.

A proper development of these psychoanalytic and Irish Studies contexts for understanding Stoker's entire body of work can only be suggested here. It is a relief, however, to see Ireland beginning to acknowledge the creator of one of the most famous characters in world literature as an important figure. Until recently, if you were to point out to most people that Ireland, the place where Stoker was born, where he was schooled, where he spent half his life, the place where he wrote his first works of fiction, where he worked in the civil service, and where he met and married his wife, has a claim on the Dracula myth and the story of its author, they would look at you with some confusion. The 'Dracula experience' is the main reason why tourists go to the Transylvania region, and the Romanian state has become increasingly active in seeing the potential cash power of the vampire myth and (after a long period where Dracula was seen as an embarrassment because of its depiction of Transylvania as a superstition-ridden melting pot of freaks and demons) many there have embraced the vampire enthusiastically. One commentator asks: 'What other land calls up such mystical visions of shrouded, misty forests; of driverless coaches pounding up treacherous, uncharted trails to hidden castles; of black-cloaked figures stalking across moonlit cemeteries in the chill of night?'[74] The answer to this should be … Ireland, of course. The connection between Dracula and Transylvania is certainly solid in the public mind, and most people seem to think that Stoker based his character on Vlad the Impaler, who

---

71 Terry Eagleton, *On evil* (London, 2010), p. 108. **72** Erich Fromm, *The anatomy of human destructiveness* (New York, 1973), pp 325–68. See also Jarlath Killeen, *Gothic Ireland: horror and the Irish Anglican imagination* (Dublin, 2005), p. 160. **73** Terry Eagleton, *Heathcliff and the great hunger: studies in Irish culture* (London, 1995), p. 187. **74** K. Browkaw, cited in Duncan Light, 'Imaginative geographies, *Dracula* and the Transylvania "place myth"', *Human Geographies*, 2:2 (2008), 14.

ruled Walachia during the fifteenth century. However, having closely examined Stoker's notes, the academic Elizabeth Miller has concluded that he knew little about Vlad other than his title Dracula, and that there is little authentically 'Romanian' about the vampire.⁷⁵ Despite this, vampire enthusiasts remain heavily invested in the Transylvanian connection, whereas Ireland had been all but forgotten. Like Romanians, the Irish have long had a rather difficult relationship with the Gothic, and the pop cultural version of Ireland as the habitation of leprechauns and fairies has clashed with the desire of Irish progressives to drag Ireland out of what they view as an atavistic backwater and into the modern world.⁷⁶ To those who wanted to emphasize a rationalist Ireland, bringing Stoker back, and highlighting possible links between this world-famous vampire and Irish culture probably seemed like an immensely bad idea (much better to celebrate James Joyce and Samuel Beckett, modernist masters of the future). That Stoker himself was a techno-fetishist as well as a supernaturalist would not have made much sense to those for whom there was a direct conflict between such categories.

A financially bankrupt Ireland needs cultural tourism, however, and in 2012 the tide appeared to turn in Stoker's favour. Trinity College Dublin, which had previously seemed rather uninterested in one of its most famous sons, held two academic conferences to 'celebrate' his ... death – one in April on 'Vampire and/as Science' under the careful guidance of Professor Clemens Ruthner, and one in June examining 'Bram Stoker: life and work', out of which the present collection grew.⁷⁷ The Irish government also released two commemorative stamps, a commemorative portrait by Aidan Hickey was unveiled, a commemorative 'festival' launched in Dublin in October, and there was even talk of naming a new bridge over the River Liffey after the great man.⁷⁸ The papers gathered here are contributions to the reassessment of Stoker and represent the current state of research on his life and his writings. The collection gathers together veterans in the field who have devoted much of their energy throughout the years to keeping Stoker alive in the scholarly and the commercial worlds, as well as relative newcomers to this enterprise. I think it is a good representation of the current range of scholarly opinion on Stoker, and should serve to encourage readers and critics to venture beyond *Dracula* and its cultural legacy, and explore the life and work of the man who first dreamed it up.

---

75 Elizabeth Miller, Dracula: *sense and nonsense* (Southend-on-Sea, Essex, 2006), pp 149–84. 76 For versions of Irish 'progressivism' see Ivana Bacik, *Kicking and screaming: dragging Ireland into the 21st century* (Dublin, 2004); Fintan O'Toole, *The ex-isle of Ireland: images of a global Ireland* (Dublin, 1997). 77 Similar conferences were held in the University of Hull, and the University of Hertfordshire in April. 78 It didn't happen. The new bridge eventually came to be named after trade unionist and activist Rosie Hackett.

Bram Stoker: the child that went with the fairies

DAVID J. SKAL

'Monster! Give me my child!'¹

I

'In my babyhood,' Bram Stoker wrote, 'I never knew what it was to stand upright.'² Mysteriously bedridden 'until nearly the age of seven',³ he would eventually grow into a robust giant of a man, a prize-winning athlete bigger and taller than his father or brothers. Stoker personally and directly attributed his uncanny growth spurt 'to long illnesses, as a child', according to his son, writing on the one hundred anniversary of his birth in 1947.⁴ No one knows if the story is true. It certainly defies science, just as it defies common sense. Nonetheless, as Stoker's late-life friend Sir Arthur Conan Doyle opined on more than one occasion through the fictional mouthpiece of Sherlock Holmes, 'When you have excluded the impossible, whatever remains, however improbable, must be the truth.'⁵ Or, at least, there might begin an understanding.

In 1847, Dublin was one of Britain's largest cities and centres of trade. Sometimes called the 'second city of the British Empire', its intractable problems with overcrowding, squalor and disease were equally oversized, and, in fact, among the worst in Europe. Death was a living presence, even if its grim vitality was expressed indirectly, through the sullen exertion of gravediggers, the unceasing procession of mourners, and the incessant writhing of worms. On 8 October, a letter from a local cleric, Richard Ardille, was published in the *Dublin Evening Mail*, addressing a perceived central issue: 'The evil to be remedied, which I think demands the serious attention of the government, and of every person, is the prac-

---

1 Bram Stoker, *Dracula: a Norton critical edition*, ed. Nina Auerbach and David J. Skal (New York, 1997), p. 48.   2 Bram Stoker, *Personal reminiscences of Henry Irving*, I (New York, 1906), p. 31.   3 Ibid.   4 Noël Thornley Stoker, 'Bram Stoker, by his son, Noël Thornley Stoker' (typewritten manuscript, November 1947). Stoker family papers, Trinity College Library Department of Manuscripts.   5 Arthur Conan Doyle, 'The adventure of the Beryl coronet' in *The adventures of Sherlock Holmes* (Oxford, 1993), p. 268.

tice that now prevails of having burial in church yards within the city, surrounded as they are by neighbourhoods densely populated, the inhabitants of which are constantly inhaling an atmosphere noxious in its character and effect'. Ardille continued with some direct observations:

> I have attended funerals where the remains of seven bodies were exhumed to make room for an eighth about to be interred; and I would ask any rational man if he could expect that a city could be healthy where such scenes were of frequent recurrence? In no country, save in Great Britain and Ireland, do interments take place within the walls of cities or towns … On the continent of Europe such an offence against propriety is unheard of. Amongst barbarous natives, as they are termed, the dead are either consumed by fire, or interred at a distance from their dwellings; but in refined and civilized England the pernicious system is yet tolerated …⁶

Actually, there was no proven connection between putrefaction in Dublin cemeteries and any disease outbreak. But crowded cemeteries did produce noxious smells, which much occupied the minds of early nineteenth-century promulgators of 'miasma theory', ever anxious to find environmental – even meteorological – causes for confounding health problems in congested urban centres. Disease, in the miasmic worldview, was best understood as the mysterious action of wafting phantoms. In the case of cemeteries, the ghostly analogy is particularly apt, for just beneath the pseudoscientific surface of miasma theory percolated ancient, stubborn superstitions about the fearful powers of the dead to reach out from their graves and weaken the living.

It is often said that death is a normal part of life, and this was certainly true in nineteenth-century Ireland. People usually died as they were born – at home, amid familiar persons and surroundings. The processes of death were not sequestered in clinical settings; in fact, a definite social stigma was attached to the very idea of dying 'in hospital'. Medical institutions were often seen, and feared, as de facto death houses to be rigorously avoided. Life expectancy in mid-century Dublin was miserably short; to live much past one's forties was an unexpected surprise in middle-class households, and among the artisan classes and the poor an impossible dream. Grimmer still were the infant mortality rates. Nearly a quarter of all children born died before the age of five, and among the poorest of the poor, the death rates could approach half. Many working-class children in Great Britain were routinely enrolled in 'burial clubs' at birth, to guard families against ruinous funeral expenses, or the shame of a pauper's grave.⁷

6 Richard Ardille, 'Prevention of diseases in Dublin', *Dublin Evening Mail*, 8 October 1847. **7** For a detailed discussion of burial clubs and death as perceived and experienced by late nineteenth-century chil-

II

At the age of twenty-nine, Charlotte Stoker, née Thornley, was an educated, forward-minded woman from a military family in the west of Ireland. She married Dublin civil servant Abraham Stoker, eighteen years her senior, in 1844; by 1847 the couple already had two children, William Thornley (born in 1845) and Matilda (born in 1846). Their third, Abraham, junior, familiarly and later famously called Bram, followed on 8 November 1847, at 15 the Crescent (now Marino Crescent), Clontarf, a seaside north Dublin parish.

Charlotte's term with Bram must have been anxious indeed. William Thornley had been born the year of a first, partial, crop failure, and Matilda during the second, worsening year. By the time she was pregnant with Bram the effects of the Famine were being fully felt, with starving and evicted tenant farmers flooding into the city slums and workhouses, and with them dysentery, famine fever and typhus. Terrifying accounts reached Dublin from Co. Mayo, where workhouses had begun the inexorable transition into death houses. About the time of Bram's conception, the *Mayo Constitution* reported the grim effects of fever:

> In Ballinrobe the workhouse is in the most deplorable state, pestilence having attacked paupers, officers, and all. In fact, this building is one horrible charnel house. [...] The master has become the victim of this dread disease; the clerk, a young man whose energies were devoted to the well-being of the union, has been added to the victims; the matron, too, is dead; and the respected and esteemed physician has fallen before the ravages of pestilence, in his constant attendance on the diseased inmates.[8]

The Stoker row house still stands. The upper two floors contain several bedrooms, though no one has ever determined which, exactly, were occupied by which of the three Stoker children. Bram might have shared a room with his brother, or may well have had his own dedicated sickroom-nursery. It has become a commonplace in Stoker commentary[9] to imagine that Bram's room might have faced the street, overlooking the handsome iron-gated park opposite, with a glimpse of the Irish sea beyond, fuelling his dreamy imagination, the park itself being the spot to which he was carried to lay 'amid cushions on the grass if the weather was fine'.[10]

---

dren, see Thomas E. Jordan, *Victorian childhood: themes and variations* (Albany, NY, 1987), pp 76–109. **8** Cited in Colm Tóibín and Diarmaid Ferriter, *The Irish Famine: a documentary* (London, 2001), pp 40–1. **9** Stoker's early fascination with the sea was first employed, rather impressionistically, by Harry Ludlam in *A biography of Dracula: the life story of Bram Stoker* (London, 1962), later echoed by Barbara Belford's *Bram Stoker: a biography of the author of* Dracula (New York, 1997), and ultimately referenced as fact elsewhere. It is a good example of the many creeping 'factoids' that complicate Stoker biography and criticism. **10** Bram Stoker, *Personal reminiscences of Henry Irving* (holograph manuscript, c.1905–6). Folger Shakespeare Library, Washington, DC. Deleted passage from vol. I, chapter II.

This is unlikely for two reasons: first, episodic memories before the age of two are universally irretrievable, subject to the well-studied phenomenon of infantile amnesia, a normal part of childhood development.[11] Second, the Clontarf waterfront, which previously attracted swimmers and sunbathers, was now an odiferous 'slobland' at a time when 'vapours' and 'miasmas' were blamed for all manner of a disease; in later years, owing to concerns about sewage dumping, the sea frontage would be completely landfilled.[12] In any event, despite its close proximity, the mouth of the Liffey was the last place a concerned parent would risk taking a sickly child.

The precise onset of Bram Stoker's debilitating illness is not recorded, but his baptism was delayed nearly seven weeks, until 30 December, and then conducted at the Anglican Church of St John the Baptist, which still half-stands in Clontarf as a picturesque ruin. The site is appropriately suggestive of the Gothic masterpiece Stoker would publish fifty years later. *Dracula* is the overwhelming reason for most people's interest in Bram Stoker today, and since Stoker chose to leave us no full accounting of his own life, only his fictions, it is not surprising that biographers, critics and essayists have long employed imaginative (and often overreaching) speculation to link the king of vampires to a sickness and symptoms initially as baffling to onlookers as those endured by Dracula's victims.

Vampirism involves blood-letting, which, in the mid-nineteenth century, was a medical practice still widely used. Henry Clutterbuck, MD, a physician, whose 'Lectures on blood-letting' appeared in *The London Medical Gazette*, told his 1838 readers that 'blood-letting is a remedy which, when judiciously employed, it is hardly possible to estimate too highly. There are, indeed, few diseases on which, at some periods, and under some circumstances, it may not be used with advantage, either as a palliative or curative means'.[13] Even a cursory look at the medical literature of the day confirms the universality of the prescription, even for conditions like childhood asthma and adolescent acne. Clutterbuck especially advocated 'prompt and vigorous application of the remedy' to 'inflammatory affections of the brain that are so common in early life'.[14] The idea of 'brain fever' in the 1800s was remarkably elastic, and seems to have comprised everything from meningitis to simple moodiness. A child so afflicted 'loses his appetite, complains of thirst, is languid and spiritless, his sleep is scanty and disturbed', Clutterbuck observed.[15]

A languid boy like Bram Stoker, showing signs of chronic motor weakness, would have been an excellent candidate for phlebotomy. Bloodletting physicians no longer invoked the principle of balancing 'humours', an idea dating from

[11] Samuel E. Wood and Ellen Green Wood, *The world of psychology* (Boston, 1999), p. 210. [12] A complete, and thoroughly fascinating account of Dublin's nineteenth-century expansion and growing pains can be found in Michael Barry's lavishly illustrated *Victorian Dublin revealed* (Dublin, 2011). For an account of the Clontarf waterfront, see p. 70. [13] Henry Clutterbuck, MD, 'Lectures on blood-letting', *London Medical Gazette*, 22 (1838), 9. [14] Ibid. [15] Ibid.

antiquity, but the similarly ancient idea of 'plethora', or excess blood, as a cause of illness was still very much in vogue.¹⁶ If Bram was treated by doctors, it would have been at home. Hospitals, especially during the time of famine fever, were resorted to cautiously, if at all. Bloodletting was performed by three means: by lancet; by "cupping" with a heated glass that created a siphoning vacuum;¹⁷ and by leeches. The demand in Europe for commercially farmed leeches was huge; in 1833, France alone imported more than 40 million from Germany, Sweden and Russia.¹⁸ Since Dracula himself is described by Stoker as 'a filthy leech, exhausted in his repletion',¹⁹ one wonders about his personal experience or observation of the bloodsucking worm. Bloodletting, then, with its happy relationship to vampires, is not only a possibility in Bram Stoker's early life, but a probability as well. For all the nineteenth-century advances in anatomical studies (considerably abetted by grave-robbing) and surgery, when it came to healing the sick, early nineteenth-century doctors had an extremely limited bag of tricks. A well-regarded doctor's reputation typically required a comforting bedside manner, a judicious dose of bluster and professional mystification, a certain generosity with opium, not to mention a surfeit of sustained good luck. And leeches.

Befitting a boy whose childhood would be shaped by fairy tales, his father, Abraham Stoker, worked in a castle – Dublin Castle, the local seat of government, where he was a career civil servant. The impressive, partly-Norman fortification no doubt carried strong legendary associations for his son; its medieval Record Tower (the oldest surviving part of the much-renovated complex, built in 1204) once displayed the freshly impaled heads of Irish traitors on its battlements. Still vigorous in middle age, the elder Stoker is said to have walked to work each day, a brisk daily journey of an hour-and-a-quarter from Clontarf, down the North Strand Road and into the commercial hurly-burly of Talbot Street, then down Sackville Street and over Carlisle Bridge²⁰ into the south bank city centre.²¹ Family accounts of Abraham's daily perambulations may well be exaggerated, however – the nearly three-mile walk would be almost impossible as a daily matter in winter, and Clontarf was one of the first Dublin suburbs to be serviced by horse-drawn omnibuses and trams, as well as trains. But the story does illustrate the Stoker family's emphasis on self-reliance and thrift.

Although Charlotte Stoker was a practical, no-nonsense woman, she nonetheless had a countervailing and lifelong weakness for things irrational, fantastic and macabre. County Sligo, where she was raised, is one of Ireland's richest reposito-

---

16 Albert S. Lyons and R. Joseph Petrucelli, *Medicine: an illustrated history* (New York, 1978). On humour theory: p. 195; plethora as concept in Greek medicine: p. 103; plethora and bloodletting: p. 513.   **17** An ingenious, Dracula-like use of this device figures in the plot resolution of Tod Browning's 1935 film *Mark of the Vampire*.   **18** Lyons and Petrucelli, *Medicine*, p. 513.   **19** Stoker, *Dracula*, p. 53.   **20** The crossing was replaced in 1880 by the present O'Connell Street Bridge, and Sackville Street renamed accordingly.   **21** Personally walked and timed by author in November 2010.

ries of folklore, and Charlotte partook of a vibrant oral tradition. She claimed to have personally heard the wail of the *Bean-sídhe* – the banshee – heralding her own mother's death.²² Like the heroine of Jane Austen's *Northanger Abbey* (1818), she came of age when popular reading material for literate young women included the Gothic novels of Ann Radcliffe (*The mysteries of Udolpho*, 1794; and *The Italian*, 1797), Matthew Lewis (*The Monk*, 1796), and the Irish cleric Charles Robert Maturin's *Melmoth the wanderer* (1820). For Irish Protestant readers, these books distilled the complicated sentiments of long sectarian strife. The Gothic novels portrayed Catholicism with a lurid – and alluring – savagery. The cruel debaucheries of villains like Ambrosio, the lustful Capuchin in *The Monk* (some of whose description and demeanour would be appropriated almost verbatim in Stoker's delineation of Count Dracula), were sensationally attractive to readers like Charlotte, and later her son, exuding all the dependable fascination of the forbidden, a dynamic the Irish historian R.F. Foster describes as 'a mingled repulsion and envy where Catholic magic is concerned'.²³

Charlotte also read the works of Edgar Allan Poe, and near the end of her life would compare her son superlatively to the world-famous author of *Tales of mystery and imagination*. 'Poe', she would write in 1897, upon the publication of *Dracula*, 'is nowhere'.²⁴ That is saying much, since the terrors of both 'The masque of the red death' and 'The premature burial' were very nearly eclipsed by the events of Charlotte's own childhood. As a thirteen-year-old girl in Sligo, she had personally witnessed the horrors of the 1832 cholera epidemic that claimed more than 25,000 lives.

> In the days of my early youth so long ago ... our world was shaken with the dread of the new and terrible plague which was desolating all lands as it passed through them. And so regular was its march that men could tell where it next would appear and almost the day when it might be expected. It was the *Cholera*, which for the first time appeared in Western Europe. And its utter strangeness and man's want of experience or knowledge of its nature, or how best to resist its attack, added if anything to its horrors.²⁵

Charlotte knew how to tell a tale, and the written version of the chilling oral account she gave to her children included the italicized inflections she must have given it vocally, building suspense and gooseflesh with equal calculation: 'But gradually the terror grew on us, as time by time we heard of it nearer and nearer. It was in France, it was in Germany, it was in *England,* and (with wild affright) we began to hear a whisper pass [:] *"It was in Ireland"*'.²⁶

22 Ludlam, *Biography of Dracula*, p. 14. **23** R.F. Foster, *Paddy and Mr Punch: connections in Irish and English history* (London, 1993), p. 220. **24** Ludlam, *Biography of Dracula* , p. 14. **25** Mrs C.M.B. (Thornley) Stoker, 'Experience of the cholera in Ireland' (typewritten manuscript; 6 May 1873, Caen, France), p. 1. Stoker family papers, Trinity College Dublin Library Manuscripts Department. **26** Ibid., p.

Sligo was one of the worst-afflicted areas. Charlotte's later reading of Poe's ruminations on live burial would no doubt have triggered memories of a specific victim: 'One I vividly remember, a poor traveller was taken ill on the roadside, some miles from the town, and how did those Samaratines tend him', she recalled. 'They dug a pit and with long poles pushed him living into it and covered him up alive. But God's hand is not to be thus stayed and severely like Sodom did our city pay for such crimes'.[27] In total, five-eighths of Sligo's citizens would perish.

Premature burial, or its threat, especially haunted her. She recollected two instances of souls who narrowly escaped the fate. One was a woman whose husband recognized her red neckerchief; she had already been piled over with corpses awaiting a mass grave. Another was a man who awoke from a deathlike stupor only when undertakers attempted to break his legs to fit an undersized coffin. 'One house would be attacked and the next spared', she wrote. 'There was no telling who would go next, and when one said "good-bye" to a friend, he said it as if forever.'[28] This was vividly demonstrated when a family the Thornleys visited one night were dead – and buried – the following morning. She remembered throwing a jug of water on a persistent coffin maker who would not stop banging at the door.

Death by cholera is especially hideous, beginning with fever and cramping, blue and puckered lips, then uncontrollable and fatal diarrhoea. The disease was all the more frightening because the exact means of transmission – contaminated drinking water – was then unknown, and would remain unknown until the 1850s. In 1832, censers of burning tar and other substances were employed, much as they were during medieval plagues, in a desperate attempt to purify the air. Plates of salt poured over with vitriolic acid were laid outside windows and doors.

All the Thornleys, including Charlotte, took a daily morning dose of ginger-thickened whiskey, and she believed the nostrum was largely responsible for her family's survival. Without this desperate, home-mixed concoction, 'no one moved a yard'.[29] The Jesuit priest Theobald Mathew of Cork, later one of the great figures of the nineteenth-century temperance movement, had nothing to offer the sick and dying but Irish whiskey.[30] Elsewhere, opium was liberally used. Those tending to the sick inexorably sickened themselves. 'The nurses died one after another', Charlotte wrote, 'and none could be found to fill their places but women of the worst description, who were always more than half drunk …'[31] The constant sound of bells attached to the cots of the dying and the carts conveying the dead would never leave Charlotte's memory. At the height of the epidemic the entire Thornley family fled Sligo and narrowly escaped death, not from the disease, but from the wrath of a mob outside of Donegal who dragged them from

---

2. See Chapter 6 of this collection for more about Stoker and the cholera epidemic of the 1830s. **27** Ibid. **28** Ibid. **29** Ibid., p. 8. **30** John F. Quinn, *Father Mathews' crusade* (Cambridge, MA, 2002), p. 45. **31** (Thornley) Stoker, 'Experience of the cholera in Ireland', p. 3.

their carriage, determined to '*burn the cholera people*'[32] in a fiery exorcism atop their own luggage.

In 1971, Tom Stoker's great-grandson Daniel Farson, a colourful London journalist and television personality, approached, or was approached by, Hammer Films, the British studio which had already produced seven *Dracula*-inspired movies, and was now interested in developing a biographical drama based on Stoker's life. Farson shared some additional family lore regarding Charlotte's cholera ordeal, omitted from her written account, but vividly recalled by Farson's own grandmother – that 'on one of the last, desperate days' of the epidemic, the Thornley family was under siege by a zombie-like hoard of cholera victims, and Charlotte was forced to take extreme measures.[33] Hammer screenwriter Don Houghton wrote a treatment involving young Bram directly in the trauma by moving the action to a fictional cholera epidemic of the 1850s in which Charlotte is already a mother, fiercely protecting her son. The climactic scene that strikingly anticipated the house-under-siege motif of countless modern horror films:

> A MAN, his face yellow, drawn and ghastly … his teeth bared in fury, appears at the window, forced forward by the mob behind him. In terrible detail the child sees the horror of what happens next. The MAN thrusts his arm through the glass to tear at the boards barring the window. The arm, white with disease, gropes into the room, like an ugly tentacle, wavering like a monstrous worm.
>
> On the table in front of CHARLOTTE there is a knife. In a fit of angry panic, she takes hold of it. The child screams as she hacks at the arm. Blood spatters over her. The fingers tear at her fingers as she continues to slash at it.[34]

In what Houghton calls 'the final, terrible picture', Bram backs away screaming from the squirming, severed arm that has fallen to the floor and his mother rushes to comfort him. But it does no good, for 'her clothes are red with gore … she is like a spectre of death …'[35]

Farson's grandmother put an axe in Charlotte's hand in place of a knife, and it's a bit surprising that Houghton chose to pull the extra visual punch. It would have been a perfect Hammer moment. But for all of its melodramatic excess, the never-filmed scene underscores a certain psychological truth. Young children can be acutely attuned to parental anxiety, with lasting emotional effect. And, in a fact previously overlooked by Stoker biographers, Bram Stoker's early bonding with his mother did take place during a cholera epidemic, one even more deadly than the

---

[32] Ibid., p. 11 (emphasis Charlotte Stoker's). [33] Daniel Farson, *The man who wrote* Dracula (New York, 1975), p. 15. [34] Don Houghton, screenplay treatment for *Victim of his imagination* (January 1972), p. 28. MS courtesy of Wayne Kinsey. [35] Ibid., p. 29.

1832 plague, reaching Dublin during the winter of 1847–8. Only days before Bram's birth, she could have read an ominous account in the *Dublin Evening News* headlined 'CHOLERA MORBUS'. The correspondent in Malta described the spread of 'this scourge of mankind' from the Black Sea, and warned that 'experience has proved the utter inutility of resorting to quarantine …'[36] More than 35,000 Irish would perish, a death toll exacerbated in a population already weakened by hunger and fever.

It is surely somehow significant that Stoker's seven-year illness coincided almost exactly with the worst years and immediate aftermath of the Great Famine, Ireland's towering trauma in a notoriously tumultuous history. Bram Stoker's birth year became known as 'Black '47', with the total failure of the potato crop. By the mid-nineteenth century, Ireland's predominantly Catholic population of rural tenant farmers had become almost totally dependent on the potato for subsistence.[37]

Scientific plant breeding was then unknown, and the tubers had no immunity against a virulent fungus, *Phytophthora infestans*, that had crossed the ocean from North America on steamships. For all that was understood about fungal life in 1847, the organism might as well have been supernatural in origin. It was believed that funguses were – impossibly – a living by-product of organic decomposition, a concept with roots in medieval alchemy (the idea, for instance, that flies were directly generated by rotting meat). The mechanisms of fungal parasitism amount to a kind of vegetable vampirism: tell-tale surface marks, easily overlooked, yield quickly to a fatal corruption. By modern consensus, a million Irish perished, most not from hunger but from diseases attacking the weakened and malnourished.[38] Over and over, those who were spared starvation would hear harrowing stories of death, and living death. In the countryside, shallow mass graves were rifled by scavenging animals. In Dublin, a few months before Stoker's birth, Cork Street Hospital was forced to close its doors against new victims.

Bram Stoker's childhood would have been filled with oral accounts of horrors attending the Famine. Most poignant and tragic were the now-legendary tales of the 'coffin ships', which carried typhus and cholera along with desperate immigrants headed for North America. Many never arrived alive; as many as 6,000 refugees were interred in one mass grave at a St Lawrence River quarantine station. Bram undoubtedly heard these stories, told and embellished like folk tales, and later could have read published first-person accounts of doomed passengers like Gerald Keegan and his new bride, Aileen, written in 1847:

> [30 April] The fever spreads and to the other horrors of the steerage is added cries of those in delirium. While coming from the galley this after-

---

36 *Dublin Evening Mail*, 6 November 1847. **37** For a comprehensive review of the potato's central role in the famine, see Cormac Ó Gráda, *Black '47 and beyond: the great Irish famine* (Princeton, NJ, 1999), especially pp 13–23. **38** R.F. Foster, *Modern Ireland: 1600–1972* (London, 1988), pp 324–5.

noon, with a pan of stirabout for some sick children, a man suddenly sprang upward from the hatchway, rushed to the bulwark, his white hair streaming in the wind, and without a moment's hesitation, leaped into the seething waters. He disappeared beneath them at once.

[13 May] ... I saw a shapeless heap move past our ship on the outgoing tide. Presently there was another and another. Craning my head over the bulwark I watched. Another came, it caught in one cable, and before the swish of the current washed it clear, I had caught a glimpse of a white face. I understood it all. The ship ahead of us had emigrants and they were throwing overboard their dead.[39]

Aileen lasted only a few days in quarantine, Gerald only six weeks. His heartbreaking journal, preserved by Keegan's uncle, was finally published in 1895 as 'The summer of sorrow'. Stoker may or may not have read it, but in any event would have known the basic story by heart from childhood. Two years later he would incorporate the log of a doomed ship into *Dracula*, in which a literal 'coffin ship' would return to British shores, haunted not by famine plague but by a spectral figure embodying both terrible hunger and pestilential dread.[40]

Outright starvation did not impact the city the way it did the countryside, but concurrent epidemics knew no geographic boundaries. A concern about unwholesome waterfront air and row-house crowding may have been the reason Charlotte and Abraham chose to move further inland, although simple financial pressure or the need for larger quarters may also have played a role. In any event, around the time of Thomas Stoker's birth in 1849, the family relocated about a mile-and-a-half northeast to Killester, and after the birth of Richard Stoker in 1851, to Artane Lodge in nearby Donnycarney. Virtually nothing is known of the Killester address, save for its entry on baptismal records, but Artane Lodge was a residential villa (in the sense of a freestanding house) set on an open parkland that is now the Clontarf Golf Club. If nothing else, the location certainly met the Victorian standards for healthy air. Abraham's father had roots in the area, and family connections may well have facilitated the move. Whether it was for Bram's immediate benefit or not, his childhood incapacitation persisted in three separate homes.

In the end, Bram never contracted cholera, or famine fever, or any other disease or condition (such as a spinal injury) that might medically account for his inability to walk. Rheumatic fever would have weakened his heart, making his later exemplary health and athleticism problematic at best. Asthma would have

---

39 Gerald Keegan, 'The summer of sorrow' in Robert Sellar's *Gleaner tales* (Huntington, Quebec, 1895). Quoted in Peter Beresford Ellis, *Eyewitness to Irish history* (Hoboken, NJ, 2004), pp 175–6. **40** The image of the vampire as a plague-spreader was not used by Stoker in *Dracula*, but would be central to F.W. Murnau's unauthorized adaptation, *Nosferatu* (1922), today regarded as a German expressionist classic and one of the most viscerally effective film versions.

created breathing problems, not immobility. Psychological or psychosomatic conditions, therefore, might offer more fertile ground for sleuthing. Since vampires circle endlessly around any attempt to uncover Stoker secrets, the phenomenon of paralyzing nightmares, long posited as the source of incubus legends, immediately comes to mind. These often manifest in children, are believed to have their roots in developmental biology, and usually disappear as the child matures.[41] Autohypnosis and forms of deep meditation can freeze the mind and body, but where does a Victorian toddler pick up the techniques? Nonetheless, we know (maddeningly) that Stoker had a lifelong interest in mesmerism and hypnosis, but little else. And somewhere in the vast spectrum of twilight consciousness called hypnagogia, there might well be the key to understanding strange states of suspended animation, but the esoteric subject is nearly as slippery and daunting as the comprehension of consciousness itself.

Sigmund Freud famously cured patients of what used to be called 'hysterical paralysis', a condition formally called conversion disorder, in which neurological symptoms such as motor weakness, muscle spasms, aphasia or even blindness manifest, all in the absence of physical disease. With Josef Breuer, Freud published *Studies on hysteria* in 1895 – the book introduced the concept of 'the unconscious' as a distinct substratum of the mind, and posited the 'talking cure' which could relieve such symptoms by bringing buried conflict or trauma to conscious examination. Although Freud's hysteria studies focused almost exclusively on women, conversion disorders now are recognized in men, but very uncommonly in young children of either sex. They are believed most often to occur in response to strict family or institutional structures in which normal emotional expression is repressed, or dysfunctional interactions denied.[42]

The idea that Bram Stoker's paralysis might have been the result of childhood sexual abuse or incest has been summoned up by a number of commentators, often achieving a near-parody of armchair psychologizing. Certainly, the argument goes, a forced glimpse of his mother menstruating would have triggered the archetypal image of the *vagina dentata* – and neatly explain his later, literary evocation of the engulfing/penetrating vampire's mouth, dripping with blood. Alternately/concurrently, could paralysis be a defence reaction to murderous Oedipal rage directed at his brothers or his father?[43]

---

[41] Patrick McNamara, *Nightmares: the science and solution of those frightening visions during sleep* (Westport, CT, 2008), p. 8. For a compete examination of the various states of consciousness between waking and sleep, see Andreas Mavromatis, *Hypnagogia* (New York, 1991). [42] For detailed discussions of conversion disorder, see American Psychological Association, *Diagnostic and statistical manual of mental disorders* (Washington, DC, 1980), pp 452–7, and W. Edward Craigshead and Charles B. Nemeroff (eds), *Corsini encyclopædia of psychology and behavioral science* (New York, 2001). [43] Maurice Richardson's insightful (and sometimes slightly tongue-in-cheek) essay 'The psychoanalysis of ghost stories' (*Twentieth Century*, 166:994 (December 1959), 419–31), included the first Freudian assessment of Stoker's novel. Stoker himself was the subject of Joseph A. Bierman's highly speculative '*Dracula*: prolonged childhood illness and the oral triad',

The attraction of Freudian theories for Stoker psychobiographers is understandable; many of the twentieth-century stage and film adaptations of *Dracula* were quite consciously moulded around Freud's ideas, but the approach can be anachronistic and off-target if one's goal is to understand the Victorian world as it understood itself. Nonetheless – ideas about menstrual exhibitionism in Victorian homes aside – much of Freud's work rests on undeniable truths. For instance, it is simple fact, not psychosexual theory, that a child first experiences his mother as food, is vulnerable to adult harm, that for centuries children have been cruelly exploited and abused, and initiated into the adult world through frightening stories of infanticide and cannibalism. A child's first smile, it should be remembered, is an automatic reflex, a survival mechanism to reinforce parental care and feeding. Parenthood in the best of circumstances is stressful, and young children can be preternaturally attuned to parental anxiety. In the case of Bram Stoker and his mother, their early bonding was clearly fraught with fearful emotions, the potential of devastating disease, and the common reality of infant mortality. The Terrible Mother can also be a Terrified Mother, and it's not surprising that a primal, interdependent gestalt of terror might thus be created.

A universal childhood custom in Ireland and throughout Western Europe was the practice of dressing both girls and boys in female attire until approximately the age of seven. The practice continued far beyond any practical utility – for instance, in toilet training. Maintaining boys in a sexually undifferentiated – or aggressively feminized – state until 'breeching' into shorts or trousers was a curious and still remarkably underexplored historical custom, especially given the enormous academic cachet of gender studies in recent decades. Laurence Sterne, in *The life and opinions of Tristram Shandy, gentleman* (1759–1767), treated the subject humorously, as a kind of tug of war between husband and wife, each rationalizing his or her own reticence in finally dealing realistically with their child's sex. 'We defer it, my dear,' Tristram quotes his father, 'shamefully.' They both try to convince themselves that the boy looks just fine dressed as he is. And might not male clothing be 'aukward'? 'When he gets these breeches made,' the father frets, 'he'll look like a beast in 'em.'[44]

Nonetheless, the breeching ritual marked the transference of a child from the mother's ethereal domestic realm to the father's beastly, worldly domain. Some mothers took proactive steps to delay this fall from grace. Not a few Victorian boyhood photographs depict shoulder-length ringlet curls and petticoats under the skirts. Whatever her conscious motivation, many a Victorian mother succeeded admirably in tricking out her darling son like date bait for Lewis Carroll.

American Imago (Summer 1972), 186–98. Daniel Lapin's *Dracula, vampires, and incest* (San Francisco, 1995) stops short of diagnosing Stoker as a victim of sexual abuse, but finds vampire metaphors everywhere in case histories of incest survivors. **44** Laurence Sterne, *The life and opinions of Tristram Shandy, gentleman*, ed. Melvyn New and Joan New (New York, 1978), pp 362–3.

Oscar Wilde, Stoker's contemporary in Dublin, later his romantic rival and a lifelong acquaintance, is a case in point. A tinted daguerreotype of Oscar at the age of two shows him dressed in an ornate, off-the-shoulder royal-blue frock, his cascading hair artificially curled. One acquaintance, especially catty, published a memoir after the death of both mother and son, maintaining that Lady Wilde, desperate for a daughter, kept Oscar in female dress until the age of ten, turning him, for all practical purposes, into 'a neurotic woman'.[45]

One Wilde family chronicler found a justification for cross-dressing in Irish folklore: he reported that in parts of rural Ireland boys were traditionally disguised as girls to protect them from being spirited off by the fairies, 'for of course, the fairies are only interested in little boys'.[46] It is intriguing that the first recorded use of the word 'fairy' as a homosexual slur occurred in 1895, the same year as Wilde's notorious trial for 'gross indecency with male persons'. In the two decades following Wilde's downfall, hundreds of years of tradition were overthrown as parents became far more vigilant for any sign of effeminacy in their sons. The practice of dressing young boys in skirts all but ended around the First World War, except for the yet-enduring custom of christening gowns.

But what does a boy think about, immobilized for years as a kind of female doll in a world coming apart at the seams? 'I was naturally thoughtful and the leisure of long illness gave opportunity for many thoughts which were fruitful according to their kind', Stoker tells us, which isn't much.[47] A healthy child would be expected to engage in normal play, but in Stoker's case he would have been a helplessly passive observer of normally abled children and adults, all of them costumed as female except his father. Among the imaginative fruits of Bram Stoker's peculiar early years may have been a lifelong fascination with gender instability and ambiguity. Indeed, near the end of his life he would devote a large section of *Famous imposters* (1910) to the theory that the 'virgin' Queen Elizabeth could have been a man, deliberately raised all her life as a girl in an elaborate plot to secure the throne – an extraordinary gambit, even by the conspiracy standards of the Tudors. Modern critical studies of *Dracula* have been dominated by psychosexual investigations into the book's multiplicity of gender transgressions that all bubble over into horror: 'new women', mannishly assertive, send the male characters into stereotypically 'female' hysterics while the title character, supernaturally frozen in an erotic limbo, absorbs and mingles transfused male fluids sucked from female veins.[48] In his fourth-to-last novel, *The man* (1905), a man obsessed with having a son tells his dying wife that the daughter she has just delivered is a boy, whom they name Stephen. The father thereafter experiences 'a certain resentment of her sex'.

45 Joy Melville, *Mother of Oscar: the life of Jane Francesca Wilde* (London, 1994), p. 79. **46** T.G. Wilson, *Victorian doctor: being the life of Sir William Wilde* (New York, 1946), p. 324. **47** Stoker, *Personal reminiscences*, p. 31. **48** See especially Christopher Craft, 'Kiss me with those red lips: a gender and inversion in Dracula', *Representations*, 8 (Fall 1984), 107–33. Excerpted at length in *Dracula*, pp 444–62.

But he never, not then nor afterwards, quite lost the old belief that Stephen was indeed a son. [...] This belief tinged all his after-life and moulded his policy with regard to his girl's upbringing. If she was to be indeed his son as well as his daughter, she must from the first be accustomed to boyish as well as to girlish ways. This, in that she was an only child, was not a difficult matter to accomplish.[49]

Charlotte's forceful personality also raises questions about her own influence on Bram's early perception of sex roles, and who, exactly, wore the trousers in the Stoker household. Although the word 'mannish' is not used in any family reference, it is clear that Charlotte was not a typical Victorian mother, was outspoken on public issues in a manner more typical of men, and had a domineering influence in her family. Nearly two decades younger and more vigorous than her spouse, Charlotte is described by Stoker editor and critic Clive Leatherdale as 'a handsome, strong minded woman who, if she could see no ambition in her husband, was determined to invest it in her sons'.[50] Abraham Stoker would be warmly remembered by family members, but not for a forceful personality or rising career achievements. The first of his family to break above the artisan class (his father, William, was a corset manufacturer), Abraham settled into decades of career complacency as a junior clerk at Dublin Castle between 1815 and 1837, when he finally became an assistant clerk, and only applied for the position of senior clerk in 1853, twelve years before his retirement. This final advancement came amid the pressures of a growing family and the births of their final three children. Certainly, Charlotte would have shared in her husband's decision, if not demanded it. According to Daniel Farson, his grandmother Enid (married to Thomas Stoker in 1891), 'was not a fanciful woman and told me that the family were in awe of Charlotte if not actually afraid of her. When one of the boys failed to come in first in an examination, Charlotte did not conceal her resentment, even though he came second out of a thousand.'[51] Charlotte's identification with male striving is further evidenced by the opinion of her grandniece Ann Dobbs that she 'didn't care a tuppence' about her own daughters' schooling[52] and her own published opinion that, to be honest, female education was mostly a practical matter of 'matrimonial speculation'.[53]

Above all, Charlotte believed passionately in the power and importance of language and literacy. A man's mind without language, she wrote, 'is a perfect blank; he recognizes no will but his own natural impulses; he is alone in the midst of his

---

49 Bram Stoker, *The man* (London, 2010), p. 17. **50** Clive Leatherdale, *Dracula: the novel and the legend* (Brighton, 1985), p. 57. **51** Farson, *The man who wrote Dracula*, p. 13. **52** Paul Murray, *From the shadow of Dracula: a life of Bram Stoker* (London, 2004), p.14. **53** Charlotte M.B. Stoker, 'On female emigration from workhouses' (printer's proof of pamphlet; Dublin, 1864), p. 9. Stoker family papers, Trinity College Dublin Library, Department of Manuscripts.

fellow-men; an outcast from society and its pleasures; a man in outward appearance, in reality reduced to the level of brute creation'.[54] Words, to Charlotte, were an essential component of Christian salvation. Take, for instance, deaf mutes (their education became one of her favourite causes), who, through their affliction, could have 'no idea of a God'.[55]

Fully half of Ireland was illiterate in the mid-nineteenth century. The Famine spurred a huge interest in the teaching of reading, which was increasingly understood as a necessity for non-agrarian employment and emigration. Outside the cities, children often learned to read under the charitable auspices of church-run 'hedge schools', so called because many classes were conducted outdoors, or in barns. In urban areas, paid tutors found themselves in high demand. A parent like Charlotte, with a keen interest in education, may well have taken on the responsibility herself.

There are few activities better suited to engaging the attention of an invalid child than reading, and it is safe to assume that Bram Stoker's early years were occupied by storytelling to a greater degree than those of his normally active siblings. Abraham Stoker proudly collected books, and all manner of reading material would have been at the disposal of Charlotte, or the nurse. The Bible, of course, was the central book in a devout Protestant home, though its vocabulary and diction would present difficulties for children of three and four; Bram was not presented with a personal copy until the age of ten. Illustrated chapbooks of all descriptions supplemented the standard textbooks, in school and out. According to William Butler Yeats, it was a rare Irish household that lacked chapbooks of fairy tales: 'They are to be found brown with turf smoke on cottage shelves and are, or were, sold on every hand by the peddlers, but cannot be found in any library …'[56] Among the most popular titles were *The royal fairy tales*, *The Hibernian tales*, and *The legends of the fairies*. By the time of Stoker's birth, most of the classic German and French fairy tales were readily available in English. Charles Perrault's *Tales of Mother Goose*, including 'Little red riding hood', 'The sleeping beauty', 'Puss in boots', 'Cinderella', and 'Bluebeard' had been in translation since 1697. 'Beauty and the beast' by Jeanne-Marie Le Prince de Beaumont appeared in English almost immediately after its French publication in 1756. Edgar Taylor had first translated the Brothers Grimm as *German popular stories* in 1823; Edwin Lane brought *The Arabian nights* to English-speaking shores in 1840; Mary Smith translated Hans Christian Andersen's *Wonderful stories for children* in 1846.

A strong current in contemporary fairy tale criticism argues that the oral versions of the classic stories were imbued with a rebellious proletariat spirit that was essentially hijacked and subverted by the bourgeoisie, the published versions repur-

---

54 Charlotte M.B. Stoker, 'On the necessity of a state provision for the education of the deaf and dumb of Ireland', *Journal of the Statistical and Social Inquiry Society of Ireland* (December 1863), 456. 55 Ibid. 56 W.B. Yeats (ed.), *Fairy and folk tales of the Irish peasantry* (London, 1888), p. 7.

posed for the indoctrination of middle-class children with a materialistic work ethic and respect for established authority.⁵⁷ The former may or may not be true, but the latter certainly would be in keeping with Charlotte Stoker's family values. The Irish folktales she shared with her children were less crafted, but often conveyed messages about miscreants and moral retribution. Irish tales don't feature vampires in the sense that Bram Stoker would later depict them, but they are replete with accounts of the returning dead (usually walking corpses encountered on churchyard roads), and the succubus-like *Leanan-sídhe*, whose draining charms prove fatal to poets who embrace her as a muse. More straightforward vampires available to young Bram included Perrault's 'Hop o' my thumb and the seven-league boots' with its evocative description of an ogre's children: 'They were yet young, and were of a fair and pleasing complexion, though they devoured human flesh like their father; but they had little round grey eyes, flat noses, and long sharp teeth set wide from each other. They promised already what they would some day grow to be; for at this early age they would bite little children on purpose to suck their blood.'⁵⁸

It would be indeed surprising if Bram did not encounter Heinrich Hoffmann's *Slovenly Peter* (also known as *Shockheaded Peter*) sometime during his childhood. First published as *Stuwwelpeter* in Leipzig in 1845, and translated anonymously into English roughly at the time of Bram Stoker's birth, the book was one of the best-selling children's titles of the late nineteenth century; the German edition alone had no less than 100 printings by the 1870s. Hoffmann's illustrated stories, written in rollicking verse, were intended to impart moral instruction by demonstrating the disastrous consequences of even the smallest misbehaviours. In 'The dreadful story of Pauline and the matches', a girl's fascination with fire leads almost instantly to industrial-strength incineration. The copious tears of 'The crybaby' loosen her eyeballs, which fall from their sockets. One of the most famous tales, 'The story of little Suck-a-Thumb', scares up a spectral tailor to perform a corrective mutilation with giant scissors. Animals and animalism are everywhere, and, perhaps most apropos to a discussion of Stoker, are the characters of Idle Fritz, whose escape from responsibility leads to his being devoured by a wolf, and Oswald, 'The night wanderer', whose repeated nocturnal ramblings transform him, permanently, into a bat: 'Oh! yes, my dears it was too true; / An ugly bat away he flew; / His parents' tears streamed down like rain; / They never saw their child again'.⁵⁹

---

57 The leading exponent of this critical approach is the prolific American folklorist Jack Zipes, especially in *Victorian fairy tales: the revolt of the fairies and elves* (New York, 1987). 58 George Cruikshank, *The Cruikshank fairy-book* (New York and London, 1897), p. 211. In this reprint compilation of his famous temperance-tract revisions of classic fairy tales (*The Cruikshank Fairy Library*, 1853–4), the writer and caricaturist follows his own sanitized version of Perrault with an afterword to parents, and takes Charles Dickens to task for championing the stories in their original, unexpurgated form: 'I would like to ask of this *peculiarity* of the young Ogres – "*Biting little children on purpose to suck their blood*", is any part of the "many such good things" to "have been first nourished in a child's heart"' (p. 212). 59 Heinrich Hoffman,

The titular Slovenly Peter was a feral-looking child with wild, matted hair and curling fingernails. He had no real story of his own; Hoffmann presented him as mostly an image and object lesson, an unforgettable distillation of the book's cautionary crusade. Victorians were already obsessed with the idea of progress as both a religious and secular ideal, and Hoffmann's supreme wild child emblemized the frightening flipside of progress: social, moral, and physical backsliding. The publication of Charles Darwin's *The origin of species* in 1859, and the monumental controversies that followed, would fuel an ever-growing preoccupation with atavism and what would come to be known as 'degeneration', a pseudoscientific catch-all term that wormed its way into every nook and cranny of late Victorian social, political, economic discourse, and is one of the most frequently discussed themes of *Dracula* today.[60] Darwin himself made no case whatsoever for reverse evolution, but no matter – the public's assimilation of evolutionary theory was a process of freewheeling osmosis, fuelled by the pervasive rhythms of repeated cultural metaphor, a dynamic closer to the mechanics of folklore than to the workings of science. To a large segment of the public, Darwin's theories had the fearful, fantastical appeal of fairy tales, complete with anthropomorphic animals and magical transformations.

For Victorian children, for the most part untroubled by Darwinian thoughts, fairy tales were only a prelude to a much more exciting experience: the annual Christmas-season pantomime, a theatrical spectacular enjoyed by young and old alike, but intended for the child in everyone. The Christmas 'panto' was in no way a religious event, didn't utilize even secular Christmas themes, but it did coincide with the holiday calendar and usually ran well into January. Producers typically found the event to be their most profitable attraction of the year. Bram's father was a stage aficionado, and would have taken pleasure in introducing his children to the yearly extravaganza at Dublin's Theatre Royal, an impressive venue with technical capabilities matching those of any stage in London.

Pantomimes had many antecedents in the theatre, most notably medieval morality plays and the *commedia dell arte*. From the morality plays came characters and stories depicting clear conflicts between Good and Evil. Malign characters – often including a Demon King – entered from the sinister stage left, and personifications of goodness from the right. A production often credited as the first recognizable English pantomime was *Harlequin Dr Faustus*, produced at Sadler Wells in 1723. In place of Bible stories were plots borrowed (sometimes very loosely) from classic fairy tales and *The Arabian nights*. From 1855 to 1864, the years between Bram's first steps and his enrolment at Trinity College, the pantomime offerings at the Theatre Royal on Harcourt Street included *Bluebeard*

Struwwelpeter: fearful stories and vile pictures to instruct good little folk (Venice, CA, 1999), p. 62. **60** For an excellent survey of degeneration theory, including a full discussion of Stoker, see Daniel Pick, *Faces of degeneration: a European disorder, c.1848–1918* (Cambridge, 1989).

(with its themes of female bloodletting, forbidden rooms and castle imprisonment), *Little Bopeep, Babes in the woods, Sleeping beauty, King of the castle, Jack the giant killer, Aladdin, Cinderella, Puss in boots* and *The house that Jack built*.[61]

One aspect of panto that may have especially resonated for a boy who had just spent years languishing helplessly in female clothing was the centrality of cross-dressing to the whole event. The tradition is usually attributed to the great London clown Joseph Grimaldi, who around 1800 introduced the travesty 'Dame' character in holiday shows at Sadler Wells and Drury Lane. To these rotund, farcical matrons he gave names like Queen Rondabelly and Dame Cecily Suet. One of the most enduring was (and remains) the Widow Twanky, a working-class laundress with a healthy disrespect for authority. The dames provided (and still provide) slapstick fun as the mothers of young male heroes – Jack the Giant Killer, Dick Whittington or Aladdin – usually played by actresses whose tights displayed more leg than would ever have been tolerated in a straight female role. These theatrical precursors of Peter Pan (not portrayed on stage until 1904, but thereafter almost always by a woman) provided dependable and provocative eye candy for adult men in attendance, be they seasoned theatre devotees like Abraham Stoker, or merely seasonal chaperones.

'Going to its first pantomime is the greatest event in the life of a child', Stoker wrote. 'It is to it a great awakening from a long dream. All the rest of life must have been nothing but one continued sleeping vision, and this is the real world in which the dawning imagination has sought and found a home to suit itself'.[62] Stoker's initiation into the world of the theatre was liberating and life-altering, coinciding with his metamorphosis from a sleeping fairy princess to a real live boy. Appropriately, the highlight of each pantomime was the 'transformation scene', in which the main characters would shed their identities and assume the personae of a traditional harlequinade, accompanied by spectacular stage effects, and in time the figures Harlequin and Columbine gave way to other displays of metamorphosis. The 'real world' Stoker discovered in the theatre was an imaginative realm of illusion; concealed, revealed, and transformed identities; strange creatures and humanized animals; a dreamy, gaslit refuge from grim realities of mid-century Dublin, and an escape from his strange affliction.

However much Stoker identified with the exuberant, shape-shifting freedom of the pantomime characters, the abject changeling of Irish legend may shed better light – or at least some illuminating dream-logic – on the enduring mystery of his illness. The special image of a child stolen by supernatural forces would remain with him for the rest of his life, to be powerfully resurrected in the image of a desperate peasant mother pounding on the door of a vampire's castle, crying

---

61 R.M. Lowry and J. O'Rorke, 'List of pantomimes from 1820', *Annals of the Theatre Royal, Dublin* (Dublin, 1880), pp 69–71. **62** Bram Stoker, 'Theatre Royal – the pantomime – juvenile nights' (unsigned review), *Dublin Evening Mail*, 10 January 1872.

'Monster! Give me my child!' Stripped of mythopoetics, changeling stories provide a filtered record of the plight and fate of sick and disabled children, and the psychological pressures thrust upon parents faced with incomprehensible childhood maladies. With no other remedies at hand, many turned to drugs.

Could Bram's paralysis have been opium-induced? The possibility is not as outlandish as it might first sound. In the mid-1800s, the administration of alcohol and opium to children, even infants, as a cure-all and prevent-all, was frighteningly common. The homespun whiskey concoctions of the Thornley family during the 1832 cholera plague had, by the 1840s, been replaced by such popular commercial preparations as 'Godfrey's Cordial', 'Infant's Preservative', and 'Mrs Wilkinson's Soothing Syrup'. Infants wasting away from 'poppy tea' and other opium preparations 'shrank up into little old men', or became 'wizened like little monkeys',[63] descriptions that could be taken almost verbatim from Irish folktale descriptions of replacement children left by the fairies, typically described as ancient, withered things. More often than not, changeling tales end sadly, as in the master Irish fantasist J. Sheridan Le Fanu's wistful story 'The child that went with the fairies' (1870). But occasionally the missing child is returned, through the cleverness of mortals or by the whim of the fairies.

Faced with the confounding and irrational nature of Stoker's childhood illness, it might be better to look for a more satisfying explanation in a realm beyond the rational. The number seven has age-old associations with luck, magic and the uncanny. The seventh son of a seventh son was believed to have occult powers. Seven-league boots were similarly enchanted. Stoker himself used the numeral in an early story, 'How 7 went mad' (1881), and used it again in the title of one of his later novels, *The jewel of seven stars* (1903).

Perhaps, in their strange wisdom, the fairies simply removed the sickly Stoker changeling from his mother's frightened charge, and replaced him after seven magical years with the fine strapping boy who would grow up to write *Dracula*.*

---

63 Anthony S. Wohl, *Endangered lives: public health in Victorian Britain* (Cambridge, MA, 1983), pp 34–5.
*Adapted from the author's forthcoming book, *Bram Stoker: the final curtain*. Copyright © 2013 by David J. Skal. All rights reserved.

Bram Stoker: the facts and the fictions

PAUL MURRAY

Few writers lived as much in the public gaze as Bram Stoker while leaving so incomplete a record of their lives. The universal recognition of *Dracula* (1897) still contrasts with the paucity of profile accorded to its creator. With so little fact, the fictions have thrived. The proliferation of fiction versions of Stoker was brought home to me when I started work on my biography[1] in the mid-1990s. While I had begun researching my previous biography of Lafcadio Hearn[2] through engagement with the primary sources in the first instance, I began my preparation for the Stoker biography – a commission – by studying the extensive body of critical comment that had developed over the preceding decades before tackling the primary sources.

The contrast between the primary materials and the differing biographical and critical approaches to which they gave rise was fascinating. Whereas Hearn, despite not having produced a globally recognized masterpiece such as *Dracula*, had been the subject of a string of substantial biographies,[3] Stoker had at that stage been the subject of just two biographies, both of them fairly short, reflecting the paucity of primary source material on a determinedly secretive subject as well as biographical approaches that were popular rather than thorough.[4] While Hearn had been a prolific letter-writer of the highest calibre, Stoker – his enormous correspondence on behalf of Henry Irving notwithstanding – had left little of a personal nature behind. It is possible to document Hearn's inner life with great exactitude whereas Stoker's remains elusive. Stoker's lifelong interest in codes and secret writing,[5] as well as the ingrained habit of secrecy that would have been a requirement of his long years of service at the heart of the British administration in Dublin Castle, ensured that little of his personal life was passed on to posterity.

---

1 Paul Murray, *From the shadow of Dracula: a life of Bram Stoker* (London, 2004). 2 Paul Murray, *A fantastic journey: the life and literature of Lafcadio Hearn* (London, 1993). 3 See the bibliography in *A fantastic journey*, pp 356–65, for a full listing. 4 Harry Ludlam, *A biography of Dracula, the life story of Bram Stoker* (London, 1962); Daniel Farson, *The man who wrote* Dracula: *a biography of Bram Stoker* (London, 1975). 5 Bram Stoker, *The mystery of the sea* (London, 1902); William Rider, London, 1913, p. 89.

This biographical vacuum was filled by a host of fictions, which took two forms: factual and interpretative. Stoker biography may have been woefully underdeveloped but *Dracula* had attracted a host of interpreters over the years who seem to have been liberated by the absence of the restraint that might have been imposed by a stronger biographical framework. Much of this criticism was written with little or no awareness of the facts of Stoker's life. For example, in possibly the most quoted of all *Dracula* interpretations, Maurice Richardson's claim that the novel 'provides really striking confirmation of the Freudian interpretation' and his description of it 'as a kind of incestuous, necrophilious, oral-anal-sadistic all-in wrestling match'[6] was published in 1959, before any Stoker biography had appeared. When serious critical attention began to be paid to *Dracula* in the early 1970s, Harry Ludlam's incomplete biography was the only one available; Daniel Farson's would not appear until 1975 and a fuller sense of Stoker's life only became available in the 1990s when Barbara Belford's biography was published in 1996 and that of Peter Haining and Peter Tremayne in 1997.[7] Neither Ludlam nor Farson consulted the massive Lyceum Theatre archives in the Brotherton Library at the University of Leeds or the Shakespeare Centre Library at Stratford-upon-Avon, not to mention many other sources of primary material. Later biographers did not access relevant material in, for example, the National Archives of Ireland and Trinity College Dublin.

A major drawback of Stoker biography is that the first, Harry Ludlam's, did not appear until fifty years after his death and, by the time that attempts were made at more scientific biography, those who would have had first-hand knowledge of the subject were dead and we are left with a vacuum that looks unlikely ever to be properly filled. Ludlam might perhaps have had an opportunity in the 1950s to interview the younger survivors of the Edwardian generation that would have known Stoker but he relied largely on the family material provided by Bram's son, Noel. By the time more specialist biographers appeared in the 1990s, Bram and his era had receded into history.

Daniel Farson had the advantage of a family connection with his subject: he was Bram's great-nephew and this should have counted for a great deal. However, Noel Stoker reportedly disliked him because of his homosexuality[8] and Ann Stoker, Bram's granddaughter, insisted to me that Farson had got it wrong in quoting her about the alleged failure of Bram's sexual relationship with his wife, Florence, on the grounds that she would not have presumed to know what went on between them.[9] I shall return to this subject later.

---

6 Maurice Richardson, 'The psychoanalysis of ghost stories', *The Twentieth Century*, 166 (December 1959), p. 994. **7** Barbara Belford, *Bram Stoker: a biography of the author of* Dracula (London, 1996); Peter Haining and Peter Tremayne, *The un-dead: the legend of Bram Stoker and Dracula* (London, 1997). **8** Farson was openly homosexual at a time when such candor was more unusual than today, a fact alluded to in the title of his autobiography, *Never a normal man* (London, 1997). **9** Conversation between the author and Ann

Apart from these specific issues inherited from the past, there are considerable difficulties inherent in any approach to Stoker biography. As already noted, his secretiveness and lack of personal correspondence makes reconstruction of his interior life difficult. The biographer therefore has a series of challenges to confront and choices to make, specifically how to:

- present the subject: limit oneself to the facts or construct an imaginary life based on the biographer's intuitive filling out of those available.[10]
- balance literary interpretation/cultural history/historical context with hard biographical fact.
- strike the correct balance between *Dracula* and Stoker's other work.
- allow the reader to appreciate the importance of understanding the formative influence of Stoker's now-vanished nineteenth-century milieu, while at the same time not succumb to modern stereotypical views of the Victorians.
- deal with misconceptions from seemingly authoritative sources such as the exaggerated claim that we know little of Stoker 'beyond the bare outline of his public career and a few hints and whispers of skeletons in his closet'.[11] This is simply not so, and the materials *do* exist for a proper – if not exhaustive – biography, although in fairness to the author of this claim, a good deal of the currently available biographical material had not been discovered or utilized at the time this claim was made.
- deal with assertions that can neither be proved nor disproved. For example, Barbara Belford claims that '*Dracula* is all about [Henry] Irving as the vampire and [Ellen] Terry as the unattainable good woman'.[12] It seems to me, however, that to say that *Dracula* is all 'about' anything is almost meaningless – it is far too complex and the range of influences too vast to be reduced to such a simple formula.
- accept the less attractive side of the subject's character: Stoker *did* emerge from childhood with a morbid streak, representing a personal duality of wholesomeness and violence, the basis of a literary duality evident in – and, indeed, central to – his fiction.[13]
- choose what is most relevant for a biography from the mass of material thrown up by research.

Stoker, 17 February 1998. It should be borne in mind however that Ann Stoker, having been born after Bram's death, was never in a position to observe Florence's interaction with her husband. **10** Barbara Belford's use of her imagination moved Professor Roy Foster to comment that she would have been better off writing a 'frankly speculative novel' about Florence Stoker rather than 'a laborious but unsatisfying biography of her elusive husband'. R.F. Foster, 'A speculative stake in the future', a review of Barbara Belford's biography of Bram Stoker, *The Independent*, 1 June 1996. **11** David Glover, *Vampires, mummies and liberals: Bram Stoker and the politics of popular fiction* (Durham and London, 1996), p. 1. **12** Belford, *Bram Stoker*, p. 106 **13** Paul Murray, 'The primrose path to Dracula', *Diabolique*, 10 (May–June 2012).

- understand the extent to which the available material can shape a biography.
- work within real-world constraints such as deadlines and a publisher's edict that may limit the length of a biography.

BIOGRAPHICAL CHALLENGES/OBLIGATIONS

The biographer also faces a series of more general challenges or obligations, including how to take a mass of often incoherent material and shape it in a way that leaves the reader with the feeling that they have experienced a coherent narrative of the subject's life. A biographer must also consider how to maintain independence and objectivity. In my view, this is best achieved by being a lone wolf: the subject's family, and dedicated societies can be helpful – I could not, for example, have written my biography without the assistance of Stoker's direct descendants, Ann Stoker and her son, Noel Dobbs, in particular – but ultimately a biographer owes a greater debt to the facts than to any other consideration.

The biographer must function as an historian who inherits inverted pyramids of fact and interpretation, to be interrogated/subjected to the test of empirical evidence; above all, the biographer must return to primary sources. One of the most insidious forms of distortion in Stoker biography is the manner in which speculation by one commentator is accepted as fact by another, who then proceeds to develop this 'fact' further, a process which can continue almost indefinitely. For example, in 1978, Penelope Shuttle and Peter Shuttle, in a book, *The wise wound: menstruation and everywoman,* speculated that Florence Stoker, 'frigid as a statue', was likely, because of her 'unsatisfactory sex life', to have had very bad menstrual disturbances, and they then ask: 'Was it some image of these that gave Stoker's subliminal mind the hint that formulated a myth of formidable power, out of the ferocity of a frustrated bleeding woman, crackling with energy and unacknowledged sexuality? It is certainly possible'.[14] There is not a shred of evidence to support this speculation but it quickly became accepted as fact by some, including Fay Weldon, who developed it into an allegation that the reason behind the Stokers' 'unsatisfactory' sex life, and therefore the 'cause' of Florence's supposed 'frigidity', was her husband's closeted homosexuality.[15]

This transformation of speculation into fact presents a challenge to the biographer who must decide how best to handle such existing misinterpretations: does s/he set out to disprove them or just write his/her own narrative? The following are some of the fictitious 'facts' about Stoker that have gained wide currency:

---

[14] Penelope Shuttle and Peter Shuttle, *The wise wound: menstruation and everywoman* (London, 1986), p. 252. [15] Fay Weldon, 'Introduction', *Bram Stoker's* Dracula *omnibus* (London, 1992), p. viii.

- as a young child, he was carried kicking and screaming to hospitals to be traumatized by men in white coats (ludicrous nonsense to anyone with the slightest knowledge of Irish hospitals of that era).[16]
- he enjoyed a life of leisure for six years at Trinity College Dublin (TCD) before graduating in 1870.
- he proposed Oscar Wilde for membership of the TCD Historical Society (the Historical Society records show plainly that Stoker did not do so and the claim that he did misrepresents his relationship with a key contemporary).[17]
- Stoker left Ireland as a young man and never looked back; he had less connection with Ireland than contemporaries such as Oscar Wilde and George Bernard Shaw (the reverse is the case since Stoker not alone spent just under half his life in Ireland but continued to engage with it politically, economically and socially for the rest of his life, to a much greater extent than the other two. He affirmed his Irishness in London, to the poet, Tennyson, for example.[18] Contrary to Belford's claim that Stoker had 'a proper British accent but often put on a Milesian brogue',[19] contemporary sources attest that he never lost his Dublin accent).[20]
- he suffered from a morbid fear of women (how then can his easy, loving relations with some of the most beautiful, accomplished and formidable women of the era, including his wife, Florence Balcombe, and the actresses, Ellen Terry and Genevieve Ward, be explained?).
- he was ruthlessly exploited by Irving and wrote *Dracula* as an act of revenge (the range of extra-curricular activities that Stoker pursued outside the Lyceum would indicate that Irving was, in fact, a fairly indulgent boss).
- *Dracula* is largely a *fin de siècle* product of 1890s, linking Stoker to Oscar Wilde, Aubrey Beardsley and decadence (this approach is an essentially lazy critical substitute for fully examining Stoker's work and, indeed, the era).[21]

Perhaps the most frustrating experience for a biographer is when facts that have been painstakingly established are cavalierly disregarded by subsequent writers on the same subject. I propose now to examine two important examples of biographical facts and fictions – from his early adulthood and the end of his life respectively – to examine this phenomenon.

16 Joseph S. Bierman, '*Dracula*: prolonged childhood illness and the oral triad', *American Imago*, 29 (1972), 186–98; see also Murray, *From the shadow*, p. 25. **17** TCD MSS, Minutes of the College Historical Society, 12 November 1873; see also Murray, *From the shadow*, p. 38. **18** Bram Stoker, *Personal reminiscences of Henry Irving* (London, 1906), i, pp 216, 231. **19** Belford, *Bram Stoker*, p. 99. **20** *The bystander*, 4 October 1905; 'Irishman's diary', *Irish Times*, 16 April 1938. **21** Max Beerbohm, that most acute of contemporary commentators wrote: 'Observe that I write no fool's prattle about *la fin de siecle*'. Quoted in Holbrook Jackson, *The Eighteen Nineties* (London, 1939), p. 18.

EARLY CAREER

Prior to my biography, the received wisdom was that Stoker had spent a leisurely six years studying for his degree at Trinity College Dublin before joining the civil service on graduation in 1870.[22] Belford added a good deal of colour to this narrative. She has Stoker graduating in 1871 and staying on to study for a Master's: 'Only Bram, now twenty-four, was reluctant to grow up; he yearned to be the eternal student, to keep his room with a view,[23] his daydreams, and his college friends'. She also has him taking 'leave of absence' (presumably from Trinity) in 1866 'to work *for a year* [emphasis added] at Dublin Castle as a clerk in the Registrar of Petty Sessions …'[24]

The records of Trinity College Dublin and the civil service – both readily available – which Belford does not appear to have consulted, tell a very different story. Stoker went up to Trinity in 1864 and was a full-time student for two years. He joined the civil service in 1866 and thereafter worked a six-and-a-half day week, under strict regulations, until he left to work for Henry Irving in December 1878. These facts accord with Stoker's own account that he spent thirteen years working in the civil service. It is not surprising that he was unable to maintain his studies at Trinity – he ceases to be listed in the student and examination records from 1866 for the rest of the 1860s, before graduating with a BA in 1870. His BA, which may have owed as much to his high visibility in college life and his familiarity with the academic staff and key members of the Dublin intelligentsia as to any academic achievement,[25] contrasts with his claim of having graduated with 'Honours in Pure Mathematics'.[26] He bought his MA in 1875, without further study, under a system that has continued into the modern era.[27] While any biographer will have sympathy with a predecessor who overlooked some primary material, those who subsequently ignore the import of the new material are more difficult to fathom. To find the old canard of Stoker joining the civil service on graduation in 1870 being recycled years after the record has been set straight is puzzling.[28]

---

22 Haining and Tremayne, *The un-dead*, p. 61. **23** Never having lived in Trinity College, Stoker never had a room with such a view! In the TCD student residence records he is listed as living at 4 Orwell Park, Rathgar from 1864 to the Michaelmas term of 1866; thereafter there are no listings for him: TCD MSS Collection, College Records, V MUN 89 3, Students Residence 1863–74. **24** Belford, *Bram Stoker*, p. 34. **25** Bram is not listed in the TCD examination records for 1869 and 1870, so he does not appear to have sat an examination in either of the two years prior to the award of his degree in 1870: TCD MSS Collection, College Records, V MUN 30 28, 1868/9 and V MUN 30 29, 1869–70. **26** Two TCD students did graduate with honours in mathematics in the spring of 1870 but Bram was not amongst them: *The Dublin university calendar for the year 1871* (Dublin, 1871), p. 123; Abraham Stoker is listed as Pensioner for Bachelor of Arts, 1 March 1870, p. 198; 'Graduates in Honours', 1870 contains no reference to Bram. Two students are listed under 'Senior Moderators', 'Mathematics', Thomas William Foster and Thomas Falkner Fleetwood, but not Stoker. **27** *A catalogue of graduates of the University of Dublin, Vol. II* (Second Edition) (Dublin and London, 1896), p. 235; *The Dublin university calendar for the year 1871* (Dublin, 1871), p. 123; see also Murray, *From the shadow*, p. 33. **28** Elizabeth Miller, 'Afterword', appended to Ian Holt and Dacre Stoker, *Dracula: the un-dead* (London, 2009), p. 391; Andrew Maunder, *Bram Stoker* (Devon, 2006), vii.

The obvious question to be asked is: does this matter? Is it simply nit-picking pedantry to expect those writing on a subject to get the facts right, after they have been clearly established? In this case, the facts *do* matter, in terms of correctly understanding Bram's formative experiences, his values and his literary output, *Dracula* in particular. If we follow Belford's logic Stoker becomes a perennial student who stayed on at Trinity not just until 1871 (she got the year of his graduation wrong – it was in fact 1870) but beyond, to study until 1875 for an MA that, in fact, required no study. In this re-construction of his Dublin years, Stoker only worked for a few years prior to leaving for London in 1878.

That a dreamy, work-shy Stoker would have been engaged by Henry Irving as his Acting Manager at the Lyceum must be open to doubt. The man selected by Irving for this challenging and complex task was actually an experienced administrator who, like himself, had started out as a clerk early in life. Stoker had proved his mettle for ten years in the civil service prior to the creation of the post of Inspector of Petty Sessions in 1876 and the authors of the report recommending its establishment had made clear the requirement for a capable and experienced official:

> The necessity for appointing a competent person to visit the different petty sessions districts, and to inspect the clerk's books and accounts, has been very clearly proved to us ... We propose that the clerk of inspection should rank next to the senior clerk, and that Mr Stoker, who is now head of the junior clerks, should be offered the appointment.[29]

Stoker was a very different individual from the one described by Belford. He was a willing workhorse from the age of eighteen, whose practical dynamism was recognized, not just by the civil service and Irving, but within his own family. It is noteworthy that it was to Bram that his family turned to handle the practical matters arising from his father's death in Italy, rather than his older brother, Thornley. Later he was made executor of his mother-in-law's will. Bram was the ever-dependable go-to man both professionally and privately in a wide range of contexts.

He also came from a more challenging environment than Belford allows and is to be located differently in the social spectrum. Belford has Stoker 'joining the ranks of the educated Protestant ascendancy'[30] when he goes up to Trinity. By contrast, my examination of the Trinity records found that his fellow students were the predominantly middle-class children of doctors, clergymen, merchants, bankers, 'private gentlemen', schoolteachers, farmers, lawyers and manufacturers.[31] Scions of the Protestant Ascendancy, with some rare possible exceptions, they were

---

29 National Archives of Ireland, 'Files of registrar of Petty Sessions Clerks', Report by Herbert Murray and Henry Robinson on the office of Registrar of Fines and Penalties, submitted to the Lord Lieutenant on 18 January 1876; see also Murray, *From the shadow*, p. 46. **30** Belford, *Bram Stoker*, p. 29. **31** TCD MSS Collection, College Records, *MSS V/26/4, Entrance Book, 1858–77*.

THE FACTS AND THE FICTIONS 63

not and no member of the Stoker family, even at the height of their considerable social success, ever belonged to that class. Instead they were part of the urgently upwardly-mobile, emerging middle-class that was displacing the Anglo-Irish aristocracy at the apex of society in nineteenth-century Ireland. Sir Thornley Stoker's position as one of the 'great and the good' in late Victorian/Edwardian Dublin, whose mansion is mentioned in James Joyce's *Ulysses* (1918–22),[32] is reflective of a social revolution that had been taking place over the preceding decades.

The correct location of the Stoker family in the social spectrum of the day was more correctly described by critics such as Chris Morash, David Glover and Roy Foster in the 1990s, with Morash explaining that 'Stoker's family were middle-class civil servants, not landowners' and Glover, who saw Stoker's middle-class Irish Protestant origins providing him with models of respectability *and penury* [emphasis added] that remained with him all his life.[33]

The period of Stoker's lifetime has been described by a leading Irish historian as that of 'the modernization of Irish society'.[34] Stoker, who rejoiced in modernity and its symbols, had no reason to mourn the passing of the Ascendancy, and did not do so: in 1907 he saw 'a strenuous, industrious spirit, spreading its revivifying influence so rapidly over the old country as to be worth more than even historical bitterness and sentimental joys …'.[35] I am among those who see no-nonsense, middle-class, meritocratic values bleeding into Bram's fiction, *Dracula* included. It is not by chance that Mina Harker, bright, sensible, skilled, down-to-earth and middle-class, should not alone survive the attentions of the Count (unlike the feather-brained, aristocratic Lucy) but should play a key role in his location and destruction.

CAUSE OF DEATH

If we jump from the beginning of Bram's adulthood to its end we encounter an even more sensitive topic, the cause of his death at the age of 64 in 1912. His GP, Dr James Browne, a fellow member of the Irish Literary Society and presumably a personal friend, wrote on the death certificate: 'Locomotor Ataxia 6 months, Granular Contracted Kidney. Exhaustion'. Harry Ludlam began a process of selective quotation from the death certificate by means of a clever formula: 'On the death certificate appeared the word "Exhaustion"'.[36] The fact that he omitted locomotor ataxia and granular contracted kidney as the primary causes of death would indicate that

---

32 James Joyce, *Ulysses* (London, 1937), p. 444. 33 Chris Morash, '"Even under some unnatural condition": Bram Stoker and the colonial fantastic' in Brian Cosgrove (ed.), *Literature and the supernatural* (Dublin, 1995), p. 112; Glover, *Vampires, mummies*, p. 9. Also, Roy Foster has commented: 'Bram Stoker was a middle-class Irish Protestant from the professional classes – not, as [Barbara] Belford repeatedly states, "Anglo-Irish"'. Foster, 'A speculative stake in the future'. 34 Joseph Lee, *The modernization of Irish society, 1848–1918* (Dublin, 1973). 35 Bram Stoker, 'The great white fair in Dublin', *The World's Work*, 9:54 (May 1907), 570–6. 36 Farson, *The man*, p. 150.

he was aware of their significance. Given that his biography was written in close collaboration with Bram's son, the question arises as to whether Noel Stoker understood the content of his father's death certificate and the connection of the suppressed wording with syphilis. As Noel was in his thirties when his father died and syphilis was then a common illness,[37] it is hard to believe that he did not understand Dr Browne's formulation. It seems to me that Ludlam began a process of evading Bram's true cause of death that continues into the present. In the context of the social climate in which the Ludlam biography was being prepared and Noel's close relationship with its subject, skirting the issue was entirely understandable; it is less so with contemporary commentators, however laudable their intentions.

The next biographer, Daniel Farson, did not share Ludlam's inhibitions. In his biography, he linked locomotor ataxia with syphilis caught, he believed, from a prostitute in Paris around the turn of the twentieth century. He presented an entirely new image of Bram as a sexual athlete with a reputation for womanizing, partly, at least, as a result of his wife's supposed frigidity. The problem with Farson's uninhibited approach is that it links the facts on the death certificate with a great deal of speculation about Stoker's private life – the basis for which has been denied by its allegedly chief source, Ann Stoker – specifically creating a connection between his final illness and prostitution for which there is no evidence.[38]

Barbara Belford argues against acceptance of syphilis as Stoker's cause of death, although she does say that we shall never know for certain whether he had it or not. She believed that it would have been sufficient for Dr Browne to have listed kidney failure as the cause of death 'but it appears that Browne was thorough and listed all the possibilities'.[39] Belford's sense of Stoker the man – which I am inclined to share – is that 'it is hard to visualize [Stoker] leaving Irving at dawn to pick up a prostitute on the Strand before arriving home for breakfast'.[40] There is no evidence that Stoker did pick up prostitutes on the Strand (which was very close to the Lyceum) or elsewhere, although had he wished to do so, his nocturnal lifestyle allied to the ready availability of prostitutes on the Strand would have made it easier for him than most.[41] It has been claimed that one house in sixty in Victorian London was a brothel, as opposed to a modern ratio of around one in six thousand.[42]

Peter Haining and Peter Tremayne, in *The undead: the legend of Bram Stoker and Dracula,* published shortly after Belford's biography, also investigated the

---

[37] It was estimated was that 13 to 15 per cent of the adult male population of Paris had syphilis at that time. Alfred Fournier, *The treatment of Syphilis* (London/New York, 1906), p. 157. [38] Ann Stoker, interview with Paul Murray, 5 April 1997. [39] Belford, *Bram Stoker*, pp 319–21. [40] Ibid., p. 122. [41] According to one account, prostitutes were rampant in the area: 'On the south side of the Strand they appeared to claim a right of way; two enormous women stood on guard at the entrance to Charing Cross station, and youths were accosted and hustled as they made their way to the trains. Further west, throughout the hours of the day and night, there was a parade in Leicester Square and detachments marched up and down the Haymarket, and towards Piccadilly'. William Pett Ridge, *A story teller: forty years in London* (London, [1923]), p. 180. [42] John Fowles, *The French lieutenant's woman* (London, 1972), p. 231.

syphilis issue in some detail. They engaged the services of a 'retired eminent pathologist', Professor Denis Baron, who consulted medical textbooks from Stoker's era and concluded that the cause of his death was 'syphilis until proven otherwise'. The authors decided on a verdict of '"unproven" in Scottish legal terms'.[43] I assume that what they meant was 'not proven', a form of acquittal that may be used in the Scottish legal system where a judge or jury feels that the evidence does not merit acquittal but is not sufficiently convinced of innocence to bring in a 'not guilty' verdict.

As someone who had been frustrated by the contrast between the caricature that so frequently emerges from critical studies of Stoker and the vital, intelligent and energetic man who emerges from the primary material, I believed that it would be possible to disprove Farson's allegations and set out to do so when preparing my biography. I met Farson before his death but found it impossible to penetrate an entertaining facade sufficiently to get answers to my questions on his Stoker biography. I next consulted three medical experts, two consultant physicians in genito-urinary medicine (Drs Siobhan Murphy and J.D. Oriel) in London and the late Professor J.B. Lyons of the Royal College of Surgeons in Ireland. The latter was both a neurologist and a distinguished author whose work had, among other things, combated the claim by Oscar Wilde's biographer, Richard Ellmann, that Wilde had died of tertiary syphilis.[44] There could be no question, therefore, of Lyons promoting a syphilitic line for sensationalist or other reasons. I was confident that these three experts would finally lay Farson's allegations to rest but, much to my surprise, the opposite transpired.

I summarized the advice of the three experts in my biography:

> In the opinion of the first, Dr Siobhan Murphy, it was unlikely that Dr Browne meant 'Locomotor Ataxia' to refer to anything other than Tabes Dorsalis, a common diseases of the nervous system, almost inevitably connected with syphilis. To the second, Dr J.D. Oriel, 'Granular Contracted Kidney' on the death certificate suggested chronic nephritis, causing scarring and loss of functions of the kidneys, consistent with the previous diagnosis of Bright's disease.[45] He concluded that Stoker died of uraemia from chronic nephritis, the balance of probability being that he also was suffering from syphilis without it being the direct cause of death. The third

---

43 Haining and Tremayne, *The un-dead*, p. 182. 44 J.B. Lyons, 'The death of Oscar Wilde: a post-mortem', *Neuroscience across the centuries* (London, 1989), pp 227–37. Also published in J.B. Lyons, *What did I die of?* (Dublin, 1991). Lyons accepts that Wilde may have had a syphilitic infection but not that he died of tertiary syphilis. 45 There was no actual medical diagnosis of Stoker suffering from Bright's Disease that I am aware of, by Dr Browne or any other doctor, only a presumed claim by Noel Stoker that the 'gout in my grandmother's ancestry in him [Stoker] took the form of Bright's Disease, and [Stoker followed] a long distressing course downhill'. Ann Stoker Collection (now at Trinity College Dublin) [Noel Stoker to Harry Ludlam?], undated, fragment of a MSS assumed to be part of a letter from Noel Stoker to Harry Ludlam.

expert, Professor J.B. Lyons, concluded: ... 'unless we are to impugn the competence of James Browne, MD, the diagnosis of "Locomotor Ataxia" resulting from syphilis must stand'.[46]

Even though I have since been described as a proponent of the syphilis theory, I refrained from comment in my biography as I felt that the three medical experts had provided the reader with the ability to make up his or her own mind. I have since had the opportunity to discuss the issue again with Dr Murphy and she made the point that with diseases such as syphilis or even diabetes, the underlying condition can be masked by a secondary but resultant illnesses. For example, a diabetic may die of kidney disease which will, however, have been caused by the underlying diabetes. It seems to me that, in the absence of records and greater specificity on the death certificate it is difficult, if not impossible, to definitively disentangle the two in Stoker's case. However, I think we need to accept that Browne *was* linking the locomotor ataxia and granular kidney as the cause of death and was describing what he believed to be a syphilitic condition although we do not know the clinical basis on which he did so. There is considerable circumstantial evidence to support Browne's presumed diagnosis. It seemed to me necessary to examine the evidence that exists in the light of the knowledge and assumptions contained in contemporary medical textbooks, assuming that Dr Browne was a good and conscientious doctor who was up-to-date in his knowledge of syphilis and related issues.

I decided to check what contemporary medical textbooks had to say on the subject of granular kidney, as this might give us a clue as to its inclusion by Dr Browne on the death certificate. Sir George Johnson, in his *The pathology of the contracted granular kidney and the associated cardio-arterial changes* (1895), deals with granular kidneys resulting both from Bright's Disease and syphilis.[47] The 1911 *Encyclopædia Britannica* states that Bright's Disease is not just one disease of the kidneys but 'may be dependent on various morbid conditions of these organs'.[48] Other textbooks of the era generally link granular kidney with alcoholism and syphilis as the primary causes. Samuel West, in *Granular kidney and physiological albuminuria* (1900), states: 'The general *post-mortem* frequency of granular kidney ranges from 11.8 to 18 per cent., so that it is a very common condition'.[49] He noted that '... the association between gout and granular kidney is extremely close ... [but] gouty kidneys and granular kidneys are not necessarily the same'.[50] West also states that the 'occurrence of chronic kidney mischief as the result of long-standing gout is well recognized; but in many cases it is quite possible that the opposite relation exists, viz., that the patients are gouty because their kidneys are granular'.[51]

46 Murray, *From the shadow*, pp 268–70. **47** Sir George Johnson, *The pathology of the contracted granular kidney and the associated cardio-arterial changes* (London, 1896), pp 12, 46. **48** *Encyclopædia Britannica*, iv, p. 571. **49** Samuel West, *Granular kidney and physiological albuminuria* (London, 1900), p. 3. **50** Ibid., p. 26. **51** Ibid., p. 119.

If Dr Browne had suspected that Stoker's 'Granular Contracted Kidney' was a result of Bright's Disease or gout, would he not have listed them on the death certificate? Stoker did say that he suffered from gout in 1894,[52] but lightning pains in the legs are common both to it and to the early stages of locomotor ataxia/tabes dorsalis, so it may be that Stoker misunderstood his own condition at the time. W.R. Gowers, in one of the most extended treatments of locomotor ataxia in a late nineteenth-century textbook,[53] has this to say on the relationship of kidney disorders to it: 'Many patients die as an indirect result of the disease. Kidney complications are the most common; they often develop most insidiously and then, as it were, explode'.[54] In the circumstances, taking into account the expert knowledge and assumptions of the era, and in the absence of any mention of other complicating factors by Dr Browne, the most logical explanation of his mention of Stoker's granular kidney was that he was linking it with locomotor ataxia.

Gowers' work is also of interest in the context of the 'six months' that Browne wrote after locomotor ataxia: 'When the disease progresses, the rate of its advance varies much. Sometimes it is slow and uniform, and the ataxy is considerable only at the end of several years. On the other hand it may be rapid, so that in a few months the patient is scarcely able to walk'.[55] In other words, the six months inscribed by Dr Browne are by no means too short for locomotor ataxia to have done its deadly work. On the relationship of locomotor ataxia to syphilis, Gowers has this to say: 'Among the individual causes, one overshadows the rest – the influence of syphilis. A very large proportion of the sufferers have had, at some previous time, constitutional syphilis, either distinct secondary symptoms or an indurated sore. The proportion is almost as large in the upper and middle classes as in the lower'.[56] Syphilis was not the only cause of locomotor ataxia and could be excluded in perhaps 10 per cent of cases.[57] This figure of 10 per cent was shared by other experts of the era: I will return to the subject later.

It is reasonable to assume that the 1911 edition of the *Encyclopædia Britannica* represented a good summary of what was known about locomotor ataxia at the time of Stoker's death. Of the three 'essential symptoms of the disease' it lists: stamping gait, swaying with the eyes shut, and the occurrence of blindness. We know that Stoker was observed walking with a stamping motion in later life and that his eyesight was failing. The *Encyclopædia* continues:

> There are three stages; (1) the preataxic, (2) the ataxic, (3) the bed-ridden paralytic. The duration of the first stage may be from one or two years, up to twenty years or even longer. In this stage various symptoms may arise. The patient usually complains of shooting, lightning-like pains in the legs …

---

52 Stoker, *Personal reminiscences*, i, p. 329.　53 W.R. Gowers, 'Locomotor Ataxia (Tabes Dorsalis: Posterior Sclerosis)', *A manual of diseases of the nervous system*, i (London, 1886), pp 287–327.　54 Ibid., p. 305.　55 Ibid.　56 Gowers, *A manual of diseases of the nervous system*, i, p. 288.　57 Ibid., p. 289.

> The ataxic gait is very characteristic, owing to the loss of reflex tonus in the muscles, and the absence of guiding sensations from all the deep structures of the limbs, muscles, joints, bones, tendons and ligaments, as well as from the skin of the soles of the feet; therefore the sufferer has to be guided by vision as to where and how to place his feet. This necessitates the bending forward of the body, extension of the knees and broadening of the basis of support; he generally uses a walking stick [as Stoker did] or even two, and he jerks the leg forward as if he were on wires, bringing the sole of the foot down on the ground with a wide stamping action.[58]

Stoker was observed stamping on the sands of Cruden Bay in 1910,[59] which would indicate that he was then in the second, ataxic state. On the subject of loss of eyesight, a contemporary authority stated: 'Atrophy of the optic nerve occurs in tabes … The course of the atrophy is usually slowly progressive, and, in most cases, it ends in total or almost total blindness'.[60]

Then there is the issue of the Wassermann test for syphilis, developed in 1906, six years before Stoker's death and which had a success rate of 95 per cent: we do not know if Browne administered it to Bram but it seems almost inconceivable that he did not do so in the six years that it was available prior to Stoker's death if he suspected that he was suffering from tabes dorsalis/locomotor ataxia. A result from a Wassermann test might help explain the lack of ambiguity with which Browne wrote his diagnosis on the death certificate.

As regards the final condition inscribed on Stoker's death certificate, exhaustion, the 1911 *Encyclopædia Britannica* has this to say of the final stage of locomotor ataxia: 'Sooner or later he passes into the *third* bed-ridden stage, with muscles wasted and their tonus so much lost that he is in a perfectly helpless condition'.[61] By the time of his death, Stoker would clearly have been in a state of exhaustion: to separate it from the other items on the death certificate is clearly misleading.

Some of the more recent books on Stoker ignore advances made in understanding the issues surrounding his death. Surprisingly, Elizabeth Miller, in *Bram Stoker's Dracula* (2009), lists most of the modern biographies in her bibliography[62] but does not take account of their findings in the section, 'The Debate about Stoker's Death', which includes only extracts from Daniel Farson and Leslie Shepard, an English-born, Dublin-based Stoker enthusiast, arranged in such a way that an extract from the former's biography dealing with syphilis is followed by a rather amateurish 'refutation' by the latter. To a reader unfamiliar with Stoker biography, it would appear

---

58 *Encyclopædia Britannica*, xvi, pp 855–6. **59** Vivienne Forrest, 'Castle Dracula', *The Leopard Magazine* (Sept. 1991), 6–7. **60** W.R. Gowers, *A manual of diseases of the nervous system*, ii, p. 298. See also Buzzard, *Clinical aspects of syphilitic nervous affections*, p. 33 and Alfred Fournier, *Syphilis and Marriage* (London, 1881), pp 116–17. **61** *Encyclopædia Britannica*, xvi, p. 856. **62** Elizabeth Miller, *Bram Stoker's* Dracula (New York, 2009), p. 377. She does not list Haining and Tremayne.

that Farson's allegations have been roundly disproved. Andrew Maunder's *Bram Stoker* (2006) takes a different tack while achieving a similar result: it reverts to the Ludlam ploy of stating that Stoker's death certificate records a verdict of 'exhaustion' with no mention of locomotor ataxia or granular kidney.[63]

The question to be asked about all this – Stoker's death and contemporary evasions – is whether it matters. In my opinion it does and it matters greatly. In fact, it is the single greatest issue in Stoker biography and has considerable repercussions for the interpretation of his life and work. It is possible to arrive at quite a different interpretation of Stoker's character and life if the claim in Farson's biography that Stoker was suffering from syphilis is separated from the other, more lurid claims associated with it – that he had contracted the illness from a Paris prostitute around the turn of the twentieth century and that he had been driven to such desperate measures by Florence's frigidity. Accepting that Stoker had syphilis when he died does not mean acceptance giving undue credence to Farson's other claims. In fact, the lengthy and flexible timeframes involved in the development of locomotor ataxia make Farson's Paris prostitute claim unlikely.

If Stoker had entered the preataxic phase of locomotor ataxia by 1894, this could project the initial infection back to the 1870s (the six months written by Browne on the death certificate in relation to locomotor ataxia could well have referred to the final, bed-ridden stage of his illness and this is in line with the facts at our disposal). This would accord with a view expressed to me by Professor Lyons in an interview in 1998, that Stoker's infection could have gone back a long way and he might have been 'at risk' in the period when he was a bachelor in Dublin. I then commented to Lyons that Stoker might well have had affairs with actresses in this period, when he was deeply immersed in the theatre.[64] We also know that Stoker was extremely popular socially in Dublin as a young man and caused many a female heart to flutter.[65] This scenario is similar to that described by a contemporary authority on syphilis in 1874:

> It is requisite to remember that as no period is too late for the occurrence of syphilitic nervous afflictions – twenty, thirty, or more years sometimes having elapsed since the primary infection – so at the earliest stage of the constitutional disorder, disturbances of the nervous system may occur, the cause of which there can be no doubt is frequently overlooked with the result that their treatment is necessarily ineffective.[66]

63 Andrew Maunder, *Bram Stoker* (Devon, 2006), pp xi, 8; other elementary errors in Maunder's these include: having Stoker joining the Civil Service in 1870 (vii); Oscar Wilde dying in 1901 (x); Florence Stoker dying at 91 (xi); Florence Balcombe married Stoker because she 'clearly reckoned Stoker a better bet' (p. 7) – there is no evidence for this pejorative claim; getting the title of one of Stoker's books wrong as *The personal reminiscences of Henry Irving* (pp 7–8). **64** Bram Stoker's health: taped interview with Professor J.B. Lyons by Paul Murray, Mercer's Library, 21 August 1998. **65** Garrick Club, London, Percy FitzGerald scrapbooks, 5:158, 'Society in Dublin' column from unidentified newspaper, no date. **66** Buzzard, *Clinical aspects*, p. 23.

If we follow this logic, Stoker may have married Florence Balcombe in 1878 unaware that he had already contracted a syphilitic infection, which may have come to light later, perhaps following the birth of their only child, Noel, in 1879. This may then have necessitated the cessation of sexual relations between the couple who, however, continued to have a loving but non-sexual relationship. On the other hand, Gowers states that: 'Loss of sexual power is an exceedingly common and often an early symptom of the disease'.[67] Thus the attribution of any lack of sexual activity in the Stoker marriage exclusively to Florence may not be entirely fair! This would provide an autobiographical explanation of the *leitmotiv* of the suspension or deferral of sexual relations between married couples in Bram's fiction, *Dracula* included. Farson's claim that the couple had ceased sexual relations after Noel's birth could therefore have some basis in fact, but not the sensationalist manner in which he presented it. To those who might contrast the sexual charge that runs through Stoker's fiction as evidence that he, at least, retained strong sexual desire, Gowers also states, somewhat paradoxically, that sexual excitement is an early symptom of the disease.[68]

Syphilis in marriage was not uncommon in the late nineteenth century, and indeed Alfred Fournier, one of the most influential nineteenth-century authorities on syphilis, wrote a book largely devoted to the subject: it was, he said in 1881, common for young, healthy girls to marry men who contracted syphilis during their bachelorhood.[69] He also noted that: 'The more recent the syphilis of the husband, the greater and more numerous are the dangers that he introduces into the marriage'.[70] To those who might wonder how Stoker and Florence could have been unaware of the possible danger prior to Noel's birth, Fournier outlines a situation in which a wife has developed syphilis 'without *having shown a primary lesion*' having been infected by her husband '*without this husband having had any contagious symptom*', or indeed even being aware of having contracted the disease.[71] Moreover, Fournier points out that 'the children born under such conditions have been able to escape hereditary syphilis',[72] so it is completely possible that Noel was unaffected by his father's condition.[73] As to whether Florence might have been affected, Gowers says: '… in married women syphilis often runs a latent course'.[74] Finally, on the subject of the advice given by doctors to syphilitic patients, Fournier makes it clear that it would have been to abstain from sexual intercourse.[75] This was echoed by the 1911 *Encyclopædia Britannica*: 'The avoidance of all stress to the nervous system … without stimulants or indulgence in the sexual passion, is the best means of delaying the progress of the disease'.[76] Gowers concurs: 'Sexual excess is also most injurious'.[77]

Not that Stoker's syphilitic condition, if that is what it was, necessarily derived from sexual intercourse. In 1906, Fournier fulminated against 'the old prejudice

[67] Gowers, *Manual of diseases*, ii, p. 296; see also pp 290–1. [68] Ibid., p. 290. [69] Alfred Fournier, *Syphilis and marriage*, p. 18. [70] Ibid., p. 91. [71] Ibid., p. 26. [72] Ibid., p. 37. [73] Ibid., p. 40. [74] Ibid., p. 289. [75] Ibid., p. 151. [76] *Encyclopædia Britannica*, xvi, p. 856. [77] Gowers, *Manual of diseases*, ii, p. 323.

among the lay public that syphilis is of exclusively venereal origin, and that it can be avoided by not exposing one's self to it. Extragenital chancres [ulcerations or sores common to the primary stage of syphilis], both by their frequency and by their situation, show the fallacy of this foolish and dangerous belief'. He reckoned that 9 or 10 per cent of the total might not be too high for extragenital chancres.[78] He went on to say that bucco-buccal contamination, through the mouth, was the most common mode of contamination: 'Bucco-buccal contamination may result from any contact between mouth and mouth ... The public have an idea that syphilis can only be transmitted by prolonged and reciprocal kissing, whereas as any labial contact is sufficient ... Contagion may follow from the respectful kiss as well as the kiss of passion'.[79] Fournier went on to list a dizzying array of possible sources of contamination, including drinking out of a dirty glass, feeding utensils, smoking utensils (pipes, cigars and cigarettes, even cigar-cutters), pens, pencils, rulers, penholders, speaking-tubes, tooth-brushes, paper-knives, toys, medical and musical instruments, body linen, old clothes and bedclothes. Contagion could be carried to the mouth by the fingers.[80] The point here is not whether Fournier was right about these myriad forms of contagion but rather that it was part of the accepted wisdom of the era and, if Bram's syphilitic condition was believed to have fallen into this category, it might explain a forgiving attitude on Florence's part.

Florence may have been aware for some time before Stoker's death that contemporary statistics for syphilitic outcomes in the era made grim reading: out of 100 cases of cerebral syphilis, 22 were cured, 19 were fatal, while 59 'survive with permanent infirmities, many of which, such as paralysis and mental decay, are almost equivalent to death'. Older patients were less amenable to treatment. The most frequent of all parasyphilitic affections was *tabes dorsalis* [*locomotor ataxia*].[81] Fournier had invented the term, parasyphilis, to cover 'the now generally accepted [fact] that certain affections which frequently occur in syphilitic subjects are the consequences of syphilis, without being syphilitic in origin ... The three principal types of parasyphilis are tabes [dorsalis], general paralysis and buccal leucoplasia ... all incurable affections with an inexorable prognosis'.[82] Fournier believed that, together with alcohol and TB, syphilis was one the 'three plagues of the present day' and called for a crusade against it.[83]

Acceptance that Stoker was suffering from syphilis at the time of his death might explain what I have long considered a somewhat overblown tribute from Bram's best friend, Hall Caine, to Florence for her care for the dying Stoker:

> Of the devotion of his wife during those last dark days, in which the whirlwind of his spirit had nothing left to it but the broken wreck of a strong

---

[78] Fournier, *The treatment of syphilis*, p. 86; a modern authority estimates that 95 per cent of syphilis is transmitted by sexual contact: see Claude Quétel, *History of syphilis* (Cambridge, 1990), p. 255, but what his contemporaries believed is what is most relevant in Stoker's case. [79] Ibid., pp 88–9. [80] Ibid., pp 89–105. [81] Ibid., p. 141. [82] Ibid., p. 158. [83] Ibid., p. 155.

man, I cannot trust myself to speak. That must always be a sacred memory to those who know what it was. If his was the genius of friendship, hers must have been the genius of love.[84]

If we think of this as a tribute to a woman who had devotedly nursed her husband through a terrible death from an unmentionable illness, then it makes perfect sense. It would also make sense that Hall Caine was one of the few who knew the true nature of Bram's illness and his tribute is a carefully coded acknowledgment of this. Finally, it makes sense of the explicitness of Browne's wording on the death certificate. There was no need to use euphemisms or evasions: Florence, a smart and brave woman, knew the truth but the nature of his passing did not diminish her affection for a man she had loved and would continue to love.[85] Of course, there is no definitive proof of this interpretation but it seems to me to fit the facts better than the alternatives.

GENERAL CONCLUSIONS

When I began to write a biography of Bram Stoker in the mid-1990s, I did not expect to be still engaged with the subject almost two decades later. What had originated as a suggestion from a fellow writer has become a subject of enduring fascination. New commentators entering the field suggest fresh possibilities, while the continuing unearthing of new material is constantly altering seemingly fixed perspectives. All of which makes Stoker a richly-rewarding field of interest. I would just make a few points in conclusion:

- Stoker remains elusive in terms of both defining him biographically and locating him culturally; dogmatism at one extreme and evasion at the other serve little useful purpose.
- there is no 'eureka' discovery that explains everything, either in terms of biographical fact or interpretation, nor is one likely to emerge.
- biography is not a zero sum game: each biographer brings new approaches, adding to an ongoing process.
- there is a need for the constant infusion of new blood (no pun intended!) to keep the subject alive.
- I keep finding new material and updating my thinking on Stoker; were I to write a new biography today, less than a decade after *From the shadow of Dracula* appeared, it would be a good deal longer with much new perspective.
- Stoker biography remains – and will continue to remain – a work in progress.

84 Hall Caine, 'Bram Stoker. The story of a great friendship', *Daily Telegraph*, 24 April 1912. **85** In conversation with the author, Ann Stoker would emphasize the continuing, fierce devotion of Florence to her late husband up to her own death.

Bram Stoker: a man of notes

ELIZABETH MILLER

> I shall keep a diary ... a sort of journal which I can write in whenever I feel so inclined. I do not suppose there will be much of interest to other people; but it is not intended for them.... It is really an exercise book. I shall try to do what I see lady journalists do: interviewing and writing descriptions and trying to remember conversations. I am told that, with a little practice, one can remember all that goes on or that one hears said during a day.[1]

Mina Murray shares with Lucy Westenra her plans for keeping a diary/journal. This is just one example of how Bram Stoker wrote himself into the characters of *Dracula* (1897). Like Mina, he made a conscious decision to keep a journal (and a diary), privately recreating conversations, recollecting descriptions and recording personal experiences.

Stoker was a prolific writer. He published not only eighteen books but also dozens of short stories and journalistic pieces, many of which have only recently been discovered.[2] He was also a keeper of copious private notes. We know of at least two sets: a journal of some 160 pages that he wrote during the 1870s when he was still living in Dublin, and a missing diary.[3]

BRAM STOKER'S JOURNAL

The Journal resides on a bookshelf on the Isle of Wight, in the home of Noel Dobbs, Stoker's great-grandson. It was among the books left to him by his grandfather Noel Stoker. For decades it languished in obscurity, its existence unknown

---

Portions of this article appeared in 'Unearthing Stoker's lost journal', *Diabolique*, 10 (May–June 2012), 46–54. **1** Bram Stoker, *Dracula* (London, 1897), p. 55. **2** See John Edgar Browning (ed.), *The forgotten writings of Bram Stoker* (New York, 2012). **3** In addition, there are 120 pages of working notes for *Dracula*. The complete set has been published in facsimile, with annotations and analysis. See Robert Eighteen-Bisang and Elizabeth Miller (eds), *Bram Stoker's notes for* Dracula (Jefferson, NC, 2008).

to the world of Stoker/*Dracula* scholars and fans alike, until it was unearthed by Dobbs about ten years ago. He then provided access to Paul Murray, who incorporated elements of it into his biography *From the shadow of Dracula: a life of Bram Stoker* (2004). In 2012, its full contents were made available for the first time, along with annotations and commentary.

The Journal comprises 310 individual entries of varying lengths written by hand on about 160 pages over an eleven-year period (1871–82). Most of the entries were recorded before Stoker left Dublin at the end of 1878 to join Henry Irving in London as his theatre manager. Indeed, Dublin stands centre-stage as one of its native sons provides details about his life in the city: his colleagues at Dublin Castle, his classmates at Trinity College, his early attraction to the theatre, his observations of the Dublin street, and above all, his rich sense of humour. There are dozens of references to friends and family, travel and office life, drunken parties, court cases and christenings. Above all, the Journal is a commonplace book, a writer's companion, a grab-bag for a variety of descriptions, anecdotes, quotations, observations and musings. Sometimes Stoker writes in the first person, while at other times he comments as a detached observer or transmits someone else's accounts. Especially noteworthy are the jottings of an emerging writer as he keeps a record of themes, plots and characters for future use in his fiction. There are even foreshadowings of *Dracula*. Many of the entries provide tantalizing insights into the man himself – his social life, his sensitivity, his character, his moral values, his Gothic sensibility and, above all, a sense of how imbedded he was in the daily life of late nineteenth-century Ireland.

Stoker began his Journal on 1 August 1871. At the age of twenty-three, he was living at the time in the family home at 43 Harcourt St, Dublin. Having graduated from Trinity College in the previous year with a BA, he would acquire the Master's degree five years later. An active student in both athletics and intellectual pursuits, he maintained his connections with the College for several years after graduation. Most significant was his continued participation in the activities of both the Philosophical and Historical societies. For example, just the year before (in 1870) he had delivered a lecture entitled 'Means of improvement in composition'. In addition, earlier in 1871 he had vigorously defended the poetry of Walt Whitman at a meeting of the 'Phil'. He kept close contact with many of his university friends, several of whom make brief appearances throughout the Journal.

In August 1871, having followed dutifully in the path towards respectability laid out for him by his father, Stoker was employed as a civil servant at the Department of Registrar of Petty Sessions Clerks, Dublin Castle. In his position at Dublin Castle, he spent many hours tediously recording and filing reports from the petty sessions courts. His Journal allowed him to express his creative side, as did his decision later that same year to begin writing regular theatre reviews for the *Dublin Evening Mail*. His first story, 'The crystal cup', appeared in the periodical *London Society* in 1872, followed three years later by *The primrose path* and 'Buried treasures', both published in serial form in *The Shamrock* in 1875.

The opening entry in the Journal is entitled 'Night fishing',[4] the earliest example of Stoker's prose writing discovered to date. Essentially a word painting, it shows an aspiring writer composing an excessively descriptive passage in flowery prose. 'Night fishing' was written in Greystones, a coastal town in Co. Wicklow, about twenty miles south of Dublin. With its long stretch of beach, Greystones was popular in Stoker's time (and still is today) as a destination for holidaymakers. Evidence from other entries around the same time indicates that he and a few friends were spending an extended weekend in the coastal town. No doubt he enjoyed the opportunity to relax, away from the stress and boredom of daily work at Dublin Castle, and to let his imagination take wing.

Years later, Stoker would draw from his Journal for two of his early books: *Under the sunset* (a collection of short stories for children, 1881) and *The snake's pass* (a novel, 1890). At one point he scribbles a memo for a story: 'A man builds up a shadow on a wall bit by bit by adding to substance. Suddenly the shadow becomes alive' (p. 37). A marginal note confirms its later use as the kernel of a story in *Under the sunset* entitled 'The shadow builder'. Another note reads: 'Palace of Fairy Queen. Child goes to sleep and palace grows – sky changes into blue silk curtains etc' (p. 38). Dreaming children make appearances in a number of stories in the collection, notably 'How 7 went mad', 'Lies and lilies' and 'The wondrous child'.

Many more notes and jottings would find their way into *The snake's pass*, his Irish novel. The book shows the influence of his frequent travels around Ireland during his tenure at Petty Sessions. Much of this material appears verbatim in the book, mostly to flesh out the comic character, Andy Sullivan. At one point Stoker even constructs a bare-bones plot for the novel:

> Mem: Irish story Torriadbreena. Shifting bog – William Haggerty makes good man exchange his land which lies lower down from bog above in hopes of finding buried treasure. Bog shifts and good man finds iron chest of money in cleft of rock laid bare – christens good man's daughter – poet and natural – young engineer who comes to find treasure by magnets etc – gombeen man – priest etc. 2nd of November, 1881. (p. 43)

We also find many suggestions for stories we assume were never written: titles such as 'The modesty of ignorance' and 'The musical liar', a story about a man married by proxy and a tale of a letter being sent in the wrong envelope. Even more intriguing are the notes of a 'web-legged girl with legs like flippers of a seal' (p. 22)

---

4 Elizabeth Miller and Dacre Stoker (eds), *The lost journal of Bram Stoker* (London, 2012), pp 17–18. Subsequent citations will be acknowledged in the text in parentheses.

and of sleeping 'under a rug of cat skins' (p. 46). At one point he planned to write a series of narratives based on modernized myths of Venus, Mars and Vulcan. He hoped to dabble in allegory, farce and comedy, and he planned a second collection of children's stories.

Stoker also tried his hand at poetry. Most of it is imitative, probing the common themes of sentimental verse such as love, longing and loneliness. His earliest surviving poem entitled 'Acrostic' (pp 48–9) is dated 1870. An acrostic is a poem in which the first letter, syllable or word of each line spells out a word, name or message. In this case, the first letters spell 'Bessie L'Estrange'. A mystery indeed!

Making entries in his Journal helped Stoker hone his writing skills in very tangible ways. Much of what he wrote is a series of reminders, items that he feared might otherwise be forgotten in the busy schedule that was his life. The reminders were, of course, to himself. One doubts he had any intention of sharing the Journal with anybody else (though his wife Florence, who survived him for twenty-five years, read it at some point and made marginal notes). Sometimes he even highlighted his *aide-mémoires* with the designation 'Mem', a technique familiar to the astute reader of *Dracula* where similar notations are made by Jonathan Harker – himself a compulsive note-taker. Harker's journal is punctuated with memos. As he records his meal of chicken at the hotel in Klausenburgh, he hastily adds in parentheses: 'Mem., get recipe for Mina'.[5] As he travels further into Transylvania and recalls how he has read of this region as a centre of superstitions, he jots down (again parenthetically) 'Mem., I must ask the Count all about them'.[6] As he records an all-night conversation with the Count at Castle Dracula, Harker makes this observation: 'Mem., this diary seems horribly like the beginning of the "Arabian Nights", for everything has to break off at cock-crow – or like the ghost of Hamlet's father'.[7] The compulsion to 'write it down' is strong.

Harker is not the only character in *Dracula* who habitually makes notes. Dr John Seward records his diary on phonograph: 'Let me put down with exactness all that happened.... Not a detail that I can recall must be forgotten'.[8] Lucy at her death leaves a memorandum. Even the lunatic Renfield 'keeps a little note-book in which he is always jotting down something'.[9] In fact, the entire novel is a patchwork of notes of various kinds: journal entries, diary entries, letters, memoranda, phonograph recordings, telegrams, newspaper reports and a ship's log. Stoker draws on up-to-date technology, having his characters take advantage of means of communication not available to him as note-keeper in the 1870s.

Several entries in the Journal show Stoker's predilection for the Gothic, such as references to Edgar Allan Poe, including a suggestion about dramatizing 'The fall of the house of Usher' (1839). Gothic elements are prevalent in his early fiction published while he was keeping the Journal, including allusions to *Faust*, a fore-

---

5 Stoker, *Dracula*, p. 1. **6** Ibid., p. 2. **7** Ibid., p. 31. **8** Ibid., p. 282. **9** Ibid., p. 71.

shadowing of the impact of that legend on the creation of *Dracula*. Even though the final dated entry in the Journal is 1882, eight years before he made his initial notes for *Dracula*, he may have had some of the entries in mind (or even at his side) while he was composing his masterpiece. There are distinct resonances in *Dracula*, indicating that the Journal could be looked at as one of the breeding grounds for his most famous book.

The Journal provides insight into Stoker as a developing writer. But it also reveals – in spades – an aspect of the author of *Dracula* that is frequently overlooked or at best, downplayed: his remarkable sense of humour. Scholars have for the most part bypassed this trait, content to psychoanalyze both the author and his characters, endlessly debating hidden sexual meanings in both his writing and his lifelong friendships. The revelations of this Journal should encourage a reassessment of the view of Stoker as an uptight, generally humourless individual. Clearly, Stoker possessed a keen sense of the comic, and excelled at recognizing incongruities around him and transmitting them to others in the form of both spoken and written narrative.

First and foremost is the man himself. He enjoyed a good laugh and raised laughter among those around him. He was always a welcome speaker at dinner parties both in Dublin and later in London. 'He had a laugh that was good to hear', noted Henry Dickens (Charles' grandson).[10] He was not averse to having a bit of fun at his own expense. Michael Holroyd records that during a winter visit to Toronto with Irving in 1884, Stoker ventured into the world of tobogganing:

> Ellen [Terry] decided to go tobogganing: Henry stood in the snow, watching her with a curiously forlorn expression. And behind him Stoker had positioned himself, hesitating between trepidation and desire until, unable to resist the iced toboggan chutes, he leapt forward, fell off the toboggan, and went somersaulting down the hillside, flapping his arms.[11]

Stoker had a special fondness for verbal humor and more sophisticated witticisms. Scattered throughout the Journal are riddles and word-games. It should therefore come as little surprise that his published writings contain a preponderance of comic elements, sometimes obvious, sometimes more nuanced. Even *Dracula* has its humorous moments.

Arguably the strongest impression one gets while reading through the Journal is the 'Irishness' of much of the content. Not only is Stoker describing for the most part Irish scenes (both in Dublin and around the countryside), he presents them with some flourish. Many of the Dublin entries record humourous anecdotes, some personal – some second-hand:

[10] Cited in Harry Ludlam, *My quest for Bram Stoker* (New York, 2000), p. 60. [11] Michael Holroyd, *A strange eventful history* (London, 2009), p. 167.

Heard a man today speak of his wife as 'My mother-in-law's daughter'. (p. 96)

Cecil Roche once in a speech of the Historical Society spoke of 'Protestants, thieves, policemen and the rest of the criminal classes'. (p. 92)

In speaking of a pending divorce case a man said, 'Oh, it is merely a case of mistaken identity.' How? 'Well you see, the lady mistook the other man for her husband.' (p. 106)

Not all entries are as light-hearted. Comedy is frequently tinged with tragedy, a blending that one frequently finds in Irish humour. Irish history is rife with irony and incongruity, qualities that lie at the core of both tragedy and comedy. Ireland's history follows a repetitive pattern of downfall and recovery, invariably followed by famine and disease. Part of the resilience of the Irish lies in their ability to laugh at themselves as well as others. No one was above using humour; no subject was too sacred; no one was spared. The results are often dark and disturbing. One such is an anecdote about a woman who judged the goodness of her husband by the fact that he had never given her a black eye (pp 195–6); or the woman who loses her breakfast after being kicked in the stomach (p. 209). We can only wonder whether Stoker actually found these incidents funny – and on what level – or if it was social commentary. We just do not know. Violence is invariably linked to drinking and drunkenness. It is not known whether Stoker was at this stage of his life a drinker, though he was well known as a 'party man'. Certainly if his early fiction is any indication, he had great reservations about alcoholic consumption and the domestic violence that could ensue. His story, *The primrose path* (1875), deals specifically with alcoholism and the inevitable domestic violence that develops from heavy drinking. It reads like a tract for temperance.

On one occasion, Stoker and two of his Trinity College friends attended the St Patrick's Ball, an annual event held on 17 March, the climax of a day of festivities hosted by the Viceroy at Dublin Castle. He provides this graphic account:

T. Martelli, Latchford, self went. There were thousands of people there and all the brass bands in Dublin. Late in the evening many men got drunk and some sick. One man got sick in the centre of Leinster Hall. The floor was waxed. Immediately a lot of fellows with one impulse rushed at the place and cut a slide. It was awful. You might see shortly after a man being brought over from the bar to get sick in the right place for the continuance of the pastime.

W. Leahy who was very obstinate would not get out of the way of a trades band which was marching up and down so they knocked him down and walked over him. The last thing he heard was, 'Hit him with the fleuwts. Hit him with the fleuwts.' (pp 199–200)

In many of the entries (and indeed in his published writing), Stoker attempted to render speech in local dialect, with very mixed results. While such recreation adds to realism, it can test the patience of the reader, especially one completely unfamiliar with the dialect. In Stoker's case, representing dialect in written prose involves phonetic spelling of what is heard: for example 'threes' for 'trees' and 'sorh' for 'sir'. Then there are changes in grammatical structure common in Irish speech: 'they do be havin' to sit' and 'What would I be after doin'.' One also finds deviation from standard pronunciation, as in 'tirty' for 'thirty' and 'dat' for 'that'. A certain rhythmic lyricism can be detected in corruptions such as 'he sez, sez he' and 'at all at all'. All of these phrases and pronunciations can still be heard in Ireland today. Of course Stoker was working with the familiar, was close enough to the scene to be able to hear the idiom, speech pattern, accent and lilt as he wrote. When writing *Dracula* many years later, he took up the rather formidable challenge of adopting an unfamiliar dialect and idiom – that of Whitby, a town on the Yorkshire coast of England that is one of the novel's major settings. He made a concerted effort to achieve accuracy, having gained access to a very useful book: *A Whitby glossary* (1876) by F.K. Robinson. From it he took four pages of notes for *Dracula*, listing localisms followed by standard meanings. He assiduously worked many of these into the comments made by Mr Swales in Chapter 6 of the novel.

Stoker's attraction to the theatre pre-dates the Journal. During his earlier years, his father encouraged this interest, taking young Bram to numerous productions and spending hours discussing with his son the actors, the sets and the performances. The two of them – father and son – would sit in the pit, where the ticket prices were in line with their finances. Paradoxically, Abraham Stoker never approved of the theatre as an occupation worthy of any of his sons. During his years at Trinity College in the 1860s, Bram actually tried his hand at acting with the Trinity Dramatic Society, appearing in two Richard Brinsley Sheridan comedies, *The school for scandal* (1777) and *The rivals* (1775). His professor and mentor, poet and Shakespearean scholar Edward Dowden, further inspired his interest in Shakespeare, whose plays would have a significant influence on *Dracula*. In 1871, he approached the proprietor of the *Dublin Evening Mail* about writing theatre reviews. The response was that the paper could not afford such a thing, to which he replied that he would gladly do it without fee or reward. And he did – for several years. This decision proved auspicious, as it began a chain of events that would result in his close association with Henry Irving, an eventual move to London, a climate in which the writing of *Dracula* would be possible.

Though he remained in his civil service job, Stoker became even more active in the theatre and as far more than a reviewer. Accounts show that he frequented Dublin's main theatres – the Theatre Royal, the Gaiety and the Queen's – not merely as a member of the audience and/or reviewer, but as a back-stage guest. During this time, he learned all he could about the inner workings of a performance: the lighting, the costumes, the staging, and offered advice and encouragement to young actors and actresses. Theatre life was (and still is) fodder for countless stories and anecdotes. Stoker, just starting to get his feet wet as a writer, indulges in a few of his own, recording them in his Journal with a humorous flourish:

> I once saw in the Queen's Theatre a cork thrown into the orchestra by some wag in the gallery. The launcher [Barrowcliff] who was very drunk stood up, stopped the band and made an oration in which he called the audience in the gallery assassins. He said, holding up the cork, 'It was only an accident and none of your fault that there was not a bottle at the end of it.' (p. 226)

He also tells a story about Frank Seymour, one of Cork's most colorful characters. Manager of the Victoria Theatre, he was usually in financial difficulties. Furthermore, he was a very poor actor. His nickname was 'Chouse' because of the way he pronounced the word 'chaos'. When he would be listed for a dramatic appearance, word would spread around Cork that 'Chouse has come again!' His creditors once posted bailiffs at the entrance to the theatre when he was to appear as the ghost in *Hamlet*. He avoided them by entering the theatre concealed in Ophelia's coffin.

A few entries record incidents about Henry Irving that occurred before Stoker joined him as his manager:

> Henry Irving told me that he once gave a reading in a town in Scotland – Dunfermline. (It was before he had played *The Bells*.) He appeared on the platform and waited there a whole hour – but not one person came! (p. 230)

> When we were in Belfast, Henry Irving, Loveday and myself (H.I. went to give a reading for the Samaritan Hospital 16/8/78), we were at supper with David Cunningham. There were many speeches giving Irving's health etc. One man said, 'Mr Irving, gentlemen, is known to you all. We know, gentlemen, whether others know that Mr Irving leads and has ever led a life of unbroken blemish.' (pp 230–1)

Bram Stoker had first seen Irving perform as Captain Absolute in *The Rivals* at the Theatre Royal in Dublin in 1867. Having watched him on stage again in 1871, Stoker was discouraged with the lack of attention given to theatrical performances in the Dublin newspapers. That was his primary motivation for offering his services as theatre reviewer. In November 1876, after he wrote a favourable review of Irving's performance of Hamlet, the actor invited the reviewer to join him at the

Shelbourne Hotel. This was the beginning of a friendship and a business relationship that would last until Irving's death in 1905. Indeed, in his own lifetime Bram Stoker was far better known as Irving's manager than as an author (even of *Dracula*).

Evidence of the influence of stage production on the text of *Dracula* lies in the theatricality of both lines and gestures. Both Henry Irving and Count Dracula are actors, practitioners of grand deceptions, both are shape-shifters who enter with ease another role, who blur the boundaries between illusion and reality. The grand sweep of Dracula's gestures mimics Irving in his finest roles – as Macbeth, as Lear, and especially as Mephistopheles (in *Faust*): 'You think to baffle me, you – with your pale faces all in a row ... My revenge is just begun! I spread it over centuries, and time is on my side'.[12] Other examples come to mind: Dracula stretching out his arm to calm the wolves, crawling face-down down his castle wall, and forcing Mina to drink from the wound in his chest. Or in this scene: 'With a fierce sweep of his arm, he hurled the woman from him, and then motioned to the others, as though he were beating them back ... "How dare you touch him, any of you? How dare you cast eyes on him when I had forbidden it? Back I tell you! This man belongs to me!"'.[13] Without the theatre – and Bram's intimate connections with it – the novel *Dracula* as we know it would never have been written.

BRAM STOKER'S DIARY

Unlike the Journal, Stoker's diary has not been found. We know of its existence because Stoker cites from it nineteen times in *Personal reminiscences of Henry Irving* (1906).[14] Most of the entries focus on Irving and/or the Lyceum Theatre. The earliest is dated 29 November 1873 (before he met Irving), an indication that for a few years he was recording in both it and the Journal. The latest entry cited was written in February 1905, just months before Irving's death. We have no way of knowing how many entries he made during that period of over thirty years.

We do, however, have a few other scraps of information about the diary. Stoker himself makes this comment: 'Lest I should forget the exact words, I wrote them then and there in my pocket-book. I entered them later in my diary'. (*Irving* 2:2). He apparently carried a small notebook (his 'pocket-book') on his person, jotting down brief notes that he could develop and elaborate on in the diary later. He considered accuracy and immediacy important.

His son Noel made these remarks about the diary:

> When he wrote 'Henry Irving' in 1906, he was able to say how many times each Play had been performed; and the Total of their Earnings. The jotted

---

12 Ibid., p. 315. **13** Ibid., p. 40. **14** Bram Stoker, *Personal reminiscences of Henry Irving*, 2 vols (London, 1906); henceforth cited as *Irving*.

Diary, which he kept, never failed him; and it is noticeable that he was never at a Loss for a Date. It is, I think, another sign of his Love and Devotion for his Friend [Irving] that, however long had been the Day – or Night, the Record in that Diary was never deferred.[15]

If, as Noel hints, Stoker wrote in his diary daily, there could very well have been hundreds of entries filling several notebooks. In any case, what we have is a small fraction of the whole.

What follows are the diary entries directly quoted by Stoker in *Personal reminiscences of Henry Irving*, arranged in chronological order. With just one exception, he includes dates.

1. 29 November 1873 (*Irving* 2:169)

Mem. Will be a great actress.

Stoker is referring to Genevieve Ward, an American-born singer who would indeed become a successful actress. Stoker first saw her perform in Dublin on 29 November 1873, was greatly impressed with her performance, and arranged an introduction. The two became very close friends. He visited her in Paris on at least two occasions and the two of them corresponded for several years. She attended Stoker's funeral at Golders Green Crematorium on 25 April 1912.

2. 14 February 1876 (*Irving* 2:96)

Spoke – I think well.

The occasion was his participation in a discussion following a lecture that was critical of the poetry of Walt Whitman. Stoker and his Trinity College mentor, Edward Dowden, both vigorously defended the American poet against his detractors. Stoker had written a lengthy letter to Whitman four years earlier but for some unknown reason he did not post it. After the lecture on 14 February 1876, he wrote a shorter one and sent both together. Within a month he received a reply from Whitman that he (Stoker) later reproduced in facsimile and inserted into copies of *Personal reminiscences of Henry Irving*. Stoker and Whitman would eventually meet in 1884, during one of the Lyceum's North American tours, and again in 1886 and 1887.

3. 22 November 1877 (*Irving* 1:54)

London in view!

Irving and Stoker first met in 1876 following Stoker's review of *Hamlet* at the Theatre Royal in Dublin. In November 1877, Irving raised the possibility that

---

15 Stoker family papers, Trinity College Dublin.

Stoker give up his position at Dublin Castle and join him in London, should he be successful in acquiring his own theatre. Stoker, eager to move to the centre of the literary world, was clearly excited. The move finally took place in December 1878, just days after Stoker's marriage to Florence Balcombe.

4. 27 March 1879 (*Irving* 1:82)

> *Stage very dismal. Ellen Terry met me in the passage and began to cry! I felt very like joining her.*

The occasion was Irving's inability to appear on stage that night due to a serious cold. Stoker notes that this was the first time in seven years that Irving had to cancel an appearance. Ellen Terry, Irving's 'leading lady', joined the Lyceum Company in 1878. She and Stoker quickly became close friends.

5. n.d. [1880] (*Irving* 1:96)

> *H. much touched at tragedy of last act, and in speaking the words wept.*

Stoker records Irving's reaction as he (Irving) read from *Romeo and Juliet*. The same night, Irving and Stoker practiced carrying the body of Paris into the tomb. Not happy with the results, Stoker consulted his brother George who had served in the Russo-Turkish War as Chief of Ambulance for the Red Crescent. George solved the problem readily.

6. 5 January 1883 (*Irving* 1:118)

> *Theatre 7 till 2. H and I supper alone. He told me of intention to play Lear on return from America. Gave rough idea of play – domestic – gives away kingdom round a wood fire, etc.*

Irving frequently discussed plays with Stoker and sought his advice on additions to the Lyceum's repertoire.

7. 30 March 1885 (*Irving* 2:259)

> *Went well. H.I. looked very distinguished.*

The reference is to a lecture that Irving gave at Harvard University. Expanding on the event in *Personal reminiscences of Henry Irving*, Stoker adds: 'Distinguished was hardly an adequate adjective. Even from that sea of fine intellectual heads his noble face shone out like a star' (2:259).

8. 14 April 1886 (*Irving* 2:147)

> *Liszt fine face leonine several large pimples prominent chin of old man long white hair down on shoulders all call him 'Master' must have had great*

> *strength in youth. Very sweet and simple in manner. H.I. and he very much alike seemed old friends as they talked animatedly though knowing but a few words of each other's language but using much expression and gesticulation. It was most interesting.*

Franz Liszt attended a performance of *Faust* at the Lyceum and was one of Irving's guests at a post-performance dinner in the Beefsteak Room.

9. 23 February 1887 (*Irving* 1:306)

> *Immense enthusiasm – remarkable – magnificent – every character given in masterly manner – consider it greatest tour-de-force of his life – even he exhausted!*

Irving's reading of *Hamlet* at Birbeck Hall brought forth from Stoker a gush of superlatives.

10. 19 April 1888 (*Irving* 2:159)

> *He is a fine actor, essentially a Comedian.*

Stoker made this entry after attending a supper party given by M.L. Mayer. The 'fine actor' is Benoit-Constant Coquelin, a French comic actor of renown. Ten years later (during the summer of 1898), Coquelin would play his acclaimed *Cyrano de Bergerac* (1897) at the Lyceum.

11. 25 November 1889 (*Irving* 1:186)

> *Theatre 7 pm till 5 am. H.I. read for Loveday and me Edgar and Lucy, Merivale's dramatization to his order of The Bride of Lammermoor. It was delightful. Play very fine. Literature noble. H.I. had cut quite one-half out.*

He then supplements from memory. This was a private reading for stage-manager H.J. Loveday and Stoker. The play entitled *Ravenswood* (based on *The bride of Lammermoor* (1819) by Sir Walter Scott) was presented the following year, with Ellen Terry playing the role of the tragic Lucy. It may be worth noting that within three months, Stoker would make his first notes for what would become *Dracula*, giving the name of Lucy to one of the female characters.

12. 10 November 1892 (*Irving* 1:119)

> *First night – King Lear. Great enthusiasm between acts. Whilst scenes on, stillness like the grave. An ideal audience. Thunders of applause and cheers at end.*

13. 21 September 1894 (*Irving* 1:249)

> *New play enormous success. H.I. fine and great. All laughed and wept. Marvellous study of senility. Eight calls at end.*

The new play was *Waterloo* by Arthur Conan Doyle. It was performed in Bristol, while Doyle was on tour in America. By this time, Doyle had achieved fame as a writer of novels and short stories. His first series of short stories featuring Sherlock Holmes was published in 1891.

14. 11 December 1894 (*Irving* 2:258)

> *H.I. got enormous reception. Cheers were startling! On leaving, students wanted to take out horses and draw carriage, but wiser counsels prevailed.*

Irving had given a lecture at the Victoria University of Manchester. Topic was 'The character of Macbeth'. Irving used the occasion to strike back at several critics whose comments about an earlier performance of *Macbeth* had been 'ridiculous … puerile … even infantile'.

15. 29 November 1895 (*Irving* 2:236)

> *Must be President some day. A man you can't cajole, can't frighten, can't buy.*

At the time Theodore Roosevelt was Commissioner of Police for the city of New York. Stoker was invited to watch Roosevelt preside over a trial of policemen charged with offenses. Stoker was very impressed with how the Commissioner handled the cases. Stoker and Roosevelt would meet again at the White House in 1903, by which time the latter was President – Bram's prophecy had come true.

16. 21 December 1898 (*Irving* 2:330)

> *H.I. looking well. Much stronger, self-possessed and evenly balanced. Arranged to tour at Easter. Lyceum season in September and October. American tour in autumn.*

Irving had been ill, missing ten weeks of stage performances as result of pneumonia and pleurisy.

17. 12 January 1903 (*Irving* 1:273)

> *Read it wonderfully well. Adumbrated every character.*

Irving performed a reading from 'Dante' (Sardou and Moreau) for the actors and actresses of the company.

18. 3 February 1905 (*Irving* 2:348)

H.I. fearfully done up, could hardly play. At end in collapse. Could hardly move or breathe.

19. [13] February 1905 (*Irving* 2:384)

H.I. very weak, but got through all right.

Irving managed to rally once more. On 2 October 1905 the Company undertook a provincial tour, including the town of Bradford. Following a performance of *Becket* on 13 October, Irving died at the Midland Hotel at the age of sixty-seven. Stoker began work on *Personal reminiscences of Henry Irving* soon afterwards, with his diary close by.

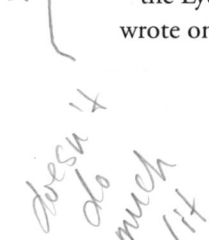

For decades, Stoker has been overshadowed by *Dracula*. There are still aspects of his life that remain obscure. But the glimpses provided by his Journal into his everyday life in Dublin, and the diary's illumination of the centre-piece of his life – the Lyceum Theatre – give us a more complete picture of the complex man who wrote one of the world's most famous novels.

Bram Stoker: Ireland and beyond

CAROL A. SENF

Although I have a long-standing scholarly and critical interest in Bram Stoker,[1] writing a book on him recently for the Gothic Authors series at the University of Wales Press and studying everything that he wrote – the short stories and the journalism as well as the novels – rekindled my enormous appreciation of the man and his work. I had first come to know Stoker through *Dracula* (1897), and had explored his other works to understand the man who could write so intriguingly about the dark corners of his own age and of our own. Reading those other works revealed to me that Stoker is far more than a Gothic novelist. Indeed, Stoker experimented with many other literary genres, including Utopian fiction, detection and romance. Although some of his works occasionally feel dated, what particularly appeals to me is his thoughtful response to the world in which he lived as well as the fact that what he wrote often touches on issues that continue to matter one hundred years after his death: the relationships between men and women, racial tensions, connections among nations – especially connections between the colonizers and the colonized, and the enormous changes created by a world that was increasingly global. In particular, even though people continue to discover smart new ways of looking at *Dracula* and some of his other better-known novels, I also want to share my enthusiasm for works that are rather less familiar. These works too deserve to be better known and studied.

Some of the lesser-known works, such as *The primrose path* (1875), 'The man from Shorrox' (1894) and *Lady Athlyne* (1908), feature Irish characters and confirm the recent critical interest in Stoker's Irishness, which is evident in Jarlath Killeen's *Gothic literature* (2009), as well as *From the shadow of Dracula* (2004) by Paul Murray and *Gaelic Gothic* (2004) by Luke Gibbons, plus practically everything Bill

---

[1] See Carol A. Senf, '*Dracula*: the unseen face in the mirror', *Journal of Narrative Technique*, 9 (1979), 160–70; idem, '*Dracula*: Stoker's response to the new woman', *Victorian Studies*, 26 (1982), 33–49; idem, *The critical response to Bram Stoker* (Westport, CT, 1993); idem, Dracula: *between tradition and modernism* (New York, 1998); idem, *Science and society in Bram Stoker's fiction* (Westport, CT, 2002).

Hughes has written or edited.² Indeed, there is no doubt that Stoker's roots were in Ireland, where he was born and educated and where he spent the first 31 years of his life. Indeed Stoker's whole family was deeply rooted in Ireland, where they were solid members of the Irish Protestant professional classes. A number of scholars have written on Stoker's Irish background, and the recently released *The Dublin years: the lost journal of Bram Stoker* (2012) edited by Elizabeth Miller and Dacre Stoker (Bram's grand-nephew) is proof of Stoker's Irish roots and includes anecdotes that eventually appeared in his fiction.³ Clive Leatherdale, Harry Ludlam, Barbara Belford, Paul Murray, and Peter Haining and Peter Tremayne observe that Charlotte Stoker's Irish folktales and stories about her ancestors are responsible for Bram's awareness of his heritage.⁴ Daniel Farson, Stoker's grand-nephew, who had access to a number of family stories, describes his grandmother's tales of her experiences during the 1832 cholera epidemic in Sligo, material that Stoker wove into several stories in *Under the sunset* (1882).⁵

While Stoker learned about his Irish heritage from his mother, his loyalty to Ireland was reinforced by his experiences at Trinity College Dublin, and his friendship with the Wilde family. Sir William Wilde, the author of several works of Irish folklore, and Lady Jane Wilde, who published under the name of Speranza, often wrote in favour of Irish independence, and indeed Speranza was deeply involved in the Young Irelanders, a separatist nationalist organization of the 1840s. Commenting on their influence, Murray observes that the Wildes and their political connections probably influenced Stoker's political views about Home Rule:

> Isaac Butt, the original advocate of Home Rule and a former Professor of Political Economy at Trinity, frequented the Wilde household, and Sir William Wilde was a Home Ruler. . . From their early days together at the Lyceum, Irving liked to rib Stoker about his Home Rule views.⁶

Despite Irving's kidding, Stoker remained a life-long supporter of Home Rule as did his wife, Florence, and his elder brother Thornley, the support in Bram's case reinforced by his friendship with William E. Gladstone, English Prime Minister and frequent visitor to the Lyceum between 1881 and 1895. An advocate of Home Rule for Ireland, Gladstone put forward legislation for Home Rule in 1885 and

---

2 Jarlath Killeen, *Gothic literature, 1825–1914* (Cardiff, 2009), pp 119–23; Paul Murray, *From the shadow of Dracula: a life of Bram Stoker* (London, 2004); Luke Gibbons, *Gaelic Gothic: race, colonization and Irish culture* (Galway, 2004); William Hughes, *Beyond* Dracula: *Bram Stoker's fiction and its cultural context* (New York, 2000). **3** Elizabeth Miller and Dacre Stoker (eds), *The Dublin years: the lost journal of Bram Stoker* (London, 2012). **4** Clive Leatherdale, Dracula: *the novel and the legend* (Wellingborough, Northamptonshire, 1985), pp 58–9; Harry Ludlam, *A biography of Dracula: the life story of Bram Stoker* (London, 1962); Barbara Belford, *Bram Stoker: a biography of the author of* Dracula (New York, 1996), pp 18–19; Murray, *From the shadow*, pp 12–16; Peter Haining and Peter Tremayne, *The un-dead: the legend of Bram Stoker and* Dracula (London, 1997), pp 44–6. **5** Daniel Farson, *The man who wrote* Dracula: *a biography of Bram Stoker* (London, 1975). **6** Murray, *From the shadow*, p. 144.

again in 1892, events about which Stoker wrote in *Personal reminiscences of Henry Irving* (1906).

Murray's excellent biography provides material on Stoker's education at Trinity and the long-term friendships that he made as a student there. Following graduation, he joined the civil service at Dublin Castle, where his father worked, and gained experience as a writer by doing unpaid theatre reviews and by writing both short stories and a manual, *The duties of clerks of petty sessions in Ireland* (1879). Working in the civil service and travelling around Ireland during the two years that he spent as Inspector of petty sessions gave him experience with rural and village Ireland (there were over 600 petty sessions or magistrates courts in Ireland during the period that Stoker was Inspector) that he ultimately used in fiction such as *The primrose path*, written while he was still in Dublin and published in *The Shamrock* in 1875, *The snake's pass*, *Lady Athlyne* (1890), and 'The way of peace' (1909). Although Andrew Smith refers to Dublin Castle as 'that most imperial of institutions' and claims that Stoker's work there reinforced his Protestant establishment background, his experience in the countryside also enabled him to rub shoulders with an entirely different kind of Irishman.[7] Indeed, Murray observes that the notebook Stoker kept during his days as a civil servant 'records travels the length and breadth of the country' during which time he witnessed first hand both Ireland's economic plight in the post-Famine years and its potential.[8] Furthermore, even though he left Ireland permanently to assume duties as acting manager of the Lyceum, Ireland had imprinted itself on his consciousness. As pointed out by David Glover, Stoker, though a part of London society, was 'always remembered as an Irishman' who never lost his Irish accent, which 'became more pronounced in the heat of an argument'.[9]

Living in England for the next 34 years and travelling widely as an emissary for the Lyceum, he continued to be interested in Ireland, arguing for Home Rule and featuring Irish characters in a number of works. *The primrose path* reveals the dangers that besiege a young Irish family when it moves to England. The first three chapters introduce its protagonist, Jerry O'Sullivan, as a happy man surrounded by a loving and supportive family. Against the advice of friends and the wishes of his mother and wife, he accepts an attractive job at a London theatre and, upon arriving in London, almost immediately falls into bad company, becomes a drunkard, and loses his job and the family's trust before murdering his wife in a drunken rage and subsequently cutting his own throat. Often read as a temperance tract, *The primrose path* also reveals the Gothic touches that are so evident in Stoker's fiction. It seems unlikely that Stoker intended it as a warning against the dangers of emigration, for the Stoker family was part of the nineteenth-century Irish dias-

---

[7] Andrew Smith, 'Demonizing the Americans: Bram Stoker's postcolonial Gothic', *Gothic Studies*, 5:2 (2003), 22. [8] Murray, *From the shadow*, 48. [9] David Glover, *Vampires, mummies and liberals: Bram Stoker and the politics of popular fiction* (Durham, NC, 1996), p. 13.

pora. Not only did Bram emigrate from Ireland, so did his parents, brothers George, Richard and Tom, and both sisters. Only his oldest brother Thornley remained in Dublin, though his sister Margaret returned to Ireland when she married a physician, Sir William Thompson, who succeeded Thornley as President of the Royal College of Surgeons.

Several later works reveal Stoker's Irish heritage in very specific ways. 'The invisible giant', from his 1882 collection *Under the sunset*, is based on Charlotte Stoker's stories of the 1832 cholera outbreak in Sligo.¹⁰ A later short story, 'The way of peace', refers to the Famine of 1845–50, when 'min an' weemin' – an' worse still, the poor childhers – was dyin' be shcores'.¹¹ The story, however, focuses on personal relationships and uses the Famine only as a backdrop. The work most often read as Irish is Stoker's first novel, *The snake's pass*, which Lisa Hopkins reads as 'a fable of reconstruction' in which the 'emblematically named' Arthur uses his own fortune to rebuild Ireland and marries Norah Joyce, who is as Irish as he is English. Hopkins explains that Stoker sees their marriage as a useful metaphor to suggest the potential harmony between Ireland and England and argues that he continues to use marriage in such a manner throughout his fiction:

> In all Stoker's fiction, Ireland plays a part, and the relationships which Stoker fantasies between his idealized men and women can indeed be seen as uneasily mirroring the harmony which this 'philosophical' but sentimental Home Ruler hoped to see between his adopted country and the country of his birth. Marriage thus becomes … a metaphor with a very wide range.¹²

However, Stoker also uses *The snake's pass* to showcase several uniquely Irish characters, including the usurious Black Murdock and the carter Andy Sullivan whose Irish brogue and genial behaviour reveal a wealth of native wisdom as well as offer comic relief. In addition, Sullivan introduces readers to Irish history, folklore and geography as well as to that uniquely Irish institution, the *shebeen*.

'The man from Shorrox', which was published in *Pall Mall* magazine in 1894, is set in Kilkenny, which had been the Irish Confederate capital until it fell to Cromwell in 1650, and narrated by a man with a decided brogue. It is a darkly humorous tale in which an Irish widow bests an impudent Manchester businessman by getting him drunk and then putting him to bed in a room where a corpse had been laid out. Told entirely in Irish dialect, it begins by suggesting the origin of Irish resentment against the English, resentment that according to the narrator could be found anywhere in Ireland:

10 See William Hughes' study of this story in Chapter 6. **11** Bram Stoker, 'The way of peace', *The Bram Stoker Society Journal*, 1 (1989), 39. **12** Lisa Hopkins, *Bram Stoker: a literary life* (New York, 2007), p. 19.

> The place was a market town in Kilkenny –r maybe King's County or Queen's County. At all evints, it was wan of them counties what Cromwell – bad cess to him! – gev his name to. An' the house was called after him that was the Lord Liftinint an' invinted the polis – God forgive him![13]

The narrator hints that the events he relates could have taken place anywhere in Ireland because Cromwell's invasion of Ireland and the brutality against its citizens led to enormous resentment.

The historical conflict between England and Ireland is reinforced by the conflict between a beautiful red-haired Irish widow and a pushy English businessman. She is briefly stunned by the forward behaviour of the man from Shorrox, 'the greatest long-cotton firrm in the whole worrld'.[14] Coming to her hotel at a time when there are no rooms available, he immediately demands the best room and then insults her personally by making advances toward her. She has the last laugh, however, when the man from Shorrox is encouraged to drink so much that he doesn't realize that he is sharing a bed with a dead man. The story concludes when the narrator finds the widow thinking about her husband, the dead man, and the Manchester businessman:

> 'Oh, but it's the crool woman I am to have such a thing done in me house – an' that poor sowl, wid none to weep for him, knocked about that a way for shport iv dhrunken min – – while me poor dear darlin' himself is in the cowed clay! – But oh! Mick, Mick, if ye were only here! Wouldn't it be you – you wid the fun iv ye an' yer merry heart – that'd be plazed wid the doing's iv this night!'[15]

This touch humanizes the widow and makes the story something more than a cruel practical joke.

If *The snake's pass* and 'The man from Shorrox' wear their Irishness on their sleeves, *Lady Athlyne* is more subtle. Probably the least known of Stoker's novels, *Lady Athlyne* was out of print in the United States for a full century until both Valancourt Books and the Bram Stoker Dracula Library released paperback editions in 2007. While the novel is set in Italy, New York, the English Lake District and Scotland, and features the early twentieth-century version of the jet set rather than Irish characters, the Irish connection is direct and obvious. Focusing on the romance of a young American woman and a Scottish lord, it begins and ends with Lord Athlyne's Irish nurse, Mrs O'Brien. She opens the novel by telling Joy Ogilvie that Lord Athlyne would be a perfect husband for the young American

---

13 Bram Stoker, 'The man from Shorrox', in *The judge's house and other weird tales* (Doylestown, PA, undated), p. 95. **14** Ibid., p. 98. **15** Ibid., pp 107–8.

heiress: 'When I seen Miss Joy come down the companion shtairs I sez to meself: "There's only wan man in Ireland – an that's in all the wurrld – that's good enough for you, me darlin'. An he'll have you for sure or I'm a gandher!"'[16] She thus becomes the matchmaker for the novel that concludes with memories of her own wedding night, when she embarrasses the usually forthright Joy by asking when there will be another generation of children for her to nurse.

Although much of Mrs O'Brien's earthy conversation revolves around parenthood and marital relations, Stoker subtly connects her to both technological development and politics. For example, the Ogilvies meet her onboard the Belfast-built *Cryptic* where she serves as a stewardess. Although she identifies herself as 'a Roscommon woman',[17] she explains that she had, like so many Irish people during the nineteenth century, left her homeland and her agricultural roots to pursue more lucrative possibilities. Furthermore, one reference reveals Stoker's awareness of contemporary Irish politics: 'I'm thinkin' that the Shinn-Fayn'll have to wake up a bit if that's the way things is going to go. Or else there'll be millea murther, from the Giant's Causeway to Cape Clear!'[18] When Arthur Griffith founded Sinn Féin (Irish for 'ourselves alone'), he suggested that Ireland might become a more equal partner with England rather than freeing itself entirely from the British Empire. At the time Stoker was working on *Lady Athlyne*, Sinn Féin was a relatively new movement that promoted the revival of the Irish language and Irish culture, and provided an outlet for the growing disenchantment with Home Rule, favouring a policy of passive resistance to England. It wasn't until after Stoker's death that the organization became associated with militant nationalism. Mrs O'Brien's cryptic comment suggests that she is aware that Ireland is changing rapidly and that Joy and her foster-son are going to be part of those changes.

When Mrs O'Brien introduces Athlyne in the first chapter, she emphasizes him as a member of the Irish nobility, 'the Right Honourable the Earl av Athlyne, Lord Liftinant av the County iv Roscommon'.[19] While Stoker apparently invented the title, Roscommon is one of Ireland's traditional counties as well as one of the counties most affected by the Famine and its after effects.[20] As Stoker probably knew, Roscommon was also the ancestral home of the Wilde family. Of course, Athlyne's background is extremely complex, for Mrs O'Brien adds that 'he's an Englishman too, an' a Welshman an' a Scotchman as well',[21] and when Joy and her

---

16 Bram Stoker, *Lady Athlyne*, rpr. ed. Carol Senf (Southend-on-Sea, Essex, 2007), p. 22. **17** Ibid., 25. **18** Ibid., 233. **19** Ibid., 22. **20** In *Quality of life and modernization in nineteenth-century Ireland* (Lewiston, NY, 2006), Thomas E. Jordan cites statistics about Ireland that were prepared by T.W. Grimshaw in 1883: 'On some comparative statistics of Irish counties, compiled from returns obtained during the late census and the census of 1841, and other publications issued by the general register office of Ireland,' *Journal of the statistical and social inquiry society of Ireland*, 61, pp 444–58; Grimshaw reveals that Roscommon was ranked 31 in 1841 and 27 in 1883. (131) Having traveled around Ireland as inspector of petty sessions, Stoker would have seen the poverty that resulted from the Famine. Even in 2012 when my husband and I traveled around Ireland, we could still see its impact. **21** Stoker, *Lady Athlyne*, p. 22.

Aunt Judy look him up in *Debrett's Guide*, they discover evidence of his wealth and his mixed background:

> Calinus Patrick Richard Westerna Hardy Mowbray Fitz-Gerald 2nd Earl of Athlyne (in the Peerage of the United Kingdom). 2nd Viscount Roscommon (in the Peerage of Ireland). 30th Baron Ceann-da-Shail (in the Peerage of Scotland). b. 6 June 1875 s. 1886 ed. Eton and University of Dublin; is D. L. for Counties of Ross and Roscommon: J. P. for Counties of Wilts, Ross and Roscommon.[22]

Even though *Debrett's* reveals that he was born, nurtured, and even educated in Ireland, Athlyne is a person who can 'pass' throughout the British Isles and is thus distinct from the many caricatures of the Irish in England.[23]

It's hard to imagine that Athlyne wouldn't have acquired a strong sense of Irish identity from his foster mother Mrs O'Brien, his biological mother having died at his birth and his father strangely absent from the novel. Indeed the only reference to the previous earl, presumably Athlyne's father, is that he identified so strongly with Ireland that he retired to the castle in Roscommon after leaving Parliament. As a result, Mrs O'Brien and her son Mick seem to be Athlyne's only family, and her loyalty to him is so strong that she urges her son to take care of his master when they go to Africa to fight the Boers and to keep 'betune him an' any bullet that's comin' his way'.[24] Regardless of his holdings elsewhere in the United Kingdom, Mrs O'Brien, who had nursed him as a baby after the death of his mother, sees him as thoroughly Irish.

Furthermore, she also identifies him as a good landlord. Not only does he understand his tenants, having been reared among them, but he expresses a desire to live among them too, as Mrs O'Brien notes: 'He has a whole lot av different houses, and he goes to them all be times. He says that no man has a right to be an intire absentee landlord – even when he's livin' in his own house!'.[25] Murray examines Athlyne's heritage and highlights the importance of his Irishness:

> The irony was that the Irish 'Ascendancy', to which the Earl of Athlyne belongs, had been in decline from the 1870s, when they moved from an assured social position to increasingly being viewed as alien by themselves and by others, while both their property and influence diminished. The central male character of *Lady Athlyne* is an Anglo-Irish hybrid, the earl of Athlyne, who is not only Irish, but also English, Welsh and Scottish, with

---

22 Ibid., p. 26. **23** David Glover describes the 'caricatures of Ireland in the English press during the troubled 1880s in which 'the Irish were depicted as monstrously subhuman, as creatures of Neanderthal stupidity and cruelty, incapable of civilized life' in *Vampires, mummies and liberals*, p. 37. **24** Stoker, *Lady Athlyne*, p. 25. **25** Ibid., pp 24–5.

corresponding lands and titles. Athlyne is no mere transplanted Briton in the Irish context; he is 'a Celt of Celts' and nationalistic rhetoric underlines his claims to true Irishness. Stoker probably derived the Athlyne name from the venerable Anglo-Irish Earldom of Athlone, which had been extinct since 1844 ... Athlyne's surname is FitzGerald, recalling ... the powerful Earls of Kildare who played a prominent role in Irish history ... If Athlyne reconciles Ireland and the rest of the British Isles politically, he is also a figure of social reconciliation at a time of divisive class tensions, having been born among his tenants and suckled by Mrs O'Brien.[26]

Stoker's emphasis of Athlyne's background reinforces his hero's ethnic background and suggests that he is capable of bridging the gulf between Irish Protestant landlords and their tenants. Equally important, because of his interest in technology (most evident in his purchase of a fancy touring car that allows him and Joy to elude their chaperones), Athlyne may, like Arthur Severn in *The snake's pass*, be capable of improving his holdings for his remaining tenants. The specifics are less clear here than in *The snake's pass* because Stoker never takes the reader to Athlyne's holdings. Nonetheless it is clear that when Athlyne returns from the Boer War he is seeking a mission in life.

Readers might be tempted to see both Mrs O'Brien and Andy Sullivan in *The snake's pass* as comic relief, but these characters provide important information about Ireland. Sullivan relates most of what the reader learns about Irish history and myth and, like Mrs O'Brien, returns at the conclusion to bless the newlyweds and wish them the best for the future. Indeed, both he and Mrs O'Brien refer to children, suggesting a definite future for each young couple (as well as a future for Ireland, which had lost half of its population to starvation and emigration). Mrs O'Brien goes so far as to offer to nurse the future offspring, noting that the newly weds should hurry and get started: 'I was a bride meself – wanst. An' I know betther nor me young Lady does now, what is what on the weddin' day afther the words is said. Though she'll pick up, so she will. She's not the soort that'll be long larnin'!.[27]

At the time he was writing *Lady Athlyne*, Stoker was also working on two essays that specifically explore Ireland's future. Written for a special Irish number of *The world's work*, 'The great white fair in Dublin' (1907) and 'The world's greatest shipbuilding yard' (1907)[28] feature Ireland's major cities, Dublin and Belfast. Murray comments specifically on the context:

> The journal devoted its May issue to Ireland in the belief that 1907 would be a special year for the country, with a royal visit in the offing, the

---

26 Murray, *From the shadow*, p. 257. **27** Stoker, *Lady Athlyne*, p. 233. **28** These essays as well as a number of other short works of nonfiction by Stoker are available in Richard Dalby (ed.), *A glimpse of America and other lectures, interviews and essays* (Westcliff-on-Sea, Essex, 2002).

prospect of Home Rule seemingly providing a solution to its political problems and a world's fair ... in Dublin. In the words of its editorial, the purpose was to carry 'a message of hope from a new Ireland' whose salvation was to be accomplished by economic regeneration and cultural renaissance, symbolized by the success of the Gaelic League, which had 'sent a new thrill of life throughout the length and breadth of the Island'. If Stoker did not write the editorial, its sentiments were close to his beliefs, as he made clear in his two articles.[29]

Both essays reveal Stoker's considerable pride in Ireland. 'The great white fair' focuses on the fair as a symbol of that pride. Indeed, while noting that Ireland is still primarily an agricultural country, Stoker points directly to the 'wonderful things' that are being done to 'start the island upon a new career of industrial progress'.[30] He notes that the fair is 'organized and arranged for the display of the direct and indirect results of learning, science and art, and illustrative of *that progress which follows in their wake*'.[31] Everything in this essay points to Stoker's hopes for a brighter future for Ireland though he would have remembered the poverty for which it was known.[32] Gary Owens describes that poverty in graphic detail:

> At the same time, there was hardly an area of Dublin where the destitute could not be found: Prunty shows them living literally in the shadows of the finest Georgian homes, in cramped courts behind the better shops, and in the dark cellars of houses on both sides of the Liffey. Unlike their British counterparts, they were not the victims of industrialization but of the absence of industry and of the general economic malaise that gripped the county from the early 1800s onward.[33]

Owens correctly notes that poverty in nineteenth-century Dublin stemmed from high unemployment when peasants, forced off the land, moved to the city. While there had always been some wealth in Dublin because it was the centre of business and government, Stoker believed that only wide-scale industrialism would make that wealth available to a significant percentage of the population.

'The world's greatest shipbuilding yard' moves from Dublin to the more industrialized north of Ireland and features the Belfast company, Harland and Wolff, which was known for its technological innovations in shipbuilding and also for its luxurious ships, one of which is featured in *Lady Athlyne*. While the com-

---

29 Murray, *From the shadow*, pp 250–1. **30** Stoker, 'The great white fair', in *A glimpse of America*, p. 146. **31** Ibid., p. 148, emphasis mine. **32** During our recent visit to Dublin Castle, a tour guide explained that a wall was erected at the castle to hide Dublin's notorious slums from Queen Victoria when she visited the city in 1900. **33** Gary Owens, 'Social history', in Laurence M. Geary and Margaret Kelleher (eds), *Nineteenth-century Ireland: a guide to recent research* (Dublin, 2005), p. 36.

pany, which was created by Edward Harland and Gustav Wolff in 1858, is recognized for its pioneering use of iron and steel for building ships, Stoker is more interested in 'the magnitude, stability and prosperity' he witnesses there, an emphasis appropriate for someone who spent his days making certain that the Lyceum operated smoothly.[34] The essay concludes with his celebration of human ingenuity: 'As there are twelve thousand people employed ... the payment of these varying accounts within *ten* minutes instances the perfection of business organization, which can hardly be exemplified in a better or more fitting manner'.[35] Stoker's emphasis here is on the number of people employed in shipbuilding as well as the speed with which they were paid. The industrialized north of Ireland did not suffer as dramatically during the nineteenth century as the agricultural south, but both articles demonstrate Stoker's belief that commerce and industrialism could eliminate the poverty that he elsewhere associates with his native land.

Thus far my discussion of Stoker's life and works might suggest that he was entirely Irish. However, it is equally important to recognize that Stoker was thinking globally from the time he was a student at Trinity College and to understand that much of his fiction demonstrates his thoughts about the world in general or occasionally about particular world events. Part of Stoker's appeal to me is that universality. For example, Bradley Dean writes convincingly that Stoker was thinking of the complicated relationship between Egypt and England when he wrote *The jewel of seven stars* (1903), and adapted the mummy fiction already established by popular writers such as Rider Haggard to address this relationship. At the time Stoker was writing, Egypt was 'nominally a vassal state of the Ottoman Empire' though the real power was 'held by the British Consul General, Lord Cromer, along with his administration of advisors and an army of occupation'.[36] Stoker's interest in Egypt is especially evident in his library. Even though he and Florence had to sell the bulk of his considerable library when they moved from Chelsea to a smaller home, 317 books were listed in the printed catalogue prepared by Sotheby, Wilkinson and Hodge in 1913. According to Leslie Shepard this catalogue 'indicates the wide range of Stoker's interests and associations', including travel and history books 'on Egypt, Asia, Canada and America'.[37]

While *The jewel of seven stars* is the only one of Stoker's novels to reveal his interest in the relationship between Egypt and England, other works demonstrate his interest in other regions of Africa. Both *Lady Athlyne* and *The man* (1905) examine the toll that the Boer War had on a generation of young people, and his final novel *Lair of the white worm* (1911), in particular his extraordinarily unat-

---

34 Stoker, 'The world's greatest shipbuilding yard', in *A glimpse of America*, p. 150. **35** Ibid., p. 153. **36** Bradley Deane, 'Mummy fiction and the occupation of Egypt', *English Literature in Transition, 1880–1920* (51:4) 281. **37** Leslie Shepard, 'The library of Bram Stoker/a note on the death certificate of Bram Stoker' in Carol Margaret Davidson (ed.), *Bram Stoker's* Dracula: *sucking across the centuries, 1897–1997* (Toronto, 1997), p. 412.

tractive portrait of the African witch doctor Oolanga, reveals his concern over racial issues and suggests that he was mulling over immigration as well.

An earlier novel, *The mystery of the sea* (1902), also touches on racial issues at the same time it reveals Stoker's concern with yet another part of the world. Writing of *The mystery of the sea*, Andrew Smith observes that Stoker uses 'images to be found in the Spanish-Cuban-American War in order to construct a possible settlement between Catholic and Protestant' and thus argues that *Mystery* is really about Ireland.[38] While Smith's reading of the conflict between Catholic and Protestant rings true, there is strong evidence that Stoker was also thinking about Cuba and about Scotland, where the novel is set, as well as about the rising power of the United States. The novel takes place in Cruden Bay, the Scottish resort community where Stoker spent many working vacations. Its American heroine Marjory Drake is passionate about the Spanish treatment of Cuban civilians, and its hero Archie Hunter sympathizes with the plight of Scottish fishermen whose livelihood is threatened by large commercial fishing operations that use dragnets to catch fish. Indeed, when Archie questions a local fisherman, he learns that 'certain fishing grounds, formerly most prolific of result to the fishers, were now absolutely worthless'.[39] That Stoker's novels touch on contemporary political issues in areas as distinct as the United States, Cuba and Scotland reveals his concern for issues taking place throughout the world.

During the time that he was writing, another one of those regions was Eastern Europe and the Balkans. Readers will think automatically of *Dracula*, which begins and concludes in Transylvania, and of *The lady of the shroud* (1909), which Stoker set in a fictional Balkan land, the Land of the Blue Mountains. Writing of Stoker's political interest in 'Bram Stoker and the treaty of Berlin (1878),' Matthew Gibson observes that Stoker's 'interest in Balkan, Ottoman and Austro-Hungarian politics ran deep'.[40] Even though Stoker did not live to see the inevitable conclusion of that treaty, the problems of boundaries, nationhood and ethnicity that it attempted to resolve would eventually result in the First World War.

Stoker's concern with the world of his own time also extends to the Western Hemisphere. While *The mystery of the sea* reveals his interest in Cuba, his fascination with the United States, based at least partially on the experiences he gained while touring North America with the Lyceum, is evident throughout his writing career. For example, in 1883 when he was organizing Irving's first American tour, he studied American customs and turned the material into a lecture that he delivered in 1885 and published the following year as *A glimpse of America*. Stoker's methodology is clear in this work. Not only does he observe America and

---

38 Andrew Smith, 'Bram Stoker's *The mystery of the sea*: Ireland and the Spanish American war', *Irish Studies Review*, 6:2 (1998), 136. **39** Bram Stoker, *The mystery of the sea*, ed. Carol A. Senf (Kansas City, 2007), p. 18. **40** Matthew Gibson, 'Bram Stoker and the treaty of Berlin (1878)', *Gothic Studies*, 6:2 (2002), p. 236.

Americans first hand, but he also relies on statistics and other published studies. *A glimpse of America* reveals the same care for details that is evident in *The duties of clerks of petty sessions of Ireland*, where he describes his methodology:

> This book ... has been compiled from all the sources of information at my disposal – statutes, General Orders, Circulars, Law Opinions, Files of Papers, Registry Books, Returns, &c. The collation of the enormous mass of such, accumulating since 1851 and following the slow growth of the splendid system now in practice, has been a work of excessive labour. Thousands of documents – entries, briefs, &c. – have been consulted, so as to ensure, as far as possible, the most rigid accuracy in the statements set forth, and to make the information given full and complete.[41]

His enormously positive portrait of the United States concludes with 'joy that England's first-born child has arrived at so noble a stature' and refers to the United States as 'so strong an ally, so close a friend'.[42]

Dracula, *The shoulder of Shasta* (1895), some of the stories in *Snowbound* (1908), *Lady Athlyne*, and 'The squaw' (1893), on the other hand, express greater ambivalence toward both the United States and American characters. A number of critics, including Franco Moretti, Elizabeth Miller and Robert Eighteen-Bisang, and James R. Simmons, remark on Quincey Morris' uniquely American character. Miller and Eighteen-Bisang observe that Stoker changed Quincey's name a number of times during the seven or more years that he worked on *Dracula* and that one incarnation of the character was as Quincey P. Adams, a decidedly more American name. They also argue convincingly that Quincey (or Brutus or simply 'The Texan') 'once played a more significant part in the novel'.[43] No matter how many changes Stoker made, however, Quincey remains distinctly American in contrast to his European colleagues. Furthermore, while neither Miller nor Eighteen-Bisang see anything sinister in Quincey's American background, Moretti and Simmons go so far as to link him to Dracula, Simmons even questioning whether Quincey might even be a vampire:

> When we consider that all actions, from his mysterious and sudden appearance in Lucy's house after her final attack, to his nocturnal habits and often-inexplicable behaviour, point to his being in league with Dracula, why couldn't Morris, too, be a vampire?[44]

---

[41] Stoker, *A glimpse of America*, v. [42] Ibid., p. 30. [43] Elizabeth Miller and Robert Eighteen-Bisang (eds), *Bram Stoker's notes for* Dracula: *a facsimile edition* (Jefferson, NC, 2008), p. 29. See also Franco Moretti, *Signs taken for wonders* (New York, 2005), pp 94–5. [44] James R. Simmons. '"If America goes on breeding men like that": *Dracula*'s Quincey Morris problematized', *Journal of the Fantastic in the Arts*, 12:4 (2002), 434.

Following in this line of thinking, P.N. Elrod, who is best known for her Vampire Files series, recently wrote a novel *Quincey Morris, vampire* (2001) that indeed depicts him as one of the undead. This is an intriguing theory and certainly an idea that would explain why he must be killed off. Like Dracula, Quincey is too primitive to exist in a Europe dominated by professionals like Harker, Seward and Van Helsing. There is no place for him in the modern world.

Published two years before *Dracula*, *The shoulder of Shasta* is the only Stoker novel set entirely in the United States[45] though one of the stories in *Snowbound* also depicts an American landscape and character, and part of *Lady Athlyne* is also set in the United States. *The shoulder of Shasta* features the rugged natural beauty of the American West, which Stoker describes at great length:

> There is something in great mountains which seems now and then to set at defiance all the laws of perspective. The magnitude of the quantities, the transparency of cloudless skies, the lack of regulating sense of the spectator's eye in dealing with vast dimensions, all tend to make optical science like a child's fancy. Up at the present height, nearly three thousand feet, the bracing air began to tell on their spirits. Even Esse's pale cheeks began … to show some colour, and her dark eyes flashed with unwonted animation, as they ranged over the splendid prospect.[46]

Not only does he comment on the rugged landscape of the United States, he also populates it with a group of equally rugged people, including the mountain man Grizzly Dick, almost certainly modelled on William Cody, a former frontier scout and buffalo hunter who had become an entertainer by the time Stoker knew him, and a tribe of Native Americans. Though the Native Americans are presented as primitive and potentially dangerous, Dick is eventually revealed as a natural gentleman who knows to stay in his place:

> Let me get back to the b'ars an' the Injuns. I'm more to home with them than I am here. Be easy, Little Missy, an' ye too, all ye ladies and gentlemen; it'll be no pleasant thinkin' for me up yonder, away among the mountings, that when I kem down to 'Frisco, meaning' to do honour to a young lady that I'd give the best drop of my blood for … I couldn't keep my blasted hands off my weppins in the midst of a crowd of women! … I ain't fit to go heeled inter decent kempany![47]

---

45 One of the other essays in this volume, Chapter 5, '*The shoulder of Shasta*: Bram Stoker's California romance' by Andrew Garavel, examines the significance of the landscape. Most of Stoker's fiction is acutely aware of the places where they are set, and I hope that someone will eventually address the importance of geography in Stoker's fiction. **46** Bram Stoker, *The shoulder of Shasta*, ed. Alan Johnson (Westcliff-on-Sea, Essex, 2000), pp 25–6. **47** Ibid., p. 124.

While very few critics have commented on *The shoulder of Shasta*, Louis S. Warren, Hopkins and Alan Johnson comment specifically on its American setting and characters.[48]

rising power of US

However, if Dick knows enough to stay in his place, other Americans are punished for taking frontier behaviour to Europe and, in Quincey's case, attempting to integrate into that society, a response that may reveal Stoker's apprehension at the rising power of the United States. 'The squaw', a short story, published the same year as *The shoulder of Shasta*, reveals a cruel and thoughtless American tourist in Nürnberg. 'Elias P. Hutcheson hailing from Isthmian City, Bleeding Gulch, Maple Tree County, Nebraska',[49] thoughtlessly kills a kitten by dropping a stone on its head. The kitten's death is certainly not deliberate, but Hutcheson's comments reveal his familiarity with cruel behaviour on the frontier:

> '[An Apache squaw] followed Splinters mor'n three year till at last the braves got him and handed him over to her. They did say that no man, white or Injun, had ever been so long a-dying under the tortures of the Apaches. The only time I ever see her smile was when I wiped her out. I kem on the camp just in time to see Splinters pass in his checks. ... Durn me, but I took a piece of his hide from one of his skinnin' posts an' had it made into a pocket-book. It's here now!' and he slapped the breast pocket of his coat.[50]

There's a kind of poetic justice at the end of the short story when the mother cat skewers Hutcheson in the Iron Maiden, one mother avenging another.

Neither as obtuse nor as cruel as Hutcheson, Quincey Morris is another resident of the New World to perish when he visits the Old. Indeed there seems to be a distinct pattern in that Stoker kills off American men when they come to Europe, and it seems not to matter which side of the law they are on. Quincey, a member of the Crew of Light that sets off across Europe in pursuit of Dracula, is killed when they all confront Dracula while the pirates in *The mystery of the sea* drown shortly after Archie rescues Marjory. American women fare better, often – like Marjory Drake and Joy Ogilvie – assimilating themselves into European culture by marrying their European lovers. Indeed, Stoker was assuredly aware of a trend at the *fin de siècle* when spunky American heiresses came to Europe and married aristocratic men. Stoker might have modelled Marjory and Joy on real women, including Jennie Jerome, who married Lord Randolph Churchill in 1874 and gave birth to Winston Churchill,[51] later prime minister of England, or

---

48 Louis S. Warren, 'Buffalo Bill meets Dracula: William F. Cody, Bram Stoker and the frontiers of racial decay', *American Historical Review*, 107 (2002), 1124–57; Hopkins, *Bram Stoker*, pp 3, 21; Alan Johnson, 'Introduction' in Bram Stoker, *The shoulder of Shasta* (Westcliff-on-Sea, Essex, 2000), pp 11–12, 16–21. **49** Bram Stoker, 'The squaw', *Dracula's guest and other stories* (Herfordshire, 2006), p. 47. **50** Ibid., pp 49–50. **51** Stoker was certainly familiar with Churchill, and his 1908 interview of the future Prime Minister is

Consuelo Vanderbilt, who married Charles Richard John Spencer-Churchill, 9th Duke of Marlborough in 1895.⁵²

Reading through all of Stoker's works reveals that he is thinking about the world around him and that he is weaving the unique characteristics of that world into his fictional world. England, Ireland, Paris, Scotland, Cuba, Egypt, the United States inspire Stoker's imagination, and he even ventures into the Pacific – specifically the Straits of Malacca – in 'The red stockade' (1894). The more I read what Stoker wrote, the more I see his universality. Neither fantasy nor a thinly veiled commentary on Ireland, Stoker's works represent his attempt to wrestle with specific problems at the *fin de siècle*.

Indeed Stoker's interest in the larger world and its politics is very much in evidence long before he started exploring that world in fiction. His 1872 Address to the Historical Society, 'The necessity for political honesty', begins by extending the human quest for truth to political endeavours:

> And as men beginning our political career, we should have ever before us … the advancement of truth, and as its perfection that truth which in public affairs is as widely different from partisanship, and class feeling and self interest, as it is from dishonesty and selfishness in private matters. As truth broadens out from individuals to nations, so should we have in view its teaching, not only to persons, but to the world at large. And to raise the nation or the individual ever so little, we must hope and work for much, and have a high ideal standard towards the realization of which all our efforts may tend.⁵³

Beginning his address with individual morality, Stoker concludes with internationalism, describing it as a modern idea that 'will sway the destinies of the future':

> What is this internationalism but the dawning of truth – the casting off of the petty chains of local prejudice, and of that quasi-nationality which is the very apotheosis of parochialism – those petty chains which … bind the soul? When will men learn that patriotism is not merely to sneer at and be jealous of surrounding nations, not to gather all the love and affection with which God has dowered the heart of men into one little spot till it becomes a garden, whilst all the rest of the world remains, for them, a waste?⁵⁴

---

included in the collection *A glimpse of America*. **52** Their stories are related in a book that supposedly influenced the recent television series, *Downton Abbey* (2010–), *To marry an English lord: tales of wealth and marriage, sex and snobbery* by Gail MacColl and Carol McD. Wallace. Originally published in 1989, it was recently released in 2012, possibly to capitalize on the popularity of *Downton Abbey*. **53** Bram Stoker, 'The necessity for political honesty' in *A glimpse of America*, p. 37. **54** Ibid., p. 43.

Fifty years before US President Woodrow Wilson posed the idea of the League of Nations and almost a century before the United Nations became a reality, Stoker was already lobbying for such an institution, powerfully insisting that: 'Men are finding out that what is best for the world is best for the nation, and that the consolidation of all countries into one common league for good is the true means of peace'.[55] This interest in a peaceful future is evident in so much of what Stoker wrote. It explains, I believe, so many of the collaborative efforts that are evident in his fiction, collaborations that involve residents of several nations working together to battle a great evil. Among these alliances is the Anglo-American alliance in *Dracula*, the Anglo-Irish alliance in *The snake's pass*, and the Anglo-Balkan alliance in *The lady of the shroud*. Such alliances were, for Stoker, often rooted in specific historical issues and problems that no longer resonate with readers of later generations. What continues to resonate is that readers today can see that similar problems remain with us today. This resonance speaks to Stoker's universality and explains why he continues to matter to us.

---

55 Ibid.

The shoulder of Shasta: Bram Stoker's California romance

ANDREW J. GARAVEL, SJ

On 17 September 1893 Bram Stoker, accompanying Henry Irving on a tour of the United States and Canada, was traveling by rail from San Francisco to Portland, Oregon, when he saw the inspiration for his one novel set in the United States, *The shoulder of Shasta*, published in 1895.[1] It is possible that his train stopped for a few minutes at the little station at Edgewood, California, but in any event Stoker would have seen Mount Shasta only once, and comparatively briefly at that.[2] Part of the Cascade Mountain Range, Mount Shasta in far northern California is the remnant of a volcano, a lone mountain rising dramatically to more than four thousand meters (fourteen thousand feet), the view of which has impressed many travellers besides Stoker. Theodore Roosevelt, for example, said 'I consider the evening twilight on Mount Shasta one of the grandest sights I have ever witnessed'.[3] And the California writer Joaquin Miller opens his book *Life amongst the Modocs* (1873) with an evocation of the mountain:

> Lonely as God, and white as a winter moon, Mount Shasta starts up sudden and solitary from the heart of the great black forests of Northern California ... It has no rival! There is not even a snow-crowned subject in sight of its dominion. A shining pyramid in mail of everlasting frosts and ice, the sailor sometimes, in a day of singular clearness, catches glimpses of it from the sea a hundred miles away to the west; and it may be seen from the dome of the capital 300 miles distant.[4]

---

[1] Alan Johnson, 'Introduction' to Bram Stoker, *The shoulder of Shasta* (Westcliff-on-Sea, Essex, 2000), p. 7. [2] Recall that in the second sentence of *Dracula*, Jonathan Harker pronounces Budapest 'a wonderful place, from the glimpse which I got of it from the train'. Bram Stoker, *Dracula*, ed. Glennis Byron (Peterborough, ON, 1998), p. 31. [3] Cited in Douglas Brinkley, *The wilderness warrior: Theodore Roosevelt and the crusade for America* (New York, 2009), p. 548. [4] Joaquin Miller, *Life amongst the Modocs: unwritten history* (London, 1873), p. 1. It is possible that Stoker decided on a novel set in the Sierra Mountains in part because of the familiarity of British readers with the locale in the writings of Miller, Bret Harte and

The 'shoulder' referred to in Stoker's title is a plateau extending from the northern side of the mountain, the setting of much of the novel's action. Stoker wrote *The shoulder of Shasta* while also at work on *Dracula* (1897), and it prefigures a number of elements of that far more famous novel, including a young heroine who has characteristics of both Mina Murray and Lucy Westenra, and a rough-hewn but kindly Westerner with clear affinities to the Texan Quincey Morris. Additionally, *The shoulder of Shasta* enacts both the sense of racial and gender anxiety found in *Dracula*.

Despite these similarities, the subject and tone of the two books are quite different: *The shoulder of Shasta* is cast in the classic mould of comedy, with a young heroine who undergoes a crisis and retires from the city to a pastoral 'green world' where her experience of Nature awakens her to the possibilities of love. Sixteen-year-old Esse Elstree has travelled from London with her widowed mother on an extended tour of the United States when she falls ill in San Francisco. Anaemia – the blood disease from which Lucy Westenra is at first thought to suffer – is her doctor's diagnosis, and the fresh air of Mount Shasta his prescription. Esse travels to the wilderness with her mother and two servants as well as her former governess, now companion, Miss Gimp. On the final leg of their journey they are guided by a hunter and trapper named Grizzly Dick who, with his Winchester rifle and long, fair hair resembles William F. 'Buffalo Bill' Cody, with whom both Stoker and his employer Henry Irving were on cordial terms.[5] In fact, Stoker explicitly mentions Cody in connection with his fictional frontiersman when Peter Blyth, a friend of the Elstree family, meets Grizzly Dick: 'Like many Londoners, his sole knowledge of the actuality of Western life was from "Buffalo Bill" and the "Wild West Show" …'[6] Bluff and good-humoured, with a natural if unsophisticated gentility, Dick speaks in a Western dialect possibly modelled on (but rather less successful than) the dialogue in Mark Twain's tales of frontier California.[7] He is also described as 'a mighty fine figure of a man', and indeed he sparks the romantic interest of both Esse and her middle-aged chaperone (47).

Even before the party reaches the mountain cottage they are to call home for the next few weeks, Esse's vitality has begun to revive. (She had been described in her illness as 'pale' and 'languorous,' terms also applied to Lucy in *Dracula*.) She is particularly sensitive to her surroundings, and the wild landscape (Stoker's descriptions of which Carol Senf rightly characterizes as 'sublime') evokes in Esse congruent emotions of awe.[8] Nature, however, is not merely uplifting, but potentially dangerous; as Dick cautions her, '[I]n the forest everythin' or anythin' may

---

Mark Twain. **5** Louis S. Warren, *Buffalo Bill's America: William Cody and the Wild West Show* (New York, 2005), p. 303. **6** Bram Stoker, *The shoulder of Shasta*, ed. Alan Johnson (Westcliff-on-Sea, Essex, 2000), p. 100. Subsequent quotations will appear in the text in parenthesis. **7** Dick and Quincey Morris speak in similar idioms, both using phrases such as 'Count me in!' in *The shoulder of Shasta*, p. 29; *Dracula*, p. 189. **8** Carol A. Senf, *Bram Stoker* (Cardiff, 2010), p. 50.

be harmful' (66). Portrayed as a Romantic, her experience of the natural world is consistently linked with her dawning self-consciousness as a woman:

> So Esse in her unsatisfied young life watched and waited at the shrine of Nature, not knowing what she sought or hoped for, whilst all the time the deep, underlying, subconscious forces of her being were making for some tangible result which would complete her life … It might be destiny, it might be fate, it might be simply the accomplishment of a natural purpose; but whatever it might be, she would yield herself to the Great Scheme, and let her feet lead her where instinct took them (38).⁹

It comes as no surprise that the destination the narrative has in store for her involves romantic love, and the opportunity for its fulfillment is, of course, dictated by place and circumstance: '… as Dick was the only male in the place, for of course Indians and servants did not count, she felt that she had to think of him now and then' (54).

And think of him she does, though at first with a mixture of gratitude for his protection and annoyance at what she regards as his frontier levity. Soon enough, however, they are teasing each other over minor faults, and Dick is teaching her to shoot. Interestingly, Grizzly Dick as a man of the wilderness is several times rendered in animal imagery (apart from his name itself), as in a doctor's description of his convalescence after having been mauled by a bear: 'His simple life, with his great energy and his plain living, make recovery seem extraordinary to town-bred men. But we must not judge of his health by the standard of the towns, but rather by the animals, who simply lie quiet and lick their wounds, and are running about again when a man is beginning to realize he is helpless!' (80). Elsewhere his powerful, easy bearing is compared to that of 'the King of Beasts'. Dick clearly is a *natural* man, indeed a kind of intermediary between the wild and civilization. And whereas he is seen as Nature ennobled, his strength and vitality at the service of the protection of the weak, the Native Americans of Mount Shasta are portrayed throughout as Nature debased. Esse quickly forms the opinion that

> the Indian [occupies] a low place in the scale of human types …. At first they amused her, and then, when she knew them a little better, they disgusted her. In fact, she went with them through somewhat of those phases with which one comes to regard a monkey before its place in the scale of creation is put in true perspective …. So she gradually came to realize that, in spite of their ragged relics of a higher civilization, they were but little

---

9 As Stoker refers to 'her being', it is worth noting that his heroine's name might well be derived from the Latin verb *esse*, 'to be'.

better than savages, and with the savage instinct that could not be altered all at once (51–2).

At least one member of the local tribe contemplates violence toward the visitors, but fortunately for the Elstrees, '[Dick's] proximity kept the Indians in order; for with the dominance of a Caucasian he made himself to some degree regulator of his neighbour's affairs. Indeed, he stood with regard to the Indians somewhat in the relation of a British justice of the peace to the village community' (49). As in *Dracula*, there is an endorsement of Anglo-Saxon or Anglo-American solidarity against the perceived threat of the racial 'other'. However, Dick's own attitude towards Native Americans is ambivalent: he holds that 'the Indian ... ain't of much account nohow', and indeed 'the cruelty of that lot of ours makes me so mad, I want to wipe them all out'; yet at the same time he asserts that the Indian 'ain't so bad as those think that don't know him', and that 'there isn't one of them, man, woman, or child, that wouldn't stand between me and death' (52). (It is possible to hear in this ambivalence an echo of the paternalistic Anglo-Irish attitude towards the Irish peasant, with its mixture of aversion and affection.) The Native Americans' rendering as potentially wayward children is seen most strikingly in their superstitious regard of a parrot belonging to Miss Gimp: because it can imitate human speech, the tribesmen conclude that the bird must be a god, so they bring gifts of game (some stolen from Dick) to Miss Gimp, the supposed priestess of the deity. Thinking that these offerings are romantic tributes from Dick, to whom she has taken a fancy, she stows the meat in her chest of drawers, where it soon goes bad. In a line that might seem to comically foreshadow *Dracula*, we are told 'a lady's bedroom is in no way adapted for the storage of dead flesh' (58). After the stench becomes intolerable, Miss Gimp and Esse bury the rotten meat under cover of darkness. When the latter relates all of this to Dick they share a hearty laugh at the older woman's foolish fancy, but that night 'Esse put her head on her pillow filled with a secret but fearful exultation that Dick and she shared a secret between them' (60).[10]

However, it is not until a near-fatal incident that their relationship develops further. Esse is painting in the forest one day when she encounters a mother grizzly bear and her two cubs. The young woman pretends to be dead, but the grizzly has come perilously close just as Dick happens along and shoots at the bear, which charges him and shatters his leg, though at the last moment he manages to kill it with his bowie knife (Quincey Morris' weapon of choice in *Dracula*). Dick urges Esse to flee, knowing that the enraged mate of the female bear will arrive shortly, but she refuses to leave him: '"Go, and leave you alone!" said Esse indignantly,

---

10 Much of Miss Gimp's role in the novel is that of a foil to Esse: the prudish, mid-Victorian spinster (she still wears the old-fashioned hoop skirts of thirty years before) contrasted with the vibrant young woman, 'modern' to a degree, but with nothing of the virago nature ascribed to the 'New Woman' by her detractors.

"and you wounded and tied down like that? Not me! What do you take me for?"' (70). The mountain man evidently knows his grizzlies because, just as he foretold, along comes the male bear at top speed making for Esse, who is able to distract it momentarily with the aid of her pocket-handkerchief, get to her revolver, and bring down the beast with an extremely lucky shot right in the eye: '[t]he good fortune which now and again attends on novices seemed to have guided her aim' (71). In its dying throes, however, the bear wounds her somewhat and shreds her dress with its claws; tellingly she notices the affront to her modesty before sensing any bodily harm, and 'a hot blush swept over her'. Pinning her clothes up as best she can, 'she set about her work with a business-like precision' (72); indeed much of Esse's demeanour recalls the brisk resourcefulness of Mina Murray.

However, the text suggests that, like her, Esse is not an example of the 'New Woman', despite the fact that she must now reverse normative gender roles by rescuing the man, just as Mina has to come to Jonathan's aid. Dick is severely injured and seems certain to die if, as he again urges her, she leaves him to seek her own safety. Consciousness of his danger 'made her efforts of feverish intensity, and she worked with an unconscious power and purpose which those who knew her would never have suspected' (72). And doubtless, too, a knack for both engineering and nursing hitherto undiscovered, as she must first extricate Dick from beneath the enormous weight of the female bear's carcass without injuring him further, which she does using a series of levers; and second, improvise a splint for his mangled leg. When she has accomplished all this, Dick yet again implores her to leave him and send for help:

> 'My dear Little Missy, I'm world-wide obliged to ye. Ye saved my life from that old grizzly, and ye've doctored me fine! Now, run off home, an' I'll be all safe here till ye return.'
> 'I'm not going to leave you, Dick!' she said decisively. 'I'm going to carry you home myself.' Dick laughed feebly, but this time it wounded the girl to the quick; she blushed up hotly, but cooled at once into a paleness, and her answer came with sudden tears into her eyes:
> 'You wouldn't leave me, Dick, if it was I who was hurt – would you, now?'
> 'Wall, I should smile!' said Dick.
> 'Then why should I leave you?' Dick scratched his head; logic and reason failed him as they have many a man when arraying them against the strength of a woman's resolve (75).

Esse posits a kind of gender equality that flies in the face of masculine 'logic and reason', temporarily rendered moot in the face of the woman's devotion.[11]

---

[11] Andrew Maunder discusses Stoker's interest in women who invert gender roles, though in the service of

Nonetheless the wounded and still-convalescent teenager must drag the helpless frontiersman down the mountain on her back: 'And, strange to say, she did carry him all the way home. It is true that the struggle seemed an endless one, and that over and over again she felt that she could have lain down and died of sheer fatigue. But it was for life and death, and to men and women who have true grit great needs give great endeavour' (75). To add to the inversion of gender roles, as Dick is being carried by the young woman, several times 'the pain overmastered him to such a degree that he swooned', but even at this stereotypically feminine moment, 'he did not make any sign, but took his swoon like a gentleman', to avoid causing Esse any further distress (75, 76). When they reach home, Dick praises Esse effusively and puts on a brave face for the onlookers, but then whispers to Mrs Ellstree's manservant, 'Take me home quick, old man! I'm racked with pain, and nigh dead, and it's torture keepin' it up afore the women folks' (78).

When she recovers, Esse helps to nurse the mountain man and realizes that their mutual life-saving 'was an important step in the growth of a romantic affection ... She was a woman now, for good or ill, and whatever she thought or did was from the standpoint of a woman, and would have to be adhered to with a woman's constancy, or abandoned with a woman's resolve' (80). When he is well enough, Dick makes a necklace for her out of the bear claws, and passes the time by recounting some of his earlier exploits: Stoker alludes to Othello's wooing of Desdemona by telling stories, though making it clear that Dick is not actively pursuing an affair (indeed, his reserve holds an attraction for the young woman). Meanwhile Mrs Elstree, like Brabantio, grows uneasy as Dick seems to become idealized in her daughter's eyes. Fortunately, from the mother's point of view, circumstances intervene in the form of the first snowfall, signaling that the city-folk must return to the city, leaving the wilderness to Grizzly Dick and the Indians.

Back in San Francisco, Esse is happily reunited with the city's shops and theatres, but something is missing, of course, as she starts to turn Dick into 'a sort of hero of romance, [and] began to exaggerate her feelings towards him' (85). She is described as lovesick in a newly scientific sense as Stoker uses the terms 'virus' and 'bacillus of love' to convey her state, and indeed her old ill-health returns: as she broods, she becomes 'pale and listless' once again (85, 86). To Peter Blyth, a friend of her late father, she confesses that: 'If I could only see him [Dick] for a moment it would be like feeling the wind blowing down from Shasta – like hearing the roar of the falling water – like the sound of the forest coming up at dawn! It all seems so little here, and he is so brave and strong, and moves through life as though he

---

love: in a chapter called 'Women as men' in *Famous imposters* (1910), Stoker 'writes admiringly of adventurous women who disguise themselves as men', because they lived under economic disadvantages precluding them from earning their own livings, but then adds that more often than not this was done in the name of love, out of a woman's self-sacrifice for her man. *Bram Stoker* (Tavistock, Devon, 2006), p. 101.

were born to rule it!' (93). Dick is more than once associated with the wilderness itself, and we are told that

> it might be that Esse's craving was for the mountain as well as the man; that the place and its possibilities, its adventures, its bracing qualities, the stimulation of the high mountain air and the whole wild, free exuberance which had come into her life at the moment her womanhood was developing ... had seized on her imagination ... In any case, the man was at present so inextricably mixed up in her mind with his surroundings that without his presence no disentanglement could take place (95).

Speaking of the friendship, her confidant insists, '[T]he whole thing is uncommon! It is not common that you should care for a man away outside the class you have been reared in; the occasions that threw you together were uncommon' (98). Blyth sees that so long as Esse associates Dick with the sublime atmosphere of the mountain, he will continue to exert a romantic fascination over her. The solution is that Dick must be summoned down to San Francisco where, out of his natural element, she can see him in a more realistic perspective: 'in the midst of her present refined surroundings, she could not help contrasting him with them ...' (96). Thus Blyth is duly dispatched to Mount Shasta to invite Dick for a visit and to convey Esse's interest in him.

Almost immediately, however, she begins to reflect that, in the words of Gwendolyn Fairfax (another lovestruck young woman from a rather better remembered work of that same year), 'It is obvious that our social spheres have been widely different.'[12] As Stoker puts it, 'Esse was beginning to feel that an unconventional attachment was not without its drawbacks' (99). Part of this change of heart is the result of an upturn in her bodily health now that she has confided her secret affection: 'When in the anaemic condition Esse's imagination was apt to run away with her, though when her system was well furnished with red blood her fancies and desires were healthy and under control'. In a better frame of body and of mind she comes to see that a picnic in the wilderness might be delightful for a time, but 'it [was] impossible for her to contemplate an isolated life in the woods or on the mountains', and the prospects of Dick moving to the city, even if he wished to, seem equally unlikely, so she wires her emissary to withhold the invitation (108).

Fortunately, less than twenty pages before the close of the novel, a more socially acceptable love interest comes along in the form of a handsome young English painter named Reginald Hampden. Though an artist, he has nothing of

---

[12] Oscar Wilde, *The importance of being Earnest* in *The complete works of Oscar Wilde* (New York, 1994), p. 364.

the aesthete about him; in fact he, too, is a hunter and a man of action, and socially adept as well: 'of a most charming personality, with gentler manners and keener refinement than might have been expected from his strength and stature' (109). He is, in other words, a figure with all of Grizzly Dick's vitality and manliness, but with the imagination and social poise the latter clearly lacks.[13] Reginald represents an ideal combination of masculinity and cultivation, just as Esse (and, even moreso, Mina Murray in *Dracula*) strike the proper balance between femininity and independence. The Englishman has come to paint the landscapes of the American West, but along with these he finds another subject: 'To him the freshness and artless simplicity of Esse was akin to those grand simplicities of Nature which had been the study of his life', and soon 'his art and human sympathies had … been united in so charming a young lady …' (110). As she is in a sense aestheticized by the painter, so in her turn she makes the memory of her former love into a work of art: '[Dick] was, and would be till the end of her life, a true and faithful friend, whose memory was set in a frame of romantic picturesqueness, as a miniature is set round with diamonds; but he did not belong to the living present at all': thus the flesh-and-blood man is transformed into a safe and sentimental icon (110). And the resourceful young woman of the mountainside undergoes a change as well, now content to let herself be addressed as 'you dear little high-minded goose!' by her beau, who has 'the amused, superior tolerance of a successful lover' (112, 111).

But complications arrive literally on Esse's doorstep: it seems that Blyth did not receive her telegram, the invitation has been conveyed, and here is Grizzly Dick, 'big as life and twice as natural', come to pay a call. Except that in the city he is no longer the natural, easy man of the mountain; instead he behaves with 'brazen impudence, this being his idea of easy deportment' (117). He has changed his appearance, too, and arrives kitted out according to the only image of city life he knows, the costume of a vaudeville comedian he has seen in a Sacramento music-hall saloon.[14] The snobs of Nob Hill society gathered at Mrs Elstree's house regard Dick as a buffoon: they make sport of him while, in the next room, Esse is mortified. As Stoker describes her position, she 'was in a way chained to the social stake' – that is, like a bear! (118). One female guest maliciously persuades Dick to declare his love for Esse and ask her to marry him in front of the whole assemblage. When he does so and Esse tearfully tells him the truth of the situation,

---

13 As Maunder points out, 'Throughout his adult life Stoker cultivated an image of a robust "manly" man, famously addicted to weightlifting, running and swimming and, whilst they are not necessarily self-portraits, he often takes such men as the basis for his novels'. *Bram Stoker*, p. 74. **14** Dick models his costume on 'the more aristocratic-looking of the Two Macs' (p. 115), one of the most popular variety acts of the day; Stoker could well have seen these knockabout comedians himself, either in the United States or in London (for example, they are described in *Punch* as 'the Two MACS belabouring each other in their old hopelessly idiotic, but always utterly irresistible style'. Anonymous, ''Tis Merry in Hall', *Punch*, 102:2 (April 1892), 157: http://www.gutenberg.org/files/14390/14390–h/14390–h.htm.

'Dick, more dangerous than any wild animal,' draws his bowie knife[15] and lashes out at the crowd around him, and then nearly throttles the newly arrived Peter Blyth, whom he thinks has tricked him into this humiliation. But Reginald coolly steps forward and restores order by pointing out that Dick is causing the young woman distress. The frontiersman is immediately contrite: 'Little Missy, forgive me if ye can! I must have gone mad! .... Let me get back to the b'ars [bears] an' the Injuns. I'm more to home with them than I am here' (124). In a flourish of self-disgust, he throws his knife into the floorboards; when several of the young San Francisco bucks are unable to pull it out again, Reginald shows his British mettle and draws forth the blade after the manner of the young King Arthur. Dick is ready to slink away in embarrassment, but the young couple and Mrs Elstree assure him that all is forgiven.

Curiously, given that the work is in the mode of romance, the reader's attention is drawn at the very end not to the happy couple, but to the rejected lover. On the final page of the novel, Reginald tells Dick, 'I've got something that will make you feel more comfortable than this Sacramento rig-out!' A few minutes later:

> there was a buzz of admiration through the room when Dick entered, clad in a hunter's outfit, something like his own, which Reginald had some time before bought from the Indians as a model for his work. There was about him something so fresh, wild and free – so noble a simplicity and manhood, that more than one woman present did not wonder that Esse had asked him to come down to 'Frisco (128).

Thus ends the book, with the mountain man dressed in an artist's model's outfit for the approval of the San Francisco crowd, much as the actual hunter William Cody becomes the buckskin-clad Buffalo Bill. Grizzly Dick is, in effect, frozen as an artifact of the West, a figure to be admired and perhaps momentarily enchanted by, as Esse was on the mountain, but not a person to be taken seriously on his own terms or to be admitted to polite society for more than an evening or two. Indeed, he excites approbation only when he keeps to his proper role as the man of the mountain, but is scorned and mocked when he foolishly tries to imitate the ways of the city. The Old West had become part of popular culture when it was hardly old, in fact during the life-times of some of the actual participants. Buffalo Bill's Wild West Show, begun seven years before the close of the frontier in 1890, presented real cowboys, Mexican *vaqueros* and Native American warriors like Chief Sitting Bull, acting out their own adventures and defeats (with whatever degree of accuracy) for the entertainment of paying audiences. Likewise, Grizzly Dick becomes transformed into an aesthetic object not long before he and

---

15 Though Stoker seems to be under the impression that a bowie knife springs open like a jackknife or switchblade.

his frontier kind are swept away, as the last of the California grizzly bears would be killed just one generation later, in 1923.

The novel ends rather abruptly and, though we are not told so explicitly, it is certain that Dick returns to the mountain, leaving the young couple to play their part in what Esse thinks of as 'the Great Scheme'. When she first beholds Shasta, she 'began to feel that in the whole scheme of Nature was one deep underlying purpose in which each thing was merely a factor; that she herself was but a unit with her own place set, and the narrow circle of her life appointed for her, so that she might move to the destined end' (38). As in comedy generally, the destined end involves marriage and procreation, though it seems here to be of a curiously impersonal sort: Esse's 'later and truer love [for Reginald] had all the unconscious, serious earnestness of the race itself, where means are forgotten and only the end is held in view', a view which includes 'no thought of Dick in her mind, no regret, no remorse, even no pity of his wasted and ruined life …' (111).

In Esse's growing realization of her true destiny as wife and as mother, and in Dick's ready acquiescence that he is not a suitable mate for her, we see the classic device of comedy in which a character is somehow saved, often at the last moment, from choosing a partner who would be regarded as unsuitable because of differences in class or temperament. (Or, as in some of Shakespeare's comedies, because the lover and the potential beloved appear to be of the same gender.) As Alan Johnson points out, in *Dracula* (which Stoker had already sketched out by the time he wrote *The shoulder of Shasta*), 'Although the pursuit of Dracula takes up much of the novel's action, the ultimate goal of the plot from its outset is the achievement of a productive union for Mina and Jonathan and for Lucy and someone'.[16] So in a strange way the Count himself becomes the *alazon* or 'blocking figure' of comedy, thwarted in the first instance, successful in his ruination of the latter. Lucy gives an indication of the social and sexual heterodoxy which will contribute to her undoing when, on the day she receives three marriage proposals, admits she might be thought 'a horrid flirt' and asks, 'Why can't they let a girl marry three men, or as many as want her, and save all this trouble? But this is heresy, and I must not say it'.[17] As in *The shoulder of Shasta*, one of these three offers of marriage is from a noble-hearted American who gallantly steps aside when an English suitor makes his presence known. But, as Carol Senf argues, 'Dick is unthreatening because he is content to remain in his place, but [Quincey] Morris … [is] punished for taking frontier behaviour to Europe and … attempting to integrate into that society, a response that may reveal Stoker's apprehension at the rising power of the United States'.[18]

Stoker refers to Esse's infatuation with Dick as 'the "preliminary canter" of her affections', as opposed to the more serious affair that lies ahead (111). As Senf goes

---

16 Johnson, 'Introduction', p. 19. **17** Stoker, *Dracula*, p. 91. **18** Senf, *Bram Stoker*, p. 50.

on to point out, in reading this slight tale of a young woman's coming to maturity it is 'difficult to anticipate the Gothic masterpiece' of *Dracula* which would follow shortly.[19] Yet the earlier, and decidedly lesser, work does display a number of the anxieties Stoker would work out more fully in *Dracula*: changing gender roles, atavism, the threat of the racial 'other', social degeneration, the need to carry on 'the race', and even blood and its disorders. And, in both texts, the heroine is at once 'brave and gallant' and full of 'sweetness and loving care',[20] a balance between the New Woman's desire for greater scope and the domestic virtues of the earlier Victorian 'angel in the house'.

Reading *The shoulder of Shasta* in some ways brings to mind a very different narrative about the American frontier: the 1956 motion picture *The Searchers* by John Ford. The film also deals with racial issues in the Old West, specifically with white anxiety about contact (especially sexual relations) with 'the Indians': a young woman who had been abducted by Native Americans and lived for years as a member of their tribe is at last restored to her family. At the final scene of reunion, however, her rescuer does not enter the house. We see him as it were from the interior of the farmhouse as he fills the doorway – it is John Wayne, of course – curiously cradling his arm as though wounded, the famous landscape of Monument Valley behind him until he turns away and the door closes behind him. He does not come in to the family home perhaps because he has done more than a few unsavoury things in his career. But more fundamentally, he cannot enter the domestic scene and the settlers' civilization it represents simply because he remains the man of the wild, a figure belonging to an earlier stage of settlement. Once his task is done, the only proper thing for him is to return to the wilderness alone. In *The shoulder of Shasta*, Stoker gives us a curious comedy in which the heroine comes to self-awareness through a place and through a man which capture her youthful imagination, but both place and man must be kept distant from the family home towards which her supposedly more mature sensibility leads her.

19 Ibid., p. 53. **20** Stoker, *Dracula*, p. 419.

'Rumours of the Great Plague': medicine, mythology and the memory of the Sligo cholera in Bram Stoker's *Under the sunset*

WILLIAM HUGHES

In *Dracula* (1897), as many modern critics have noted, meticulously fictionalized medical practice serves a function characteristic of the cultural polemic of the Victorian *fin de siècle*.[1] Cultural anxiety, for example, seemingly motivates the novel's pointed allusions to the scientific criminology of Cesare Lombroso and Max Nordau.[2] Their fables of criminality and degenerate contagion perceptibly combine, in Stoker's novel, with contemporary fears of both invasion from beyond national (or racial) borders and an impending domestic cultural decline.[3] Elsewhere in *Dracula*, the specific naming of David Ferrier and Sir John Burdon-Sanderson as touchstones for the speculations of the vivisectionist asylum-keeper John Seward occludes a more protracted encounter with the practice of another British physician, William B. Carpenter, now widely acknowledged in academic criticism.[4] Carpenter's theory of 'Unconscious cerebration', which is repeatedly cited in *Dracula*, underwrites the habituated, purblind empiricism which distracts the unwary and unimaginative specifically from the dangers posed by the unprecedented phenomenon of vampirism but implicitly, also, from many other more subtle and conventional threats.[5] In *Dracula*, as critical consensus seems now to

---

1 See, for example, the interpretations of Victor Sage, *Horror fiction in the Protestant tradition* (Basingstoke, 1988), pp 180–5; Daniel Pick, '"Terrors of the night": *Dracula* and "degeneration" in the late nineteenth century', *Critical Quarterly*, 30:4 (1988), 71–87; and Valerie Pedlar, 'The zoophagous maniac: madness and degeneracy in *Dracula*' in *'The most dreadful visitation: male madness in Victorian fiction* (Liverpool, 2006),' pp 134–58. **2** Bram Stoker, *Dracula*, ed., William Hughes and Diane Mason (Bath, 2007), p. 385. **3** Jules Zanger, 'A sympathetic vibration: *Dracula* and the Jews', *ELT*, 34 (1991), pp 33–43; Clive Leatherdale, *Dracula: the novel and the legend*, third edition (Westcliff-on-Sea, 2001), pp 207–9, 228–31. **4** Stoker, *Dracula*, p. 115; David Glover, *Vampires, mummies and liberals: Bram Stoker and the politics of popular fiction* (Durham, 1996), pp 76–9; William Hughes, *Beyond* Dracula: *Bram Stoker's fiction and its cultural context* (Basingstoke, 2000), pp 141–8. **5** Stoker, *Dracula*, pp 112–13; cf. Sage, *Horror fiction*, p. 54.

readily accept, Stoker is a knowing participant in both the practical and the polemical applications of the discourses of Victorian medicine.

Less, though, has been said of the incorporation of medical thought into the author's other writings, even though some of these works are more clearly the product of the period which Stoker spent, for better or worse, in at times humble Dublin lodgings rather than in London's fashionable Cheyne Walk. In these early years, when he was associated with both Trinity College and Dublin Castle, he lodged with the three of his brothers – William, Richard and George – all of whom chose medicine as a profession. Again, Stoker sought the social company of Dublin clinicians such as Sir William Wilde and John Todhunter – these being medical gentlemen who enjoyed literary as well as pathological pursuits.[6] Criticism has characteristically emphasized Stoker's interest in *speculative* medicine, most notably through his explicit fictional acknowledgment of Lombroso, Nordau and Jean-Martin Charcot in *Dracula*. It should be understood, though, that the author's most protracted encounters were with *practical* clinicians rather than established theorists; and even if two of his brothers ultimately published their own speculations upon topics as diverse as hysterectomy and diseases of the pharynx,[7] the author's biography amply demonstrates his familiarity with such practical matters as the treatment of blood poisoning, resuscitation and trepanning.[8]

Stoker's interest in practical symptomatology can be traced to his earliest published volume of fiction, the 1881 short story collection *Under the sunset*.[9] A volume of macabre allegories, ostensibly for children, this intriguing collection of moralistic fables has for many years been dismissed, or at best marginalized by academic criticism.[10] Where acknowledged in criticism at all, *Under the sunset* is characteristically interpreted as a sort of preliminary exercize in the anticipation of horrors to be fully realized later in *Dracula*. 'A crucial stage in the writing of *Dracula*', Joseph Bierman's 1998 psychobiographical reading of the relationship of *Under the sunset* to Stoker's other writings is, perhaps, representative of this tendency. In *Under the sunset*, Bierman discerns traces of authorial infantile anxieties associated in part with the birth of younger siblings, but also with later, ostensibly unconscious, fears regarding the integrity of the author's independent masculinity. These infantile

---

6 Peter Haining and Peter Tremayne, *The un-dead: the legend of Bram Stoker and Dracula* (London, 1997), pp 62, 91. **7** See, for example, Anon., 'Obituary: Sir William Thornley Stoker, Bart, MD', *British Medical Journal*, 15 July 1912, p. 1399; George Stoker, *Clergyman's sore throat and post nasal catarrh: causes, symptoms and treatment* (London, 1884). **8** Barbara Belford, *Bram Stoker: a biography of the author of* Dracula (London, 1996), pp 128, 136–7; Robert Eighteen-Bisang and Elizabeth Miller (eds), *Bram Stoker's notes for* Dracula: *a facsimile edition* (Jefferson NC, 2008), pp 171–85. **9** Though dated 1882 on the title page, *Under the sunset* was actually released in 1881 in order to take advantage of the lucrative Christmas gift-book market. See Richard Dalby, *Bram Stoker: a bibliography of first editions* (London, 1983), p. 9. **10** There are a few notable exceptions to this consensus. The earliest is an unpublished doctoral dissertation by Douglas Oliver Street entitled 'Bram Stoker's *Under the sunset*: an edition with introductory, biographical and critical material' (University of Nebraska, 1977), while Phyllis Roth devotes an entire chapter to 'The fairy tales' in her *Bram Stoker* (Boston, 1982).

fears, Bierman suggests, are translated by Stoker into recurrent fantasies capable of psychologically processing both the fear of personal debilitation and the threat to selfhood posed by more needy or successful siblings, fantasies which may be revisited and expressed at times of unconsciously perceived threat later in life. Hence:

> Once he had put his childhood fantasies into the form of the eight stories of *Under the sunset*, Stoker would then use references to those stories, both directly and covertly, to express his fantasies in subsequent stories and novels, even those he wrote 30 years later.[11]

If materialist criticism is less readily inclined to accept an interpretation of *Under the sunset* as the earliest of many expressions of the author's repressed sibling rivalry, one assertion by Bierman would seem to be almost beyond reproach: that *Under the sunset* is – possibly more than any other work of Stoker's – a product determined by its author's earlier years.

This small concession, perversely, has greater implications than might first appear. Immediately, it distances *Under the sunset*, and the discourses it embodies, from the pervasive unease of *fin de siècle* London. Stoker had been resident in London for just under three years at the time *Under the sunset* was published, and during this period he was almost certainly preoccupied not merely with the establishment of the Irving regime at the Lyceum Theatre but also with his family: he had married in December 1878, just five days prior to joining Irving in Birmingham, and his son Noel – the dedicatee of *Under the sunset* – was born in December 1879.[12] Stoker's Dublin journal likewise infers that he was at least planning *Under the sunset* some time *before* his move to London: the germ of a tale which became 'The shadow builder' is sketched out within its pages, accompanied by the (possibly later) marginal note, 'Idea used in Under the Sunset' [sic], while a second entry is headed 'Mem for story in "Under the Sunset"' [sic], though this latter – 'The king of the spiders' – was never realized in the volume.[13] If *Dracula* is saturated with the fearful discourses of the 1890s, *Under the sunset* is, by contrast, far less polemical than any work subsequently published by the author, and its characters, mythic in their compass, keep a due distance from any contemporary embodiment of social concern, be it connected with gender, imperial or racial politics.[14] Yet, even in the midst of this, Stoker's abiding interest in medicine, as a

11 Joseph Bierman, 'A crucial stage in the writing of *Dracula*' in William Hughes and Andrew Smith (eds), *Bram Stoker: history, psychoanalysis and the Gothic* (Basingstoke, 1998), pp 151–72 at p. 151. **12** Paul Murray, *From the shadow of Dracula: a life of Bram Stoker* (London, 2004), pp 77, 91. **13** Elizabeth Miller and Dacre Stoker (eds), *The Dublin years: the lost journal of Bram Stoker* (London, 2012), p. 37. Two undated references to *Under the sunset* appear on p. 118 of this private notebook in its original pagination. Assuming that Stoker filled the book's pages chronologically, this would date the conception of the volume to a time before 24 November 1877, for the latter date appears on an entry on p. 123. **14** The author's interest in those topics had, admittedly, already been expressed in a nascent form as early as 1872, by way of Stoker's Auditor's

moral discourse as well as a diagnostic and curative practice, peculiarly intrudes, and in a manner notably discrete from its later deployment in *Dracula*. This is nowhere more evident than in the depiction of disease and mortality contained in 'The invisible giant', the third story in *Under the sunset*.

The connection between 'The invisible giant' and Stoker's mother's written memoir of the Sligo cholera epidemic of 1832 has long been recognized.[15] Charlotte Stoker's personal reminiscences, which were first made available to the general reader in Harry Ludlam's 1962 biography of Stoker, are a telling account of how the spread of cholera was perceived and comprehended before the satisfactory microscopic isolation of the Comma bacillus by Robert Koch in the 1880s.[16] Bram Stoker's recension of this family resource maintains a certain quantum of the moralism of the earlier account, but is further tempered with an appreciation of the *causes* as well as the *symptoms* of cholera, in that it engages knowledge not available to Charlotte Stoker at the time of her experience. 'The invisible giant' is, in effect, a palimpsest whose implications are as distant from the early nineteenth-century Protestant cosmology of the author's mother as they are from the late-Victorian cultural polemic adopted by her son at the *fin de siècle*. It thus presents to the reader a quite different aspect of the latter's medical interests.

Charlotte Stoker's account of the Sligo cholera epidemic alternates between her non-clinical observation and a theologically determined commentary which arises out of her own Protestant upbringing.[17] It opens by recounting the wholly alien nature of what she called the 'new and terrible plague which was desolating all lands as it passed through them'. Knowledge of this pestilence came fitfully and in an imperfect form:

> Rumours of the great plague broke on us from time to time, as men talk of far-off things which can never come near themselves, but gradually the terror grew on us as we heard of it coming nearer and nearer. 'It is in France', they said. 'It is in Germany', and 'It is in England'.

---

address to the Historical Society of the University of Dublin, this being a work in which he issued possibly his first polemic regarding eastern-European immigration and an early statement whose implications linked the Anglo-Saxon populations of Europe and the United States. See Bram Stoker, 'The necessity for political honesty' in *A glimpse of America and other lectures, interviews and essays*, ed. Richard Dalby (Westcliff-on-Sea, 2002), pp 31–47 at p. 45. **15** Harry Ludlam, *A biography of Dracula: the life story of Bram Stoker* (London, 1962), p. 32. **16** Christopher Wills, *Plagues: their origin, history and future* (London, 1996), p. 116; Ann G. Carmichael, 'Cholera: pandemic pestilence' in Kenneth F. Kiple (ed.), *Plague, pox and pestilence: disease in history* (London, 1997), pp 142–7 at pp 145–6. **17** Such cosmologies – which are based upon an assumed divine cause or else a corresponding solution to visitations such as plague and famine – punctuate Irish history. Among many such reactions to the Famine may be found a report, penned by a Protestant clergyman from County Cork and quoted in a London newspaper, which stresses the fatalities within a number of Roman Catholic households in that county before concluding 'May a God of mercy look on us, and on this most miserable land': see Anon., 'Horrors of Famine in Ireland', *Bell's Life in London and Sporting Chronicle*, 14 February 1847, p. 3, cols 1–2 at col. 1.

Then, with wild afright, we began to hear the whisper passed, 'It is in Ireland!'[18]

Cholera was, indeed, a relatively new pandemic disease in Europe.[19] The earliest recorded, though probably not the first, pandemic outbreak of cholera began in Bengal, near Kolkata, in 1817, and lasted till around 1823. This relatively localized pandemic – which, nevertheless, claimed the lives of around 10,000 British troops in the Subcontinent as well as hundreds of thousands from among the native populations of India and Java – was succeeded by a second pandemic in 1829. Starting again in India, cholera this time spread both north and west along what was by then a greatly enhanced trading and military network. Reaching Russia by 1830, the pandemic entered Poland and Finland, and then raged for two years from 1831 across the cities of England. From England, cholera quickly and inevitably spread to Ireland, and from Ireland and via the English ports, it reached the US, Canada and Latin America by 1833.[20] There was little warning, other than sudden death and a spectacular display of morbid symptoms. There was no cure, and no sure explanation nor any understanding of how the fatal complaint might be transmitted from person to person across apparently open countryside or between afflicted and cholera-free conurbations.

In Charlotte Stoker's experiential recollection, a false sense of security is temporarily granted to the citizens of Sligo, if not to the population of Ireland as a whole, by spatial distance. The cholera is perceived as being far away, and if it is *has* reached native soil, then its presence is something fearfully communicated but still not readily perceived, its existence being confirmed only by what it does – and how, and who, it kills.[21] Likewise, in *Under the sunset*, temporal distance, and the transformation of history into myth brings the plague personified as 'The invisible giant' within the compass of 'far-off things which can never come near' to the soon-to-be afflicted population. In *Under the sunset*, 'The invisible Giant' immediately follows 'The rose prince', a tale of literal giant–killing, deeply laced with morality, which draws heavily upon the biblical story of David and Goliath.[22] In 'The rose prince',

---

18 Reprinted in Ludlam, *Biography of Dracula*, pp 25–31 at pp 25, 26. **19** Indeed, British newspapers infer the presence of cholera (and name that complaint explicitly) in the symptoms of an epidemic afflicting Liverpool, north-west England and north Wales at the turn of the eighteenth century. See Anon., 'Ship news', *The Morning Chronicle* (London), 6 October 1801, p. 3, col. 3. **20** The four cholera pandemics which affected Europe and the United States took place between 1817–23, 1829–51, 1852–9 and 1863–79. The fifth pandemic was isolated from the European and North American populations primarily because of the conscious adoption of hygienic measures and mobility restrictions, the latter partly a consequence of Dr John Snow's findings in London between 1849 and 1854. For a history of cholera in the period, see Dhiman Barua, 'History of cholera' in Dhiman Barua and William B. Greenough III (eds), *Cholera* (New York, 1992), pp 1–36. **21** Consider here the tone of, and the statistics which accompany, contemporary newspaper accounts of the Sligo cholera: Anon., 'The cholera', *Belfast News-letter*, 28 August 1832, p. 2, col. 3; Anon., 'Cholera in Sligo', *Freeman's Journal and Daily Commercial Advertiser* (Dublin), 31 August 1832, p. 3, col. 3. **22** This much was disparagingly recognized by the 'special child critic' in the *Punch* review of

a bestial, fanged and naked giant ravages the Land Under the Sunset, destroying without distinction the natural world, peaceable human communities and armies mustered 'in the pride of their strength', until the young Prince Zaphir slays him with a stone projected from a sling.[23] Zaphir's victory is styled as one based upon trust and humility rather than pride: he discards his bejewelled armour, repents his former misdeeds, and prays fervently for strength.[24] The great – but historically distant – victory by Prince Zaphir recounted in that story has, however, become nothing more than a myth to later generations. As the narrator sadly observes, the passage of time has made the Country Under the Sunset less than idyllic, its new condition being as perfect a breeding ground for cynicism as it is for disease:

> All the beautiful Country was sadly changed, and changed was the life of the dwellers in it. The people had almost forgotten Prince Zaphir, who was dead many, many years ago ... Those who lived now in the Country Under the Sunset laughed at the idea of more Giants, and they did not fear them because they did not see them. Some of them said,
> 'Tush! what can there be to fear? Even if there ever were giants there are none now.'
> And so the people sang and danced and feasted as before, and thought only of themselves.[25]

Indeed, in this mythic simulacrum of the purblind modern world, only one individual – an innocent and selfless child – actually perceives the slow progress of the plague from the distant wildernesses to the heart of the conurbation in which she dwells. Zaya, whose name teasingly recalls the long-dead giant killer Zaphir, gazes out from her garret window:

> There she saw a terrible thing – something so terrible that she gave a low cry of fear and wonder, and leaned out of the window, shading her eyes with her hand to see more clearly.
> In the sky beyond the city she saw a vast shadowy Form with its arms raised. It was shrouded in a great misty robe that covered it, fading away into air so that she could only see the face and the grim, spectral hands.
> The Form was so mighty that the city below it seemed like a child's toy. It was still far off the city.

A scene has been set in 'The invisible giant' that is not dissimilar to the opening paragraphs of Charlotte Stoker's reminiscence. In this account, indeed, cholera attains an almost physical presence despite its obscure origins and nature, and a

---

Under the sunset. See Anon., 'Christmas books', *Punch*, 81 (1881), p. 261. **23** Bram Stoker, 'The rose prince' in *Under the sunset* (North Hollywood, 1978), pp 13–44 at pp 26, 38. **24** Stoker, 'The rose prince', pp 36–7. **25** Bram Stoker, 'The invisible giant' in *Under the sunset* (North Hollywood, 1978), pp 45–71 at p. 46.

transmissibility which is intimate, implicated even in the bodies of those it silently touches. Charlotte Stoker's account begins:

> In the days of my early youth ... the world was shaken with the dread of a new and terrible plague which was desolating all lands as it passed through them, and so regular was its march that men could tell where next it would appear and almost the day it might be expected. It was the cholera, which for the first time appeared in Western Europe. Its bitter strange kiss, and man's want of experience or knowledge of its nature, or how best to resist its attacks, added, if anything could, to its horrors.[26]

The plague is literally walking towards the city at the heart of the Country Under the Sunset. Its steps are measured, predictable, irrevocable, but its nature remains obscure, even to the perceptive Zaya. Her immediate conclusion that 'The Giants, then, are not dead. This is another of them' prefaces her desire to communicate the impending doom to her neighbours.[27] They heed it not.

Curiously, though, Zaya appears to wish to confront this fearful apparition, despite the fatal associations of giants in Stoker's mythic kingdom. Her encounter with the giant is notably tactile. The narrator recalls her sensations as she approaches 'the great form before her in the air':

> As she went on, and got nearer and nearer to the Giant, it grew a little darker. She could see only the clouds; but still there was visible the form of a Giant hanging dimly in the air.
>
> A cold mist closed around her as the giant appeared to come onwards towards her ....[28]

That 'cold mist' is a constant associate of the Giant's pestilent progress, yet its roots are to be found less in the fairy tale and more in contemporary views regarding the spread of cholera – views that persisted even after Dr John Snow associated the spread of the disease with contaminated drinking water during the 1854 epidemic in London.[29]

The pre-Victorian attitude to the spread of cholera is amply displayed in Charlotte Stoker's account. If cholera is not a 'Giant' as such in this lay account of subtly approaching pestilence, it certainly partakes of the qualities of a miasma. Charlotte Stoker recalled how

> On some days the cholera was more fatal than on others, and on those days we could see a heavy sulphurous looking cloud hang low over the house, and we heard that birds were found dead on the shores of Lough Gill.[30]

---

26 Ludlam, *A biography of Dracula*, p. 25. **27** Ibid., p. 51. **28** Ibid., p. 52. **29** Consider here, for example, Max von Pettenkofer's theory that cholera was associated with some activating chemical agent present in the soil of affected areas. See Carmichael, 'Pandemic pestilence', pp 145, 147. **30** Reprinted in Ludlam,

1: W.V. Cockburn's illustration to 'The invisible giant'

This draping of a vaporous body across (and, implicitly, *through*) the permeable walls of domestic architecture strikingly anticipates W. V. Cockburn's disturbing 1880 illustration to this story (fig. 1), and the 'cold mist' of Stoker's allegory is paralleled also by the peaking of the cholera, according to the author's mother, 'on a damp, drizzling morning' – the point at which the family finally flee the plague that has now come 'amongst and around them'.[31]

A report from an English provincial newspaper, dated 30 April 1818 and derived from an earlier source in British India verified by 'high medical authority', likewise notes how 'a sudden blast of cold air from the hills, which came down the course of the Ganges, produced so fatal and violent a *cholera morbus* that twenty thousand persons perished in the course of three or four days'.[32]

The contemporary prophylactics recorded in Charlotte Stoker's account indicate that cholera was regarded as an air rather than water-borne complaint at the time. In addition to 'a constant fumigation' by way of 'Plates of salt on which vitriolic acid was poured from time to time', she recalls how 'At night many tar barrels and other combustible matters used to be burned along the street to try to purify the air, and they had a weird, unearthly look, gleaming out in the darkness'.[33] The cutting of trenches across the roads, 'for the purpose of stopping all intercourse with the affected districts' appears pointless if cholera is considered miasmatic in transmission, but sensible if its containment by human and soluble isolation were to have been understood.[34] Elemental mists, like Giants and uncontained water, respect no human boundaries.[35]

Stoker commissioned the 33 original illustrations for *Under the sunset* probably around 1880 from his Trinity associate, William Fitzgerald, and a professional illustrator, W.V. Cockburn.[36] The two illustrations of giants – that slain by Zaphir, and that perceived by Zaya – were drawn by Cockburn, and appear prominently within the first edition as tissue-faced plates. The second of these is particularly relevant to the specific association of the Invisible Giant with cholera, given that it participates in the graphic conventions by which the disorder was personified in popular discourse across the nineteenth century. As early as 1831, in an illustration for *McLean's Monthly Sheet of Caricatures*, the British artist Robert Seymour had personified cholera as an enshrouded skeletal figure, its face obscure, towering over modern armies engaged in battle (fig. 2).[37]

Biography of Dracula, p. 29. **31** Ludlam, *Biography of Dracula*, p. 29. Stoker, 'The invisible giant', p. 63. The illustration is reproduced in Belford, *Bram Stoker*, p. 140. **32** 'East India intelligence', *Trewman's Exeter Flying Post or Plymouth and Cornish Advertiser*, 30 April 1818, p. 3, col. 1. **33** Reprinted in Ludlam, *Biography of Dracula*, p. 28. **34** Reprinted in Ludlam, *Biography of Dracula*, p. 26. Such actions by local troops are recorded in the contemporary press: see Anon., 'Cholera in Sligo', *Freeman's Journal and Daily Commercial Advertiser* (Dublin), 3 September 1832, p. 1, col. 4. **35** Cf. Stoker, *Dracula*, pp 283, 302. **36** Murray, *From the shadow*, p. 151. Correspondence and illustrations by Fitzgerald for *Under the sunset* were sold at Christies on 28 January 1994. See http://www.christies.com/LotFinder/lot_details.aspx?intObjectID=3691359 accessed on 22 June 2012. **37** Robert Seymour, 'Cholera tramples the victors and the vanquish'd both',

2: Robert Seymour, 'Cholera tramples the victors and the vanquish'd both' (1832)

A subsequent woodcut of the approaching cholera, published by Seymour a year later in 1832, maintains the skeletal outline, though the now visible face is fanged, horned and demonic (fig. 3), and bears a greater resemblance to Zaphir's corporeal giant rather than the spectral one perceived by Zaya.[38]

Cockburn, though, is not merely drawing in these illustrations upon the caricatural conventions of the time of Charlotte Stoker's youth. Indeed, his work is well within the temper of those cartoon illustrations which personified cholera in its fifth pandemic – the first in which consciously deployed strategies of hygiene, containment and exclusion kept the contagion out the United Kingdom and the United States. If these illustrations of the 1880s were frequently racist – F. Fritz Graetz's 1883 cartoon for *Puck*, entitled 'Cholera on the Bowsprit', which crowns cholera with a fez, is perhaps the best known of these (fig. 4)[39] – Cockburn does

---

McLean's Monthly Sheet of Caricatures, 1 October 1832, p. 2. Illustration available on-line at http://ihm.nlm.nih.gov/luna/servlet/detail/ NLMNLM~1~1~101393375~148816:Cholera—Tramples-the-victors-&-the?qvq=w4s:/what/Cholera/;lc: NLMNLM~1~1&mi=6&trs=53 accessed on 22 June 2012. **38** Robert Seymour, 'The cholera morbus', in *The pegasus and harmonic guide: a collection of all the most popular and favorite songs, duets, medleys, parodies, glees and chorusses* (London, 1832), unpaginated. Illustration available online at http://scdp.uky.edu/vic/0016.html, accessed on 22 June 2012. The relevant plates are to be found between pp 38–9 and pp 50–1 in the first and second editions of *Under the sunset*. **39** Graetz, 'Cholera on the bowsprit', *Puck*, 18 July 1883, available online at http://www.pandemicportal.ca/photos/custom/pp28%20cholera%20obwsprit.jpg, accessed 3 January 2013.

3: Robert Seymour, 'The cholera morbus' (1832)

not associate the impending plague with immigration in *Under the sunset*, just as Stoker himself makes no such gesture in his own rhetoric.

Other caricatures published *after* the circulation of *Under the sunset*, though, seem to echo the conventions of Cockburn's Giant. T. Bernhard Gillam, for example, depicts disease in general as a semi-transparent (though not gigantic) crowned ghost, infiltrating the bodies and the streets of New York in an 1881 cartoon in *Harper's Weekly*.[40]

Most striking, though, is Kendrick's trenchant 1883 cartoon 'Is This a Time for Sleep?', which depicts an enshrouded and menacing cholera looming over New York while science sleeps, failing to perceive the impending danger (fig. 5).[41] Published in the US journal *Life*, the central figure's resemblance to Cockburn's earlier giant is noteworthy, and given that *Under the sunset* enjoyed a severely limited currency in the United States – its first American edition was released only in 1978 – one can only assume that a transatlantic grammar for this sort of personification was already well established by the 1880s. Stoker did not visit the United States until 1883, and

---

[40] T. Bernhard Gillam, 'The streets of New York', *Harper's Weekly*, 26 February 1881. Reproduced in Bert Hansen, 'The image and advocacy of public health in American caricature and cartoons from 1860 to 1900', *American Journal of Public Health*, 87:11 (1997), 1798–1807, fig. 3, p. 1801.   [41] Charles Kendrick, 'Is this a time for sleep?', *Life*, 2 August 1883. Reproduced as the cover to Dhiman Barua and William B. Greenough III (eds), *Current topics in infectious disease: cholera* (New York, 1992).

4: F. Fritz Graetz, 'Cholera on the bowsprit' (1883)

no extensive and detailed correspondence has yet come to light between Stoker and Cockburn to parallel that between the author and Fitzgerald. Thus, there remains no reliable guide as to how much input the author had with regard to the illustration of the 'invisible giant'. One thing, however, is evident. If the Land Under the Sunset is mythical and atemporal, at least one of its embedded illustrations is, like the technology which Jonathan Harker deploys in archaic Transylvania, 'nineteenth century up-to-date with a vengeance'.[42]

Just as Science slumbers at the watery portal to New York in Kendrick's illustration, so too do the dwellers in the Land Under the Sunset perceive no danger from beyond the curtilage of their crowded city. Indeed, they are indignant at Zaya's attempts to warn them about the spectre which only she can see. This encounter, during which Zaya – in the company of a fellow believer, the elderly sage Knoal – is physically menaced by her fellow citizens, is the point at which the fairytale logic of 'The invisible giant' turns conclusively towards a representation of medical symptoms horrific, no doubt, to the child reader but almost certainly familiar to any adult with memories of any of the first four cholera pandemics. With the giant no longer visible to Zaya, because he is now *both* within the city *and* the bodies of its inhabitants, the narrative bespeaks a range of identifiable

---

42 Stoker, *Dracula*, p. 77.

5: Charles Kendrick, 'Is this a time for sleep?' (1883)

symptoms literally and graphically written upon those who seek to punish the child and her associate by ducking them within the marketplace fountain:

> ... they advanced closer to lay hands on them both.
> The hand of one who was a ringleader was already outstretched, when he gave a low cry, and pressed his hand to his side; and, whilst the others turned to look at him in wonder, he cried out in great pain, and screamed horribly. Even whilst the people looked, his face grew blacker and blacker, and he fell down before them, and writhed a while in pain, and then died.[43]

43 Stoker, 'The invisible giant', pp 61–2.

This sudden and unanticipated death is followed first by a vocal wave of panic – 'All the people screamed out in terror, and ran away, crying aloud, "The Giant! the Giant! he is indeed among us!"' and then by further carnage among the general population, for 'before they could leave the market-place, in the centre of which was the fountain, many fell dead, and their corpses lay'.[44]

Two things are particularly stressed in Stoker's fictional account: the symptomatology associated with sudden death and the constant presence of water. The former, though not specifically referenced in Charlotte Stoker's memoir, was doubtless familiar to her; the latter is relevant to later visitations of the cholera and, in fact, represents again the absolute timeliness of Stoker's ostensibly fairy-tale narrative. Stoker is more likely to have gathered his impressions of sudden choleraic death from Victorian medical sources, oral or written, rather than from the document written by his mother. He may well have consulted his brothers William, Richard and George, all of whom trained as doctors: William Stoker, notably, was to provide surgical information ultimately deployed in *Dracula*.[45] Whatever the source of Stoker's imagery, its verisimilitude to the contemporary consciousness of cholera symptomatology is undeniable. Home medical guides, as much as clinical accounts, display a consensus regarding the likely symptoms and possible duration of cholera in the individual. These represent the lingering images of cholera in the Victorian popular mind. Those from the latter part of the nineteenth century, when cholera was effectively controlled within the United Kingdom, but still represented a threat which *might* return, are characteristically the most detailed, even if they offer relatively little practical hope to the lay practitioner.

Such popular works are invariably emphatic regarding the sudden onset of the final stages of cholera, even if this is usually described as taking somewhat longer than the demise of the fictional assailant of Zaya. *Cassell's family doctor*, for example, warns 'The disease may come on in two ways – either suddenly, without any warning symptoms, or with a premonitory period varying from a few hours to a few days'.[46] This is, certainly, in keeping with Charlotte Stoker's recollection that one family in her locality were 'left ... all well at 9 pm' only to have been 'dead and buried' by 9 the next morning.[47]

Though the abject evacuations of cholera – vomiting and the so-called 'rice-water stools' – are not mentioned in either the fiction or the memoir, the demise of Stoker's fictional ringleader embodies another physiological development associated with the progress of cholera. A brief but chilling account of a cholera seizure in *Bell's Life in London and Sporting Chronicle*, dated 12 August 1832, makes reference to the victim's 'violent cramps followed by every other symptom of cholera'.[48]

44 Ibid., p. 62.   **45** See Bram Stoker, *Bram Stoker's Notes for* Dracula: *a facsimile edition*, ed. Robert Eighteen-Bisang and Elizabeth Miller (Jefferson, NC, 2008), pp 178–83.   **46** A Medical Man, pseud., *Cassell's family doctor* (London, 1897), p. 641.   **47** Reprinted in Ludlam, *Biography of Dracula*, p. 28.   **48** Anon., 'Cholera', *Bell's Life in London and Sporting Chronicle*, 12 August 1832, p. 2, col. 4.

Cassell's family doctor is more explicit regarding the bodily location of the former, something which provides an obvious explanation for the comparatively crude line-drawing which illustrates this episode in Stoker's work:

> Cramp of the muscles of the arms, legs, and abdomen sets in, producing the most exquisite pain. This stage, which may last from two to fifteen hours, passes on to the stage of collapse, or cold stage. The temperature falls very low, the pulse gets very weak, and the urine becomes very scanty, or may cease to be excreted at all.[49]

The 'ice-cold hand' of the giant is indeed repeatedly noted in the story.[50] The black face of Stoker's victim likewise has its parallel in cholera literature, albeit with a chromatic variation. An account originally published in the *Fife Herald*, quoted ironically in the London periodical, *The Age*, on 3 July 1831, describes a ship's master stricken with cholera as being 'cramped all over the body' while alive, but notes that 'after his death his hands and arms, up to his elbows, were of a dark blue colour'.[51] An alleged testimony of a supposed cure of cholera through patent medicine again indexes, in the words of the victim, the 'cramp in my limbs, being all drawn up' and a body which was 'all over a blue colour'.[52] Popular medical guides published later in the century confirm this dramatic change of complexion, Thomson and Steele's *A dictionary of domestic medicine and household surgery* (1899) depicting the sufferer's skin as variously 'cold, blue, bathed in sweat' and 'markedly bluish'.[53] Twentieth-century writers for the popular market are inclined to be more dramatic: Christopher Wills, for example, contends that 'Victims of cholera often turn black as the blood congeals and the skin collapses'.[54]

In such an environment as the fictional Land Under the Sunset, the ready transmission of complaints so familiar in nineteenth-century Ireland seems hardly surprising. Contemporary reports of the Sligo cholera dwell long upon the tendency of the local population to remain in close company with the afflicted, and to indulge also in wakes following the death, 'thus making every cabin and private house, a nucleus for the pestilence'. Hence, 'In almost every case where the sick person died in his own house, three or four of the same family have been attacked'.[55] In Stoker's fiction, a moral dimension is imbricated with the development of overcrowding. The narrator notes how the population of the Land 'had become more selfish and more greedy, and had tried to grasp all they could for

---

49 *Cassell's family doctor*, p. 641. The line drawing, signed 'WVC', is identical in both the first and second editions: see Stoker, *Under the sunset*, p. 62. **50** Stoker, 'The invisible giant', pp 63, 65. **51** Anon., 'Cholera and the judge advocate', *The Age*, 3 July 1831, p. 211, col. 3. **52** Anon., 'Cholera morbus cured by Morrison's universal medicines only' [advertisement], *The Satirist; or, The Censor of the Times*, 8 January 1832, p. 16, col. 3. **53** Spencer Thomson and J.C. Steele, *A dictionary of domestic medicine and household surgery* (London, 1899), pp 124, 717. **54** Wills, *Plagues*, p. 105. **55** Anon., 'Cholera in Sligo', *Freeman's Journal and Daily Commercial Advertiser* (Dublin), 31 August 1832, p. 3, col. 3.

themselves. There were some very rich and there were many poor'. Such a situation has an effect upon the very structure of the mythical city, making it resemble the tenement-infested conurbations in which the second and third cholera pandemics found their ready breeding place. As the narrator notes: 'Houses had grown up close around the palace; and in some of these dwelt many persons who could only afford to pay for part of a house'.[56] Zaya dwells in such a garret, but is spared specifically because of her demonstrable selflessness. The giant's parting words are: 'Innocence and devotion save the land'.[57]

The presence of water, finally, is the element that again affirms Stoker's acquaintance with contemporary, rather than pre-Victorian, theories regarding the spread of cholera. The decision of Dr John Snow to remove the water pump at the centre of the Broad Street epidemic in London in 1854 represented the first systematic understanding of the role played by ingestion and excretion in the spread of cholera. Cholera is spread most virulently when its bacilli enter the drinking water supply through its contamination by the liquid faeces of those who are already afflicted. This was *not* known in Sligo in 1832, hence Charlotte Stoker's images of miasma and airborne infection. In 'The invisible giant', though, Zaya and Knoal are menaced by a crowd gathered around a marketplace fountain, and the cry goes up that the citizens 'should put her under the fountain and duck her, as a lesson to liars who would frighten us'.[58] If this were a visitation of the cholera such an action would doubtless expose the two to the contagion, and though Zaya is subsequently – and fancifully – protected by the wild birds whom she feeds and who 'pecked of her bread and drank of her cup', it is plain from the final illustration to 'The invisible giant' that Knoal expires beside that same fountain, the pestilential waters of which still continue to flow (fig. 6).[59] He, presumably, has somehow partaken of the infected water, and lacking resistance expires as the others.

What is clear about 'The invisible giant' is that its medical script is as thorough and as detailed as that later inscribed in *Dracula*. In the latter novel, Stoker's deployment of medical symptoms and speculations is closely imbricated with the social, political and racial critique of a novel that is not so much nineteenth century as *fin de siècle* – 'up to date with a vengeance'. In 'The invisible giant', though, the polemic is less pointed and, indeed, less time-specific. If it is a tirade against greed, it is not focused upon any individual or indeed group. There is no verbal or illustrative distinction that demarcates Zaya's attackers as elite or proletarian, no suggestion that they are 'othered' by racial or religious difference. The plague, again, lacks direction from any deity, and moves seemingly at random, killing without reference to virtue or to vice. If there is a redemptive function, it is gained through the human agency of Zaya and Knoal, who remain in the city as a physical comfort to the afflicted, the herbal-

56 Stoker, 'The invisible giant', p. 45. **57** Ibid., p. 71. **58** Ibid., p. 61. **59** Ibid., p. 69. This unsigned but paginated plate was redrawn for the second edition: see Richard Dalby and William Hughes, *Bram Stoker: a bibliography* (Westcliff-on-Sea, 2004), p. 48.

6: Unsigned plate for 'The invisible giant'

ist's skill being instrumental in the recovery of some. The narrator's coda to this – that those who were rescued 'were very thankful, and henceforth ever after lived holier and more unselfish lives'– seems rather glib and unconvincing.[60] The connection between this aside and the giant's parting words is never properly made. On the one hand, it is an oblique *homage* to the earlier example of Zaphir, one whose 'heart was purified by repentance for all wrongs done in the past, and by high resolves to be good in the future'.[61] As is the case so often in fable and fairytale, however, the final destiny of those affected is rendered implicitly rather than explicitly. There is no closure, for it is not vouchsafed that the chastened state of the surviving populace will endure throughout their retrieved lives, nor whether its tenets will be transmitted to future generations. The remainder of the stories in *Under the sunset*, notably, eschew the city of Zaphir and Zaya and its teeming population in favour of more intimate studies of singular children and young adults. In conclusion, the moral context of 'The invisible giant', the centre of its brittle polemic, remains open and nebulous, the implications of the story being far less clearly demarcated than the more complex and extensive *Dracula*. 'The invisible giant', though, is suggestive at least of the importance that medical topics, whether as symptomatologies or as moral indices, were to play in Stoker's writings from the 1880s to his final novel in 1911.

60 Stoker, 'The invisible giant', p. 64.   61 Stoker, 'The rose prince', p. 37.

'The sport of opposite forces': Bram Stoker's generational anxiety

DAVID FLOYD

This chapter examines how Bram Stoker's fiction articulates a sense of generational anxiety. The first part discusses various conventions Stoker used to underscore his generation's interstitial predicament, with challenges to the paradigms of 'modern' protagonists, examples and contestations of clear delineations of 'traditional' and 'modern' females, and the theme of degenerating communication. The second part focuses on Stoker's engagement with the Victorian myth of the ideal family as imaging an endangered traditional world, examining depictions of exile from normative contexts, the disruption of familial structures, and threats to the domestic space.

Bram Stoker's work is in many regards exemplary of its time, resonating with irresolution and incertitude. Kate Hebblethwaite states it is 'in tune with the cultural zeitgeist', with its experimental nature, its pronouncements of contemporary thought and creativity, and its demonstration of the author's awareness of the cultural significance of late nineteenth- and early twentieth-century Britain.[1] Sos Eltis notes Stoker's intentional engagement with the late nineteenth-century world of 'technological advance, gender instability and proliferating discourses'.[2] Stoker's perception of the *fin de siècle*'s pivotal position in human history was, however, not without its unease. The period is notable not only for what James Wilson calls the 'bewildered sense' of a world preparing for a significant realignment of religious belief[3] but for scepticism regarding the traditional world in general. Louis James points out that the era marked 'the transition from the "modern" of the Victorians to the "Modernism" of the next century'.[4] This modernism was characterized by a 'decidedly eschatological impulse', as well as growing negativity and despair that

---

1 Kate Hebblethwaite, 'Introduction' to *Dracula's guest and other weird stories* (London, 2006), pp xiii and xxix. 2 Sos Eltis, 'Corrupting of the blood and degeneration of the race: *Dracula* and policing the borders of gender' in John Paul Riquelme (ed.), *Dracula* (Boston, 2002), p. 451. 3 James Wilson, 'Landscape with figures' in Andrew Noble (ed.), *Robert Louis Stevenson* (London, 1983), pp 73–95. 4 Louis James, *The Victorian novel* (Malden, MA, 2006), p. 8.

seemed to 'herald the coming of a new age'.[5] Stoker was no exception to this impulse, writing of 'a changing world he feared'.[6]

Stoker certainly did have an appreciation for the achievements of the modern era. Jenny Bourne Taylor observes the writer's fascination with the technological and scientific accomplishments of the nineteenth century, stating that Stoker even saw in them the potential to save humanity.[7] But his regard was weighed down by the concern that the materialism, scientism and naturalism attending that progress would imperil the spiritual, religious and moral scaffolding associated with some aspects of the traditional past that Stoker also held in such high regard, and which modernism threatened to displace. Indeed, Stoker's interest in technological progress seems to have been haunted by worries of the loss of traditional morality, that the values he felt so crucial to society would be a casualty of the modern world.

The final decades of the century indeed seemed a tenuous synthesis of opposing paradigms. Some facets of the culture lamented the disintegration of the old world, particularly as that disintegration was demonstrated in scepticism and incredulity concerning the family; others advocated an emphasis on materialism and scientism, disparaging 'outdated' concepts like traditional family structures and religious institutions. Stoker himself clearly 'looked in two opposing directions': imminent modernity and the past it threatened to forfeit.[8] We see this duality played out in the variety of his fiction. Stoker's collection of children's stories, *Under the sunset* (1882), presents a fantastic realm that is only discernible in dreams; the Gothic *Dracula* (1897), meanwhile, offers such technological achievements as vocal recorders and flashlights. Second sight is the main theme of the initial chapters of *The mystery of the sea* (1902); but dynamite is used to destroy Diana's Grove in *The lair of the white worm* (1911). Throughout most of Stoker's work, romanticized, stereotypical templates determine predictable masculine and feminine characters; however, questions of identity, including gender inversion, frequently undermine those generalities. Caught between the fading traditional world of presumed stability and virtuous integrity, and the advent of a modern world tinged with uncertainty and even immorality, Stoker indeed perceived his generation as interstitial.

'A SORT OF VAGUE BEGINNING OF CONSCIOUSNESS': CHALLENGING THE MODERN

One manner by which Stoker demonstrates this generational anxiety is by problematizing his typical male protagonist's materialist, scientific facility with the

---

5 Stephen Arata, *Fictions of loss in the Victorian* fin de siècle (Cambridge, 1996), p. 1; Joseph Warren Beach, *English literature of the nineteenth and the early twentieth centuries, 1798 to the First World War* (New York, 1962), p. 195. **6** Barbara Belford, *Bram Stoker: a biography of the author of Dracula* (New York, 1996), p. xv. **7** Jenny Bourne Taylor, 'Psychology at the *fin de siècle*' in Gail Marshall (ed.), *The Cambridge companion to the* fin de siècle (Cambridge, 2007), p. 28. **8** Carol Senf, Dracula: *between tradition and modernism* (New York, 1998), p. 6.

implications of the unexplainable events with which he comes into contact. Challenges frequently engage the protagonist's capacity for rationale, his moral integrity or the certainty of his identity and his logic proves incapable of assessing certain phenomena with which he comes into contact. This predicament often results in an epiphany effecting the protagonist's slippage from his stature as the most educated, stable or 'civilized' – that is, modern – of the story's characters. Ultimately, the paradigm to which he typically defers proves deficient in qualifying, defining or apprehending the occult, unearthly or supernatural entity or event and he is compelled into a kind of stunned acceptance. John Reed points out that, with *Dracula,* Stoker 'implicitly denounces its sceptical and selfish age' and that the implication of the Count's invasion and potential reproduction are a 'warning' to a world of 'materialistic and therefore soulless men' who are 'unable to value life'.[9] Despite his regard for modernity's progress, Stoker clearly maintained that its methodologies were limited, insufficient to account for the whole of reality, and should therefore co-exist with the spiritual impulse, never displace it.

Offering analogs of the dislocation and irresolution that characterized the fin-de-siècle, Stoker protagonists are often situated in foreign countries with which they are unfamiliar or circumstances to which they are unaccustomed. One is reminded of the Poet of 'The castle of the king', one of the stories collected in *Under the sunset,* to whom, as he wanders, 'even solid things lost their substance, and melted in the dark and cold mists which swept along'.[10] Similarly, in his jaunt further into the unknown countryside, the narrator of 'Dracula's guest' (1914) encounters numerous modes of detachment from the familiar and recognizable. His journey conveys the shift from the familiarity and presumed reliability of materialism to the less certain realm of the mythic, legendary and unknowable, and such variance's definite effect on the traveller. He notes the landscape's 'desolation' and its unconscious impression on him. Having been compelled by his immoderate – one could say 'modern' – curiosity, once gone a distance that he perceives as too far afield, the narrator finds himself disoriented, the snow 'falling so thickly and whirling around me in such rapid eddies that I could hardly keep my eyes open'.[11] The narrator of 'The burial of the rats' (1891), while not necessarily portrayed as an academic, is clearly of the leisure class that affords him the opportunity of roaming Paris for an extended period. In his journey to the environs of the city, he also enacts the abandoning of a 'civilized' or 'modern' space to explore what he calls a '*terra incognita*', a 'social wilderness', an 'Ultima Thule of social exploration'[12] which he engages with the same bemused curiosity – and carelessness – as Harker or the narrator of 'Dracula's guest'. As he moves daily deeper

---

9 John Reed, 'The occult in later Victorian fiction' in Peter B. Maessent (ed.), *Literature of the occult* (Englewood Cliffs, NJ, 1981), pp 89–104. **10** Bram Stoker, *Under the sunset* (London, 1882), p. 108. **11** Bram Stoker, *Dracula's guest and other weird stories*, p. 10. **12** Ibid., p. 95.

into the unknown world of the chiffonier, one of a 'heap of rags' and a 'heap of bones' that he 'penetrated' 'despite reason', he does so with the acute sense of leaving one world behind and entering another, and ultimately, 'the torturous course shut out the path behind me'.[13]

In Stoker's work, irrationality on the part of the superstitious initially reduces them to curious cultural artefacts whose 'simplicity' warrants the disdain of a rational narrator, but is eventually proven correct. The coachman Johann, who 'always got excited and broke into his native tongue', 'jabbered away in his native German', and whose imagination 'had got hold of him',[14] demonstrates the same kind of anxious nature of the townsfolk who try in vain to prevent Harker from travelling on St George's Eve. In 'The judge's house' (1891), the landlady of the Good Traveller Inn, Mrs Witham, is reminiscent of the woman who offers Harker her rosary and the folk who offer their prayers. Like Johann's unintelligible babble, the superstitious woman's 'pent-up emotions found vent in a shriek'.[15] She 'threw up her hands in amazement' upon hearing of Malcolmson's choice of residence, and elicits 'some exclamation' at his report of the house's strangeness.[16] Often, though, the seemingly irrational, emotional and hyper-sensitive nature of the superstitious belies a wisdom that, though not discerned by the protagonist, ultimately proves accurate.

In *Dracula*, employing the scientific approach to which he is accustomed and which, as Van Helsing points out, actually stunts his capacity for enlightenment, Dr John Seward ineptly endeavours to diagnose the lunatic, Renfield, while never really successfully comprehending the full measure of the patient's idiosyncrasies. Jonathan Harker attempts to describe the bucolic elements of Bistritz in an analytical manner that renders the scene as a diorama or museum piece observed through Western eyes in a bemused fashion and discounts the superstition presented to him. Harker 'constantly tries to normalize the strange into the discourse of the nineteenth-century travelogue'[17] but he clearly fails to do this successfully, and ultimately, his nonchalance leads him to imprisonment within the Count's castle. The narrator of 'The squaw' (1893) refers to the Nurnberg landscape as similar to the work of the painter Claude Lorraine, who, as Kate Hebblethwaite notes, 'chiefly concerned [himself] with the picturesque'.[18] In doing so, the narrator renders his surroundings as though they might be merely quaint curiosities of little bearing, overlooking any suggestions of the unnatural, while the same story's Hutchesson bears an overt ignorance of the area's unearthly aspects.

The narrator of 'Dracula's guest' is an Englishman in a strange land peopled by the 'picturesque' and superstitious. Carelessness colours the narrator's actions and eventually leads him to encounter forces far beyond his understanding or control.

---

13 Ibid., pp 95–8. **14** Ibid., pp 6, 8. **15** Ibid., p. 29. **16** Ibid. **17** David Seed, 'The narrative method of *Dracula*', *Nineteenth-Century Fiction*, 40:1 (1985), 64. **18** Hebblethwaite, 'Introduction', p. 384.

'Walpurgis-nacht doesn't concern Englishmen',[19] he declares. As though to indict what he perceived as his generation's decline in faith and its regard for spiritual matters as mere sport or entertainment, Stoker observes the narrator's admittedly 'light heart' as he journeys for the span of hours, notably regardless of the lapse of time and distance, heedless of 'signs of a coming storm'.[20] Furthermore, indicating the less distinct character of the supernatural that aggravates, challenges, even bewilders the 'modern' mind, the narrator strays from the path through an alien landscape the boundaries of which 'were not so marked'.[21] But just as the characters of 'The squaw' are confronted with disturbing consequences of Hutchesson's disregard, and Harker finds St George's Night to be more than he expected, the narrator of 'Dracula's guest' too falls victim to the realities of Walpurgis-nacht.

Similarly, in 'The Judge's House', Malcolmson finds the town of Benchurch to be amusingly idyllic and idiosyncratic. Immersed in his academic studies, he is more concerned with the more modern phenomena of 'Harmonic Progression, Permutations and Combinations, and Elliptic Functions'[22] to concern himself about the 'somethings' and 'bogies' of the mysterious house he is renting. The unusual nature of the haunted space, however, proves capable of subverting the logic of mathematics. In an image underscoring his academic approach's insufficiency in understanding the supernatural forces around him, Malcolmson resorts to throwing at the mysterious rat a 'badly aimed' book of logarithms.[23] Ultimately, his collection of mathematical tomes is reduced to the status of weapons haplessly and impotently employed.

When faced with the superstitious mysteries of gipsy fortune-tellers, Joshua Considine and his friend Dr Gerald Burleigh, of 'A gipsy prophecy' (1914), are sarcastic and dismissive. In reference to the mysteries of the stars, Considine states that 'we commonplace mortals want something more definite',[24] concrete facts, not cryptic supernatural ramblings. When a gipsy girl offers to tell Considine's fortune, and he accidentally slights her by not offering her silver, Burleigh cynically states, 'You must cross her hand with silver' as that is 'one of the most important parts of the mystery'.[25] Having 'met warning with scorn, and appeal with levity', Considine scoffs to his wife, Mary, 'The juris-imprudent stars have announced their fell tidings that this hand is red with blood – your blood!'[26] But his dismissal of the prophecy does not prevent its coming true, however benignly.

When demonstrated by townsfolk and other 'picturesque' individuals, superstitious fear is typically regarded as humorous or endearing, but often eventually possesses the Stoker protagonist. These realizations tend to render the previously somewhat egotistical, on occasion snide, protagonist physically weakened, virtually impotent. Malcolmson's fear causes him to falter intellectually, so that upon seeing

19 Stoker, *Dracula's guest*, p. 8. **20** Ibid., pp 8 and 9. **21** Ibid., p. 10. **22** Ibid., p. 20. **23** Ibid., p. 26. **24** Ibid., p. 67. **25** Ibid., p. 65. **26** Ibid., p. 67.

the painting of the Judge he 'expected to find some strange presence behind him'; he eventually fears he 'shall become a crazy fool' and that his nerves 'must have been getting into a queer state'.[27] Upon seeing the Judge materialize from the painting, Malcolmson abandons his clinical disposition and 'began to shake and tremble like a man with palsy'.[28] When he beholds the ghost of the Judge, '[h]is strength seemed to have left him, and he was incapable of action or movement, hardly even of thought'; and when the Judge approaches him, the mathematician is rendered immobile, as there is 'something paralyzing in [the Judge's] very presence' that causes Malcolmson to stand 'rigid as corpse'.[29] Harker worries from time to time whether or not he is losing his sanity, noting that his newly acquired nocturnal existence is 'destroying my nerve', causing him to 'start at my own shadow' and filling him with 'all sorts of horrible imaginings'.[30] Like Harker, whose experience as Dracula's prisoner permanently affects him, the narrator of 'Dracula's guest' is rendered emasculated, inept and psychically traumatized. He describes Johann's behaviour as ending 'in a perfect paroxysm of fear', but uses the same term, 'paroxysm', to describe his own reaction to the realization that Walpurgis-nacht is real. In *The lair of the white worm*, when confronted with the disturbing staring contest between Edgar Caswall and Lilla, Adam Salton is reduced to a mute and ineffective witness, held in 'bonds of will' that 'held me inactive' and 'numbed all my faculties, except sight and hearing'.[31] Interestingly, it is at the point where he relinquishes his materialist scientific paradigm, acquiescing to the insistence of the quaint or superstitious, that the Stoker protagonist often discerns the truth of the matter.

Another convention Stoker employed to represent the contest between variant ideologies as experienced by his generation is found in the gradual disintegration of discernible, identifiable sounds; the conflict of speech and supernatural phenomena; and the narrator's degeneration from logical and articulate Englishman to bewildered mute incapable of comprehending his predicament. The narrator of 'Dracula's guest' encounters difficulty communicating and eventually arguing with Johann due to his ignorance of the coachman's language. 'The advantage certainly rested with him', states the narrator, to whom Johann's speech seems to disintegrate, becoming 'so mixed up that I could not understand what he said'.[32] But even this incomprehensible babble is outdone by the haunting, indefinite sounds that follow. The narrator's journey is notably marked by an increasing din of indefinable aural effects. He recalls hearing something 'between a bark and a yelp',[33] an indication of the indeterminate sounds he will continue to encounter. As he dismisses Johann, a 'sighing sound' and a 'muffled roar' come upon him, followed by a 'far-away rushing sound, through which seemed to come at intervals' the cry of what he presumes is a wolf, as well as 'the rush of high winds overhead'.[34]

27 Ibid., pp 32 and 33. 28 Ibid., p. 34. 29 Ibid., pp 34 and 36. 30 Stoker, *Dracula*, p. 57. 31 Stoker, *Dracula's guest*, p. 218. 32 Ibid., pp 6–7. 33 Ibid., p. 6. 34 Ibid., pp 9–10.

Animal noises blend with those of a tempestuous nature in a manner in which they are indistinguishable, seemingly imitative of one another. The 'weird sound of the wolf' appears to be 'echoed by many similar sounds' and the 'fierce sigh of the storm' is likened to a 'long low howl, as of many dogs or wolves'.[35] The 'bitter scream of pain' of the woman rising from the tomb is 'drowned in the thunder-crash'; this is followed by a 'mingling of dreadful sound' and the 'howling of wolves'.[36] Even upon the arrival of the horsemen who retrieve the narrator and return him to the normalcy of a social construction, human spoken communication is intermingled with the indefinable din of the haunted environs, as though the rationale and logic conveyed by articulate speech is incapable of overcoming or suppressing the implications of the narrator's otherworldly experiences. The wolf's yelps continue, almost competing with the horsemen's 'Holloa! Holloa!' and understandable sentences are complicated by the uttering of 'frightened exclamations' and the gibbering of one man 'whose wits had plainly given out for the moment'.[37] A few utterances are discerned at this point, but those actually result in the fabrication of the lie that the men 'found an English stranger, guarded by a large dog'.[38] Here Stoker uses the notion of contending noises of varying degrees of lucidity to convey the disorienting juxtaposition of the traditional and the modern.

In 'The burial of the rats' there is a notable degeneration of communication that becomes a disturbing silence the further the narrator goes. As he enters the realm of the chiffonier, his comments to a threadbare soldier initially go ignored, and then are followed merely by a 'very queer expression', after which the soldier simply drops his head and looks away; a second soldier 'did not notice me while I was passing'.[39] The narrator wishes to ask directions, 'but could see no one'.[40] The old woman and man of the shanty do engage the narrator in conversation, but their 'fascinating' talk is merely to entice him to remain in their world past dusk, and eventually disintegrates into harsh, offensive sounds; the narrator remarks that 'the sound of [the old woman's] voice … jarred upon me' and that she breaks into 'a chuckling fit of the ghastliest merriment'.[41] The narrator's mental state deteriorates at certain moments despite his repeated references to the cerebral acuity of the hunted; as he begins to feel fearful of his circumstances, he feels 'that whirling condition of mind' and 'a sort of spiritual drunkenness'.[42]

Once he is properly pursued by the group of chiffoniers, he describes a silence 'which shrouded and appalled' him, 'a silence which was more dreadful than any sound' and that his pursuers move 'in deadly silence'; when he shouts in hopes of attracting the attention of someone to help him, 'not even an echo rewarded my efforts'.[43] What voices he does hear are inarticulate, 'the fierce whirr of a muttered "Sacre!"', after which 'sounds came thick and fast', including 'the fiercest whispers',

[35] Ibid., pp 10–11. [36] Ibid., pp 12–13. [37] Ibid., p. 15. [38] Ibid., pp 14–16. [39] Ibid., p. 97. [40] Ibid., p. 97. [41] Ibid., pp 101–2. [42] Ibid., p. 100. [43] Ibid., pp 112 and 106.

a shout, and 'muttering curses'.⁴⁴ Even the discernible 'Halt la!' and 'Qui va la?' of his rescuers are notably in a language foreign to him, and are quickly followed by the 'clink and rattle of arms' and 'loud, harsh voices'.⁴⁵ Upon the narrator's return to the city, he engages in the normalcy of conversation with the Parisian police; but this dialogue contrasts starkly with the 'hollow boom', 'muffled cry', shouted orders, calls made 'harshly and loudly'⁴⁶ and other disorienting sounds that ensue upon returning to the chiffoniers' realm. What conversations take place there are brief, even fragmentary, and it is only with the restoration of order, with the command, 'Form!', that the narrator senses the alleviation of the disorder, confusion and danger he has encountered in his journey into the unknown.

If Stoker's male protagonists typically fall into notable categories and behaviours, his female characters do as well. The notion of problematic women that reached its apex at the end of the nineteenth century emerges in Stoker's fiction in very distinct ways. Clearly representative of tradition, Stoker's older women tend to be maternal, nurturing and selfless. Lucy Westenra's mother is well-meaning, if unaware of the immensity of her daughter's situation, and wills her fortune to Arthur, whom she presumes to be her future son-in-law. The old lady who receives Harker is concerned for his safety and even bestows upon him her crucifix. Mrs Witham warns Malcolmson of the strangeness of the Judge's house. She projects the comforts of her own domestic space onto Malcolmson's ruined provisional space with the comforts of various accoutrements associated with the home; 'with much kind forethought she had sent from her own kitchen sufficient provisions to last for a few days'.⁴⁷ She also attempts to employ Dr Thornhill to evaluate Malcolmson's well-being.

Younger women, however, tend to fall into two categories that further stress Stoker's distinction between the traditional and the modern. 'Traditional' younger females are typically unbelievably virtuous, hyper-sensitive and in need of saving, conforming to Stoker's romantic, near chauvinistic idealism of the genders. Amelia, wife of the narrator of 'The squaw', is consistently rendered as fainting and crying out in horror. The emotional Mary Considine immediately doubts her husband and grows paranoid from the ravings of the fortune-teller. Mina Harker, though certainly possessing intellectual capacity beyond the parameters generally permitted within Stoker's works, nevertheless is consciously self-depreciating, compliant and on occasion even subservient not only to her husband but to the other male protagonists.

The 'modern' female, meanwhile, displays aggressiveness, sometimes conflated with overt sexuality, notably stepping beyond appropriate boundaries and at times even threatening male characters with the implications of their propositions. Sarah of 'The coming of Abel Behenna' (1914) is somewhat reminiscent of Lucy Westenra

---

44 Ibid., pp 112–13. **45** Ibid., p. 114. **46** Ibid., p. 116. **47** Ibid., p. 21.

not only with her numerous suitors, but in her indecision as to which to chose. She is 'vain and something frivolous'; while Abel is away, Sanson's presence 'determined purpose over the woman's weaker nature'; Sarah is also an opportunist; she considers 'more of what she might lose, than of what she might gain'.[48] Falling outside Stoker's usual model of maternity, Sarah's mother is as much an opportunist as her daughter, attempting to exploit all she can from both of her daughter's suitors, 'to so arrange matters that Sarah should get all that was possible out of both men'.[49] The undead woman of 'Dracula's guest' is described as 'beautiful' and with 'rounded red cheeks and red lips', indicating a kind of threatening, unnatural sexual attraction that echoes that of the vampirized Lucy Westenra.

Despite the ease with which many Stoker characters fall into these categories, the notion of sexual ambiguity and the suggestion that identity is a malleable construct, ideas that were some of the primary preoccupations of the *fin de siècle*, persistently present themselves to challenge the author's own evident definitions and assumptions. Female characters often display 'masculine' qualities. Despite her misleading name, Stephen Norman, of *The man,* is a woman. Mina Harker, though embodying the chaste and maternal attributes of the ideal Victorian woman, possesses the 'masculine' traits of mental prowess and adventurous vitality in enough measure to assist in the defeat of Dracula, including the bearing of a firearm.[50] Male characters, meanwhile, are often emasculated, described as having 'feminine' traits such as hyper-sensitivity and physical weakness. As his wife is defiled by the Count, Harker simply lies inert, 'as though in a stupor'.[51] When Caswall, Lady Arabella and Oolonga engage Lilla and Mimi in their bizarre staring contest, Adam is relegated to immobile observer, mute and ineffectual. The narrator of 'Dracula's guest' notes how he felt 'quite faint' upon his discovery of the Countess Dolingen's sepulchre, and states that he must have either fallen asleep or 'swooned' afterwards; like Harker, the narrator is emasculated by powers beyond his ken, and is rendered 'powerless'.[52] With passive enjoyment he describes as 'delicious' the warmth of his submissiveness to the wolf and echoes the 'wicked burning desire' and 'languorous ecstasy'[53] Harker describes in his account of his experience with the 'weird sisters' in the Count's castle. Even after being rescued, the narrator's tongue 'refused its office' and he appears to fall asleep; he 'crie[s] out in pain' when he touches the wound on his throat and reels when reading Dracula's letter, so that had the maitre d'hôtel not caught him, 'I think I should have fallen'.[54] The narrator of 'The burial of the rats' claims at one point that he 'must have fainted'[55] and at another that he falters, so that a guard must catch him. Stoker demonstrates definite assumptions about the specificity of gender, of the

---

48 Ibid., pp 83 and 76. **49** Ibid., p. 77. **50** Kathy Casey, 'Note' in *Dracula* by Bram Stoker (Mineola, NY, 2000), iv. **51** Stoker, *Dracula*, p. 282. **52** Stoker, *Dracula's guest*, pp 11, 13–14. **53** Stoker, *Dracula*, pp 61–2. **54** Stoker, *Dracula's Guest*, pp 16–17. **55** Ibid., p. 114.

stability of identity and other previously unquestioned paradigms; but those assumptions are constantly being scrutinized by the author himself, in characters who do not conform to such prescribed qualities and who image the *fin de siècle*'s challenge to traditional modes of thought.

STOKER'S FRACTURED FAMILIES

Despite his immersion in *fin de siècle* culture, Stoker differed from his contemporaries in several respects. One of the prominent characteristics that distinguished his fiction from that of many other writers of the time was his esteem for the ideal Victorian family. The late nineteenth century in many ways dislocated the family from its previous status as a site of acceptance, belonging, and identity, relegating it to a place of limitation, suppressive to the individualistic impulse intrinsic to modernism. As early as 1869, John Stuart Mill cited 'the modern view of the family', a place of oppression, license and selfishness.[56] By the century's end, the familial myth so often associated with Victoria's reign had in large measure become an object of scrutiny and even ridicule, derided as a hindrance to the development of the individual; for it was the family wherein supposedly 'outmoded' and 'restrictive' morals and normative definitions were formulated, nurtured and exhibited.

However, whereas numerous late-century writers pictured the family as anachronous, inhibitive, even unsafe, and exacted the dissolution of the family primarily to suggest its shortcomings, Stoker offered ruptured or endangered portraits of this most basic and fundamental of social structures to demonstrate its importance to both cultural stability and individual well-being. Furthermore, he considered the family to be intrinsically connected to, and representative of, the fading traditional world of moral, religious and social paradigms for which he felt such a notable nostalgia. These were paradigms contrastive to elements such as the decadence, moral ambiguity and degeneration associated with the emergent new world that had the potential to render the family fractured, endangered or even non-existent.

Stoker's fiction is remarkable not only for its representation of generational anxiety in the form of threatened or ruined domestic spaces and familial relationships, but, too, for portrayals of the suffering of those exiled from social and family structures. By depicting this disjunction, and in each case the resultant configuration being something undesired, even tragic, Stoker emphasized the advantages of maintaining the family ideal. Repeatedly in his novels and short stories, he depicts incidences such as the disruption of family unions, betrayal of family

---

[56] Peter Keating, *The haunted study* (London, 1989), p. 161.

trust, marriages in peril, and intrusion into domestic spaces, all which reflect the late-Victorian notions of society's moral and psychic dissolution with which his generation wrestled.

In Stoker's work, the familial relationships are crucial, and existence outside of their context inevitably proves hazardous. The narrator of 'The burial of the rats' is refused communication with his fiancé for a probationary period of a year. He furthermore mentions the absence of anyone in his own family to inform him of her well-being during this interim. His exile and its resultant wandering are factors that contribute to his near-death experience in the environs of Paris. In 'A dream of red hands' (1894), Jacob Settle is haunted by dreams of a previous crime, a predicament notably exacerbated by his estrangement from society. Underscoring Stoker's conviction that the exiled suffer, Settle contrasts himself with 'people who live in comfort with those they love around them' and states that it is '1,000 times worse for those who live alone and have to do so.'[57] Malcolmson pursues 'the sense of isolation from his kind' in order to study for his final honours examination; he wants 'to read by himself', and 'wished to avoid friends', and even 'obliterated his tracks' so as not to be found; indeed, his choice of places to read is so remote 'that everything in the world, except the problem which he was trying to solve, passed away from him'.[58] While not exiling himself to another country, Malcolmson does seek the isolation of the town called Benchurch, which he calls 'attractive as a desert'.[59] *Under the sunset* is notable for its emphasis on parent-child fidelity and brother-sister relationships, an attribute contrasting with the Delandre family of 'The secret of the growing gold' (1892), who suffer the severance of brother and sister, 'not merely on the terms of armed neutrality but of bitter hatred'.[60] In *The watter's mou'* (1895), Maggie MacWhirter's family stability is jeopardized when her father and brothers get involved in smuggling, and the deaths of Maggie and the protagonist, William Barrow, result from the former's attempt to warn her family. In *Dracula*, one of Van Helsing's imperatives is that the 'band of light' will fail if they do not maintain the unity of their provisional brotherhood. *The lair of the white worm* features Richard Salton's great-nephew, the orphan Adam, whose existence had been unknown, and who had to be tracked down in remote Australia and brought to Britain, 'the place of your forbears.'[61] The same novel relates the dysfunction of Edgar Caswall's family, which is plagued by a six-generation antagonism, a history couched in an ancient account of Wulfere, king of Mercia, whom Stoker writes murdered his two sons for embracing Christianity.[62]

It is notable that several of Stoker's tales end with the convention of marriage, the foundation of the ideal family and the structure so crucial to the perpetuation

---

[57] Stoker, *Dracula's guest*, p. 119. [58] Ibid., pp 18, 22–3. [59] Ibid., p. 18. [60] Ibid., p. 52. [61] Ibid., p. 161.
[62] Wulfere was actually a Christian who supported the religion and married a Christian Kentish princess, Eormenhild. Despite this evident error on Stoker's part, the tale underscores the theme of generational conflict.

of civilized society. *The shoulder of Shasta* (1895) concludes with Esse's replacing of the burly mountain man, Grizzly Dick, by marrying the more sophisticated, domesticated Reginald Hampden; *Dracula* concludes with the reestablishment of the marital stability of Jonathan Harker and Mina Murphy, including the birth of their son; *Miss Betty* (1898) ends with the marriage of Rafe Otwell and Betty Pole. But in addition to this convention of the happy ending, the return to the status quo, Stoker frequently portrayed the institution of marriage as imperilled. In 'The fate of Fenella' (1892),[63] the marriage of Frank and Fenella Onslow is scandalized when Onslow, believing his wife to be having an affair with one De Murger, falls into a trance and unknowingly murders De Murger. Fenella, an unwilling object of De Murger's lustful intentions, takes the blame for the murder, but is acquitted. Onslow, however, thinking her an adulteress, shuns his wife, severing communication with her and endangering their marriage. In 'The secret of the growing gold', Geoffrey Brent murders his first wife. 'A gipsy prophecy' relates the threat posed by the ominous fortune-telling of a gipsy queen to the stability of the marriage of Joshua and Mary Considine, with the gipsy queen's insistence that Considine leave his wife at once and sever the sacred bond of marriage. The prophecy proves a disrupting influence in the formerly peaceful domestic space, severing for a time at least, the bonds of trust between husband and wife; while Considine insists on telling Mary about the prophecy, against the advice of Burleigh, Mary keeps from her husband the fact that she herself visits the gipsy camp. Mary even goes to the trouble of dulling all of the knives in the house, for fear of her own spouse. Stoker portrayed such troubling discord among married characters, resulting from notably avoidable immorality or supernatural elements, to emphasize the importance of preserving this foundational aspect of civilization.

Anxieties of the Victorian period were often articulated through interpretations of the domestic space,[64] that structure that symbolizes, encompasses and protects the family. Stoker's fiction is remarkable not only for its representation of that anxiety in his treatment of familial relationships, but also of threatened or ruined domestic spaces. There is sacredness to the domestic space the removal of which results in tragedy and the undoing of the social fabric, incidences of which are redolent throughout Stoker's fiction. One of the most unsettling notions of *Dracula,* for instance, is the Count's infiltration of domestic spaces such as Lucy's home and the Harker's bedroom, in a manner that prevents Lucy's wedding to Arthur and their potential procreation, and threatens the sanctity of Mina and Jonathan's marital union, respectively. In *The lair of the white worm* Oolanga's potential savagery and Caswall's unsettling staring disrupt the civility of Lilla and

---

63 'The Fate of Fenella' was part of a serial novel in *Cassell's Magazine,* with different authors writing each of the twenty-four chapters. Stoker's was the tenth of these chapters. **64** Gail Marshall, *The Victorian novel* (London, 2002), p. 108.

Mimi's home, while Caswall affects the social order by contriving the dependence of the agrarian populace on his kite to allay the plague of birds that threaten their means of survival. 'The dualatists; or the death doom of the double born' (1886) features the Bubbs, a childless couple who are ultimately blessed with twins. Their domestic equilibrium, however, is menaced by two neighbouring youths, Harry and Tommy, whose insidious and violent escapades are largely perpetrated on Bubbs' own property. In addition to invading Bubbs' domestic space, Harry and Tommy not only cause the death of Bubb and his wife, but of their offspring as well, altogether unmaking the Bubb household and dooming their lineage. The household of Joshua and Mary Considine is one 'of rest and quiet happiness, as though the outward type of the peacefulness and joy which made a heaven of the home of the young married folk'.[65] Their pleasant domestic setting, imbued with cigars, *La Tour*, and Mendelssohn, is juxtaposed against the nomadic and unstable nature of the gypsies encamped nearby.

In a text particularly concerned with the creation of a domestic situation, even if a conspicuously contrived one, 'The coming of Abel Behenna' begins with idyllic descriptions of portside domestic cottages emblematic of fruitful and joyous homes.[66] But Sarah's house becomes a place of deception and failed promises when she falls for the wiles of the jealous and impatient Sanson in Abel's absence. And Sanson's becomes a criminal's refuge in which he locks himself away from society; in fact, the haunting memory of Abel's murder pervades the confines of his home, rendering him sleepless, looking haggard and as though having aged over the course of only days. And it is notably at Sanson's house that the murdered body of Abel appears to seal his murderer's doom.

One of the narrative dynamics of 'The squaw' is the contrast of marital union with reckless individualism. The travelling couple and their companion, the American, Hutcheson, are situated so that they can see the town of Nurnberg, but also the environs dotted with towns and gardens. The town itself, 'happy in that it was never sacked',[67] is undefiled, and surrounded by pastoral images of tranquillity, imaging the implications of marriage and the social stability to which it contributes.[68] The landscape, however, is marked by the ominous presence of Max Tower, used for torture during the Inquisition. This contrast emphasizes the distinction between the union of the married couple with the cruel, not to mention

---

65 Stoker, *Dracula's guest*, p. 64. **66** 'At either side of the river was a row of cottages down almost on the level of high tide. They were pretty cottages, strongly and snugly built, with trim narrow gardens in front, full of old-fashioned plants, flowering currants, coloured primroses, wallflower, and stonecrop. Over the front of many of them climbed clematis and wisteria. The window sides and door posts of all were as white as snow, and the little pathway to each was paved with light coloured stones. At some of the doors were tiny porches, whilst at others were rustic seats cut from tree trunks or from old barrels; in nearly every case the window ledges were filled with boxes or pots of flowers or foliage plants' (Stoker, *Dracula's guest*, p. 75). **67** Stoker, *Dracula's guest*, p. 38. **68** That the narrator of the story actually seems to have quickly tired of his fiancé has biographical and psychological implications that are beyond the scope of this chapter.

spontaneous and irresponsible, Hutcheson, whose actions colour the rest of the story and determine his own fate. While the couple admires their surroundings, it is Hutcheson's recklessness that results in the death of a kitten and the destruction of a family unit of mother and offspring, putting into motion events that not only cause his death, but result in the branding of the newlyweds' offspring with a birthmark, a permanent reminder of Hutcheson's misdeeds.

'The Judge's house' offers a contrast between a provisional and household setting and the actuality of its state as a haunted space. Malcolmson seeks to establish a pseudo-domestic area wherein he may attend to his academic pursuits. In doing so, he chooses the uninhabited ruin of the Judge's house, a place of 'desolation', which exceeds the solitude he seeks, and which is described as 'more like a fortified house', set apart from society. The charwoman, Mrs Dempster, endeavours to refashion the house into a semblance of domesticity, with 'the room swept and tidied, a fire burning in the old hearth, the lamp lit, and the table spread for supper with Mrs Witham's excellent fare' and a 'delicious, voluptuous ease'.[69] But despite the fact that it is 'bright and tidy with a cheerful fire and a well-trimmed lamp',[70] Malcolmson senses the place is yet haunted. Like the imprisoned Harker in *Dracula*, Malcolmson begins a nocturnal existence, working throughout the night with the stimulus of strong tea. In an appropriate symbol of such inversion, the great rat that troubles him appears on the high-backed carved oak chair by the fire-place, imaging the usurpation of normalcy in the scope of a contrived home-like space.

In 'The secret of the growing gold', Brent's choice to inter his murdered wife, Margaret, in the hearth, that venerable symbol of domestic serenity, serves as an affront to the notion of 'home', an indignity answered with the exposure of Brent's crime. It is important to note that the majority of Brent's previous immoral escapades are confined to London and Paris and Vienna, 'anywhere out of sight and sound of his home', where 'opinion was silent'.[71] What evils he perpetuates, as long as committed outside the realm of his home, go unnoticed. It is when, through murder, he instigates the disruption of his own home that his wrongdoings catch up with him. Accordingly, when Brent brings into his home a new mistress, 'a small army of workmen invaded the house; and hammer and plane sounded, and a general air of size and paint pervaded the atmosphere';[72] Brent endeavours to recreate his home as though to conceal his crime. In the same story, Delandre's home, reflective of his growing hatred and the nursing of his revenge, becomes 'little better than a ruin, without dignity or picturesqueness of any kind'.[73]

To Stoker, the ideal family was an emblem of tradition, and furthermore the preservation of the family ideal was essential not only for social stability but for the well-being of the individual. Existence outside the context of that institution,

---

[69] Stoker, *Dracula's guest*, p. 22. [70] Ibid., p. 30. [71] Ibid., p. 52. [72] Ibid., p. 55. [73] Ibid., p. 56.

that is, existence beyond the confines of tradition, therefore, inevitably proves hazardous. Indeed, to regard the family is to consider exclusion from it, and Stoker's intense concern with the belonging and identity associated with it frequently led him to write of characters either ostracized from the family or rendered parentless at some point in the narrative. His fiction frequently features actual orphans or those characterized by the conventions traditionally associated with orphanhood, to impart the hazards of abandoning traditional paradigms.

Entities of questionable origin, orphans are characterized by lack of family and exile from society, and as such, embody the kind of incertitude and ambiguity that marked the *fin de siècle*. Because of his or her detachment from the stabilizing integration and certainty that attends inclusion into the traditional family, the orphan embodied Stoker's generation's interstitial predicament. In Stoker's work, the orphanic condition becomes an analog of the loss of the traditional world and the advent of a modern one characterized by uncertainty, apprehension, iconoclasm, even immorality. Defined by his or her exclusion from the family structure, devoid of an identifying context, the orphan type imaged a generation that advanced inevitably – perhaps irretrievably – toward an unsure future.

Locating many of his narratives in contemporary Britain, Stoker situated his orphan characters within the transitory environment of the late nineteenth century, insinuating them into cultural predicaments to which their condition alluded and endowing them with particular metaphoric import in regard to his generation's psychic state. The orphan condition therefore performed a vital role in Stoker's negotiation of the advent of modernism, since the orphan functioned as a figure severed from the very institution that, to Stoker, had the capacity to salvage the late Victorians from the perils they faced.

One telling aspect of Stoker's orphans is the sense of legacy that often attends them. Frequently posited as recipients of vast fortunes or inheritances from either actual or adoptive familial associations, Stoker's orphans convey the sense of being endowed with the heritage of the past and the charge of preserving those traditions for the future. These inheritances represent the burden of engaging the degeneration, decadence and nihilism Stoker believed could only be deterred by the unity, support and totality found in the family and imaged by the bequeathal of fortunes. *Under the sunset,* for example, features the orphaned Princess Bluebell, of 'The rose prince', who is adopted by the king. In the romance, *The snake's pass* (1890), Arthur Severn, whose parents have died and who is reared by his great aunt, inherits a vast fortune. In *Dracula*, Harker, a 'surrogate son' is bequeathed the fortune of Hawkins, '[a] kind of ideal bourgeois father';[74] in the same novel, Arthur inherits the fortunes of both his father and Mrs Westenra upon their

[74] Richard Astle, 'Dracula as totemic monster: Lacan, Freud, Oedipus and history', *SubStance,* 8:4, issue 25 (1979), 100.

respective deaths. In *The man*, which features the female orphan Stephen Norman, another orphan, Harold An Wolf, is adopted into Stephen's home as a son. Rupert, of *The lady of the shroud* (1909), reared by his aunt after the death of his mother, inherits his uncle's fortune. Betty Pole has inherited a fortune from her grandfather. These recipients of material wealth from either actual or adoptive familial associations form a narrative convention showing Stoker's sense of being endowed with the heritage of the past and the preservation of its traditions.

CONCLUSION

Seeing his generation as positioned within a kind of spectrum, with the traditional world of certain moral values and reliable paradigms on one end, and the modern world of scientism, materialism and iconoclasm on the other, Bram Stoker conveyed the anxiety of a generation in flux. The belief systems and methodologies of his protagonists, often doctors, attorneys and other highly educated Victorian professionals, are frequently compromised by supernatural phenomena that cannot be explained away by their 'modern' approaches. The conflict of vying ideologies emerges in Stoker's manipulation of speech and sound: modes of communication are interrupted or compromised; the origin of sounds, even voices, remains uncertain; and the previously articulate protagonist is rendered bewildered and inarticulate. Despite a romanticized notion of gender, the ambiguity of identity, sexual and otherwise, emerges to complicate such assumptions. Stoker also underscored the advantages, indeed the necessity, of maintaining the traditional family, portraying familial constructions as endangered, and in each case the resulting disjointed configuration being something unwanted. In doing so, Stoker stressed the significance of the ideal and the traditional attributes attached to it, further entrenching the notion that it was upon the family that late nineteenth-century civilization depended for its moral integrity, its unity and perhaps even its survival.

'See how the bog can preserve': bogs, snakes and Irish stereotypes in *The snake's pass*

VALERIA CAVALLI

While still in Transylvania, Count Dracula confides to Jonathan Harker his worries about moving to London, especially highlighting his fear of being recognized as a foreigner: 'Here I am noble [...] and I am master. But a stranger in a strange land, he is no one; men know him not – and to know not is to care not for'.[1] As Paul Murray has pointed out in his biography of the author, to a large extent, Bram Stoker '*was* Dracula'.[2] With the Count he shared a privileged background, but also the ability to turn his hand to all sorts of different jobs that the role of manager to actor Henry Irving may have demanded. Above all though, like Dracula, he was a stranger in London, his Irish brogue identifying him as a perennial outsider. Bram Stoker belonged to a middle class Protestant family whose Irish heritage could be traced back in centuries. Although he was not part of the landowning Ascendancy, R.F. Foster has argued that he shared the sense of isolation which became typical of this class due to the rise of Catholic nationalism through the nineteenth century. Like his contemporaries W. B. Yeats, Lady Gregory and Standish O'Grady, Stoker suffered from this feeling unwelcome on both sides of the Channel.[3] Being a Protestant in Catholic Ireland meant being stereotyped as an English invader, while an Irishman in England was considered as a 'mere' Irish, that is, as part of what Joseph Valente calls 'the residuum'.[4]

As Foster has pointed out, political upheavals and land agitation in the late nineteenth century were instrumental in the destruction of Irish Protestant political power. Irish Protestants had been sinking into an increasingly deep sense of marginalization since the 1830s, after the granting of Catholic Emancipation. 'In an age when their right to be "Irish" was beginning to be questioned by the new wave of Irish nationalism', many Protestants attempted to re-assert their Irish

---

1 Bram Stoker, *Dracula* (London, 2003), p. 27. **2** Paul Murray, *From the shadow of Dracula: a life of Bram Stoker* (London, 2004), p. 3. **3** R.F. Foster, *Paddy and Mr Punch* (London, 1995), p. 220. **4** Joseph Valente, *Dracula's crypt: Bram Stoker, Irishness and the question of blood* (Urbana, IL, 2002), p. 38.

identity by reclaiming a legendary past going back to pre-colonial times as the basis of a single, non-sectarian Irish national culture.⁵ As Oona Frawley has argued, in post-colonial cultures and in cultures which have suffered from social disruption and consequent emigration, such as nineteenth-century Ireland, populations tend to react to a general sense of unrest and insecurity by sinking into nostalgia. Nostalgia, which is defined as a condition of homesickness (derived from the Greek *nostos*, home, and *algos*, pain), induces what Frawley describes as 'a reverie-like state of remembrance for experiences which, as past, are unrecoverable, [by] remind[ing] individuals, generations and entire cultures of times that, because of their distance from the unsettled present, seem safer and more stable'.⁶ During the 'rise' of the Irish pastoral, the Literary Revival, powered by O'Grady, Yeats and Lady Gregory among others, re-proposed for consideration the ancient legends and sagas of pagan Ireland along with the traditions of early Christian Ireland, where the Irish could be represented as one noble people before the onset of sectarian division. Many believed that the heroic and aristocratic nature of the past, in sharp contrast with a present age characterized by defeat and compromise, could revive in the Irish a sense of lost pride and cultural independence.

In this context, Stoker's first novel, *The snake's pass* (1890), positions him within the Celtic Revival of the late nineteenth century, its story depending heavily on a noble Irish past preceding religious divisions, when the Irish population was spiritually united under the common faith of Christianity. Moreover, Stoker's return to the marriage plot bringing together an Irish beauty and an English hero (a trope that gained increasing importance after the Act of Union of 1800, best exemplified in the work of Maria Edgeworth and Lady Morgan) is proof of his moderate, or (as he called it) 'philosophical', version of Home Rule for Ireland.⁷ *The snake's pass* is Stoker's only novel explicitly set in Ireland. As early as September 1889, Stoker had revealed to the English press that he was working on a story inspired by a holiday spent in the West of Ireland, which he would later describe as 'my book [...] of Ireland [...] dealing with Irish ways'.⁸ It was not until July 1890 that the novel began serialization in the weekly *People*, after being warmly publicized as comparable to 'the best novels of modern times', its 'scene being placed in Ireland, while the plot [being] interwoven with a local tradition which dates back to the very long ago'.⁹ *The snake's pass* was eventually published in book form in November 1890, between Gladstone's Home Rule bills of 1886 and 1893.

---

5 Foster, *Paddy and Mr Punch*, p. 216. **6** Oona Frawley, *Irish pastoral: nostalgia and twentieth-century Irish literature* (Dublin, 2005), pp 3–4. **7** For an excellent reading of *The snake's pass* as part of the Celtic Twilight and on the marriage plot, see Nicholas Daly, 'Irish roots: the romance of history in Bram Stoker's *The snake's pass*', *Literature and History*, 4:2 (1995). **8** Bram Stoker, *Personal reminiscences of Henry Irving*, 2 vols (London, 1906), ii, p. 29. As Paul Murray points out, the elements of the plot had instead been in his mind for years, as proved by the reflections contained in his notebooks, p. 157. **9** Murray, p. 157.

The story is set in Co. Mayo at the time of the Land War. Arthur Severn is a young Englishman who has just come into possession of a great inheritance and is now enjoying a few weeks of holiday in the west of Ireland. Here, he falls in love with a native beauty, Norah Joyce, and although starting off as a mere visitor and admirer of the rough landscape, he becomes involved with the dispute opposing her father Phelim to the greedy moneylender Murtagh Murdock. 'Black' Murdock has evicted the Joyces in order to become the sole proprietor of a vast bogland which is believed to hide two treasures, whose origins can be traced to the abortive insurrection of 1798 and to the legendary deliverance of the island from the snakes at the hands of St Patrick. History and legend intertwine in the novel's nostalgic recreation of a glorious past, but their messages of hope and resurgent power are stifled by the sterile bog. The bog, I argue, symbolizes the misjudged representations which were holding Stoker's class in a liminal position on both sides of the Channel. In fact, while the Catholics of Ireland tended to stereotype Irish Protestants as colonial invaders, the British public did not distinguish them from the clichéd image of the violent and rebellious 'Paddy' or the uncivilized 'bog-trotter'.[10] Bram Stoker seized these negative stereotypes with the express intention of subverting and overcoming them, so as to project a more positive version of Irish identity and contemporary Ireland to both his fellow-countrymen and to the potential English readers of his tale. At the end of the novel, Black Murdock, who is the embodiment of the stereotypical Neanderthal Paddy of the British press, is swallowed up by the quaking bog. The Joyces are rewarded with the treasures, and, through Norah's marriage to Arthur, the kind and entrepreneurial landlord, they are restored as owners of a fertile new land.

The story begins with Arthur listening eagerly to the natives of the area recounting the origins of the peculiar names that characterize the region. Legend has it that in ancient times the King of the Snakes defied St Patrick on the nearby mountain and, by hiding his crown at the heart of the mountain (after which the village of Knockcalltecrore is named), he managed to save himself from the saint's wrath until better times would come around, and allow him to return and claim his land:

> 'I'm King here, an' I'm not going.'
> 'Thin', says the Saint, 'I depose ye!'
> 'You can't', sez the Shnake, 'while I have me crown.'
> [...] 'An' till ye git me crown I'm king here still, though ye banish me. An' mayhap *I'll come in some forrum what ye don't suspect*, for I must watch me crown. An' now I go away – iv me own accord.' An' widout one word

---

[10] On the figure of 'Paddy' see Foster, *Paddy and Mr Punch*, pp 171–94; on 'bog-witticisms' see Bruce Stewart, 'The old bog road: expressions of atavism in Irish culture', *Writing Ulster*, 6 (1999), 162–93, 165 and William Hughes, *Beyond* Dracula (Basingstoke, 2000), p. 60.

more, good or bad, he shlid right away into the say, dhrivin' through the rock an' making the clift that they call the Shleenanaher – an' that's the Irish for the Shnake's Pass – until this day.'[11]

The belief shared by the villagers is that the King of the Snakes has indeed returned, in the shape of the shifting bog and the gombeen man, whose common sterility and violence allow them to merge in a terrifying metamorphosis in Arthur's nightmares:

> Presently, as I dreamed, the whole Mountain seemed to writhe and shake as though the great Snake was circling round it, deep under the earth; and again this movement changed into the shifting of the bog. [...] Suddenly Murdock's evil face, borne out on a huge serpent body, writhed up beside us [...]. And then over the cliff poured the whole mass of the bog, foul-smelling, foetid, terrible, and of endless might. [...] The whole mighty mass turned into loathsome, writhing snakes, sweeping into the sea! (pp 176–7)

The snake, the bog and the moneylender, then, are different forms of the same monster. As its human embodiment, Black Murdock retains the bog's suffocating power over the inhabitants of the area. In fact, in his greedy accumulation, Murdock proves totally indifferent to the needs of the farmers, showing how one man's rapacity can feed on the welfare of many. Similarly, Murdock boasts the snake's unruliness, bestiality and paganism, characteristics which were commonly associated with the 'Celt' in the British press.

Murtagh Murdock represents a new breed of merciless, ambitious entrepreneurs, a 'hard man' of whom the villagers of Knockcalltecrore are in awe, since rumour has it that he 'has done some cruel things among them' (p. 20). In his selfish plan to become the sole possessor of the hill and of the treasures it hides, Murdock shows no scruples in using his money and his authority to threaten and bribe honest people out of their land. He is described as a wolf, preying upon his tenants like a prototype of Count Dracula; in fact, as one of the farmers explains, 'he would take the blood out of yer body if he could sell it or use it anyhow' (p. 19).[12] Just as the King of the Snakes refused to take orders from St Patrick, 'because [...] this is my own houldin' [...]. I'm the whole government here, and I put a nexeat on meself not to lave widout me own permission' (p. 14), Murdock imposes

---

[11] Bram Stoker, *The snake's pass* (Chicago, 2006), p. 15, my italics. All further references to this edition will be parenthesized inside the text.   [12] Also note that Murdock is frequently associated with the wolf, in *Dracula*, one of the several metamorphosis of the Count: 'in the clutches iv that wolf', 'that human-shaped wolf', 'the wolf that ye are – fattening on the blood of the poor', 'Murdock turned at once with a scowl and a sort of snarl', pp 24, 72, 96, 181. Furthermore, like Dracula, Murdock has a vivid scar on the face, p. 27.

his selfish will with the same force: 'I've had in me hands, wan time or another, ivery inch iv this mountain, bit be bit, all except the Cliff Fields, and thim I wanted for purposes iv me own. [...] Ye had betther have a care wid me. I've crushed ye wance, an' I'll crush ye again' (pp 145–6). Murdock is not afraid of breaking God's commandments in the oppression of his neighbours, because the only god he seems to venerate is Mammon, in the shape of the treasure:

> It certainly was filthy. It was a shapeless, irregular mass, but made solid with rust and ooze, and the bog surface through which it had been dragged. The slime ran from it in a stream; but its filth had no deterring power for Murdock, who threw himself down beside it and actually kissed the nauseous mass, as he murmured: 'At last, as last, me treasure! All me own!' (p. 132)

Murdock's animalistic representation, monstrous, vampiric and serpentine, recalls the stereotypical figure of the Irish, and particularly of the Irish nationalist, as represented in British culture. The Irish were thought to be the dangerous issue of an atavistic race whose religious beliefs were rooted in paganism and superstition.[13] In his *On the study of Celtic literature* (1867), Matthew Arnold had defined the Celts as 'violent stormy people', 'undisciplinable, anarchical and turbulent by nature', a people best characterized by their quality of sentiment, 'quick to feel impressions, and feeling them very strongly', lacking 'the skilful and resolute appliance of means to ends which is needed both to make progress in material civilization, also to form powerful states', culturally 'poor, slovenly, and half barbarous', mere savages.[14] Fenian activity and Parnellite agitation in the late nineteenth century, in particular, were met with denigrating caricatures of the reptilian Irish in the English press, reinforcing the deep-rooted belief that the English and Irish were separated by insuperable racial, religious and cultural barriers. The figure of the serpent, as a representation of cunning and sin, was frequently associated with land agitators, and particularly with Parnell, in Victorian magazines like *Punch* and *Judy*.[15] One of the favourite themes of British caricature became the legendary battle between St George and the Irish dragon, labelled 'Fenianism' or hidden behind the mask worn by many 'Moonlighters' during their nocturnal raids (fig. 7).

Similar cartoons represented St Patrick, chasing away hordes of snake-like agitators from a suffering Ireland. Just after the Phoenix Park murders in 1882, 'The Irish Sea Serpent' was represented in *Judy* as a hybrid and indefinable creature of massive dimensions, to symbolize both the physical strength of Irish nationalism and its simultaneous lack of human, as well as humane, characteristics (fig. 8).

13 See Edward R. Norman, *Anti-Catholicism in Victorian England* (London, 1968), particularly Ch. 1. **14** Matthew Arnold, *The study of Celtic literature* (London, 1867), pp 82, 100, 105. **15** For a detailed study of the Irish in Victorian literature, see Lewis Perry Curtis, *Apes and angels: the Irishman in Victorian caricature* (Washington, 1997).

7: William H. Boucher, 'At last' (*Judy*, 26 October 1881)

In *The snake's pass*, Stoker exploits these stereotypes to show the unwholesome effect that they have on the land and its people. In the aftermath of the Land War, when the novel was published, the shifting bog comes to represent the unstable national identity of a country in turmoil, an image still in operation some forty years later when Daniel Corkery complained that '[e]verywhere in the mentality of the Irish people are flux and uncertainty. Our national consciousness may be described, in a native phrase, as a quaking sod. It gives no footing'.[16] As long as Black Murdock lives, and the stereotype of the slippery and serpentine Irish persists, both the natives and their English friends are at the mercy of the bog: while 'the Hill holds us all' (p. 118), the land remains barren, and even the landscape engineer Dick Sutherland cannot find a way to 'heal' the bog until he breaks free from Murdock. In fact, although Dick recognizes the great potential of the land, his expertise initially amounts to nothing:

---

16 Cited in Luke Gibbons, '"Some hysterical hatred": history, hysteria and the Literary Revival', *Irish University Review*, 27:1 (1997), 7–23 at 13.

8: William H. Boucher, 'Another triumph for Jonathan – biggest reptile in the universe' (*Judy*, 17 May 1882)

> You will hardly believe that, although the subject is one of vital interest to thousands of persons in our own country – one in which national prosperity is mixed up to a large extent – one which touches deeply the happiness and material prosperity of a large section of Irish people, and so helps to mould their political action, there are hardly any works on the subject in existence. [...]
> You can imagine how devoid of knowledge we are, when I tell you that even the last edition of the *Encyclopædia Britannica* does not contain the heading 'bog'. (pp 43–4)

Dick's scientific approach to the bog reveals it as a treacherous 'carpet of death' (p. 47). It appears like 'a film or skin of vegetation of a very low kind, [...] floating on a sea of ooze and slime [...] of an unknown depth', and is capable of swallowing a body, and forever keeping it 'with the existing vegetation somewhere about the roots, or [...] among the slime at the bottom' (p. 47). The bog represents a fatal threat, which will eventually claim the life of Black Murdock, just as it had taken those of entire families in Ireland, as Stoker may well have been aware, having travelled in the Irish countryside as a civil servant for thirteen years (1866–78). Certainly, cases of lethal bog-slides frequently appeared in the daily newspapers: for instance, in October 1873 the *Irish Times* reported that in Belwell, Co. Galway, the shifting of the Gor bog caused 'great destruction', overwhelming two houses and 300 acres of pasture.[17] In December 1881, the village of Garrycastle, in Co. Westmeath, suffered a similar catastrophe, in which the house of the railway gatekeeper was 'turned half-way round', while in the following year the moving of some hundred of acres of bogland in east Clare 'actually swept away the main road to Limerick', almost killing one of the men who intervened to repair the damage.[18] Another two houses were swamped in Co. Roscommon in January and February 1883, and eight families were made ready to evacuate their homes at a moment's notice.[19] More cases followed in the years preceding the publication of *The snake's pass*, showing how the dangerous bog could strike at any time and anywhere.

The bog as murderous monster haunts the novel until Murdock is washed away with it as a result of his own evil nature. It is after the destruction of the negative stereotype that the land renders up its riches, in the form of material treasures, fertility and a noble national identity. As well as being a hideous version of the simian Paddy of the British press, Murdock *also* resembles the clichéd Protestant landlord, a figure that historian J.E. Pomfret defined in his book *The struggle for land in Ireland* (1930) as part of 'a class [...who] had little interest in the welfare of the peasants or in the improvements of their property'.[20] It is crucial that Stoker positions Murdock in the new stock of *Catholic* landowners, and further represents the stereotypical 'Paddy', the ruthless, greedy and serpentine usurper, as the exception rather than the rule, in what otherwise appears to be a religious, honest, hard-working and progressive community. Once the cliché is destroyed, the bog turns from a stifling, undefined mass into a natural museum, the preserver of the glorious past of a pre-colonial culture.

In *Irish pastoral* (2005), Oona Frawley points out that this view of nature as a repository of ancient history is common in colonial thinking, so that, while the colonizer sees the wilderness of the colonial landscape as an antidote to the sense of dissatisfaction and alienation resulting from industrialization, the colonized turn to their rough lands and ruins in search of their own lost identity.[21] Luke Gibbons also argues that the bog 'has the capacity to retain history in its most disruptive and turbulent manifestations', and contends that Stoker uses the quagmire as a symbol of the political guilt which was now haunting his class.[22] Gibbons points out that the

---

[17] 'A moving bog', *Irish Times*, 7 Oct. 1873, p. 5. See also 'Moving bogs in Ireland', *Irish Times*, 24 Oct. 1873, p. 7. [18] 'A moving bog', *Irish Times*, 5 Dec. 1881, p. 5; 'A moving bog', *Irish Times*, 30 May 1882, p. 5. [19] 'A moving bog', *Irish Times*, 27 Jan. 1883, p. 5; 'The moving bog', *Irish Times*, 1 Feb. 1883, p. 7. [20] J.E. Pomfret, *The struggle for land in Ireland, 1800–1923* (Princeton, 1930), quoted in William E. Vaughan, *Landlords and tenants in mid-Victorian England* (Oxford, 1994), p. v. [21] Frawley, *Irish pastoral*, p. 43. [22] Gibbons, 'Some hysterical hatred', 14.

little knowledge of bogland that Dick Sutherland possesses comes partly from William King's 'Of the bogs and loughs of Ireland' (1685), where the archbishop affirms that bogs are 'a shelter and refuge to tories, and thieves'. Capitalizing on these 'subversive associations' of nature in the colonial thought, Gibbons believes that '[t]he bog, in fact, stands for those aspects of the Irish past which will not go away', but rather come back, like revenants, in Irish Protestant fiction.²³ Bruce Stewart, however, warns that nationalist critics are often too keen on reading the works of the Irish Gothic as articulating 'a burden of secret guilt' and correctly points out that although 'Stoker does indeed furnish his sensational novel with skeletons of French soldiers dutifully regurgitated by the Shifting Bog when Black Murdock is swallowed up in the final cataclysm', 'Dick Sutherland is perfectly cheerful about the macabre spectacle'.²⁴ In *The snake's pass* the corpses and the treasures revealed by the bog do not symbolize the 'return of the repressed', but rather offer a point of departure to those who wish to start afresh, in line with Stoker's moderate idea of Ireland as one nation within the Empire.

The novel opens with Arthur being struck by the peculiarity of the Irish landscape, to whose savagery his English eyes were unaccustomed:

> In the wide terrace-like steps of the shelving mountain there were occasional glimpses of civilization emerging from the almost primal desolation which immediately surrounded us – clumps of trees, cottages, and the irregular outlines of stone-walled fields, with black stacks of turf for winter firing piled here and there, far beyond, was the sea – the great Atlantic – with a wildly irregular coast-line studded with a myriad of clustering rocky islands. [...]
>
> Earth, sea, and air all evidenced the triumph of Nature, and told of her wild majesty and beauty. (pp 3–4)

The sight of the Irish sublime provokes an awakening of Arthur's senses and an increasing interest in the place and in its people: 'I felt exalted in a strange way, and impressed at the same time with a new sense of the reality of things. [...] My foreign tour had been gradually dissipating my old sleepy ideas, or perhaps overcoming the negative forces that had hitherto dominated my life' (pp 4–5). By getting to know the natives, Arthur begins to appreciate their ways, until he finally realizes that despite superficial differences he shares the same values, and is ready to fight for them. Thus, rather than being haunted by the ghosts of the past, as suggested by Gibbons, Arthur is let partake in the extraordinary discovery of the treasures on the basis of his very closeness to the inhabitants of the land.

The first treasure that emerges from the bog is a chest full of gold dating back to the abortive insurrection of 1798, when Catholics, Protestants and Dissenters

---

23 Ibid. 24 Stewart, 'The old bog road', 171, 172.

had united under the name of Irishmen to fight together for independence as one nation. Since the end of the Williamite wars, Ireland had been controlled by a Protestant Ascendancy on behalf of the British Crown, governing the predominantly Catholic population by means of sectarian Penal Laws. The example of the American and French Revolutions induced some in the Irish ruling class to seek common cause with Irish Catholics in order to achieve reform and greater autonomy from Britain. The Society of United Irishmen was founded in 1791 with the specific aim of fighting for Irish self-rule, and by 1797 it counted more than 100,000 volunteers.[25] The rebellion started in Dublin in May 1798 and quickly spread all over the country under the leadership of General Theobald Wolfe Tone, with the support of the French officer Jean Joseph Amable Humbert and his army, and counting among the many soldiers Stoker's extravagant great-uncle George Blake.[26] The brother of Stoker's maternal grandmother Matilda, Blake was the protagonist of a number of local legends, which the author's mother Charlotte did not fail to recount to her children.[27] When the French army of General Humbert landed in Ireland, Blake set out to join them, although he knew that the mission would have never prove successful. Blake fought in both the 'Races of Castlebar' and the final Battle of Ballinamuck, and it was rumoured that his battalion was the only effective one at Ballinamuck. As the story goes, he was even protagonist of a duel at the side of Humbert on the eve of the final battle.[28] The incredible adventures of George Blake find a vivid echo in Stoker's works, and in *The snake's pass* the insurrection resurfaces to teach a lesson of pride and loyalty, the time being ripe for Ireland to re-interpret those events as evidence of a common past for the divided peoples of the island, and to encourage them to finally unite as one people:

> At each end of the chest lay a skeleton, the fleshless fingers grasping the metal handle. […] 'they did their duty nobly; they guarded their treasure to the last.' […] 'see how the bog can preserve. […] they were brave fellows all the same, and faithful ones; they never let go the handles; look, their dead hands clasp them still. France should be proud of such sons. It would make a noble coat of arms, this treasure-chest sent by *freemen to aid others*, and with two such supporters.' (pp 206–7, my italics)

The second treasure hidden in the bog is the ancient crown of the King of the Snakes, who was defeated by St Patrick at the dawn of Christianity. As Bridget McCormack has pointed out in her *Perceptions of St Patrick in eighteenth-century Ireland* (2000), from early in that century, 'the greatest monster which Patrick was

---

25 R.F. Foster, *Modern Ireland, 1600–1972* (London, 1989), Ch. 12. **26** Murray, *From the shadow of Dracula*, pp 9–10. See also Elizabeth Miller and Dacre Stoker (eds), *The lost journal of Bram Stoker: the Dublin years* (London, 2012), p. 160. **27** Murray, ibid., pp 9–10. **28** Ibid.

expected to banish in [...] Ireland was party and division'.²⁹ In fact, while St Patrick was adopted as patron saint by both Catholics and Protestants, the two groups nuanced his image to bring him closer to their own doctrines. Protestants saw Patrick as the founder of a church which was independent of Rome, thus affirming the historical legitimacy of the Church of Ireland in the country; Catholics, contrariwise, insisted on Patrick's loyalty to Rome. In *The snake's pass* the discovery of the ancient crown of the King of the Snakes serves the purpose of reminding the opposing factions of a harmonious past as Christians before the Reformation. And at this point, Stoker goes even further and rewards the community with a third, unexpected treasure which dates back to a pre-Christian era: 'Ogham! – one of the oldest and least known of writings', exclaims Dick Sutherland in stupefaction at the discovery of indecipherable inscriptions indicating the existence of an ancient literate culture (p. 208). Of course, as Nicholas Daly has pointed out, 'this historical affiliation is baseless', since it is hard to justify the desire manifested by Irish Protestants to partake of a pre-Christian past and ignore more recent history.³⁰ However, from a symbolic perspective, Stoker succeeds in offering his class a noble past to share with the natives of Ireland, thus allowing the creation of one common national identity.

The ancient treasures from a heroic past position *The snake's pass* within the Celtic Twilight of the late nineteenth century. The marriage plot, though, makes the novel part of a wider project, which extends beyond national boundaries. Once Catholics and Protestants have rediscovered the basis for a common identity, Stoker moves on to find for Ireland a privileged place within the British Empire. Stoker was well known for being a proud Irishman. When *The snake's pass* appeared, he had been living in London for over ten years, working as an acting manager at Henry Irving's Lyceum, but he was still recognized as 'a big, cheery, handsome Irishman', with his 'very flippantly sarcastic tongue' and his unmistakable brogue.³¹ His affiliation with 'philosophical' Irish nationalism dated back to his early years as a student at Trinity College, when he met the Home Rule leader Isaac Butt, literary Revivalists such as Standish O'Grady, Alfred Perceval Graves and John Todhunter, and became friendly with the Wilde family, whose deep knowledge of Irish folklore influenced *The snake's pass*.³² In later years Stoker would associate himself with John Dillon, one of the organizers of the Plan of Campaign for the reduction of rent, and would even try to help another nation-

---

29 Bridget McCormack, *Perceptions of St Patrick in eighteenth-century Ireland* (Dublin, 2000), p. 29. **30** Daly, 'Irish roots', 63–4. **31** Murray, *From the shadow of Dracula*, pp 220–1. **32** Ibid, pp 33–4. Murray points out that both Sir William and Lady Wilde wrote on legends about a giant serpent and that in the novel, Stoker remembers Sir Wilde's commitment to science and dedication as an antiquarian through the praise of the character of Andy. After Dick Sutherland has explained the process of drainage of the bog, Andy exclaims: 'Musha, but Dochter Wilde himself (rest his sowl!) couldn't have put it aisier to grip', p. 44; see Murray, pp 158, 65. On the Wildes' influence on *The snake's pass*, see also Stoker enthusiast John Moore's comment in Miller and Stoker, *The lost journal of Bram Stoker*, p. 159.

alist, William O'Brien, to stage a version of his Fenian novel *When we were boys* at the Lyceum.³³ However, Stoker's more moderate political views encouraged his identification with Gladstone's non-violent politics for an autonomous Ireland within the Empire.³⁴

When Stoker published *The snake's pass*, between the two Home Rule bills proposed by Gladstone, he was conscious of the political message contained in his novel. For this reason he tried hard to find an audience among those who supported the cause of Home Rule for Ireland, sending a copy to Gladstone himself, 'whose magnificent power and ability and character I had all my life so much admired'. He also sent a copy to the former Land Leaguer Michael Davitt, editor of the *Labour World*.³⁵ Davitt kept the promise of saying a 'not unkindly word' in his newspaper, and actually described the novel as a 'fresh, powerful, dramatic, intensely interesting story', but Stoker's greatest satisfaction came from Gladstone's positive comments.³⁶ He was 'more than pleased' to see that, despite the fact that 'in the interval between his getting the book and when we met, had occurred one of the greatest troubles and trials of his whole political life [...] yet in the midst of all he found time to read – and remember, even to details and names – the work of an unimportant friend', and judge it 'very fine indeed'.³⁷ Stoker's support of Gladstone went beyond the plan for a united Ireland flourishing through the exploitation of its natural potential for its own welfare. As an Irishman in England, Stoker recognized the importance of being part of the Empire, whose world-wide power and dimensions fascinated him, proved by the fact that in an address to the Historical Society in May 1872 he opposed a motion concerning England's preparation for an early emancipation of her colonies.³⁸

The marriage plot then, comes to embody this desire for a union based on mutual respect and understanding. For this reason, Stoker did not limit himself to exploiting the common trope of having the English colonizer wed the Irish peasant of Catholic faith, but went further by representing both parties as perfect mixes of the two cultures. Norah is described as a rare beauty. She is 'tall and beautifully proportioned', her neck 'long and slender, gracefully set in her rounded shoulders, and supporting a beautiful head [...] crowned [...] with a rich mass of hair as black and as glossy as the raven's wing' (p. 61). She is 'the living evidence of the truth of the hearsay' that along 'the west coast of Ireland there are traces of Spanish blood and Spanish beauty' (ibid.). However, she is said to be 'all the more perfect for being tempered with northern calm', that is, her Catholic blood having

---

33 David Glover, '"Dark enough fur any man": Bram Stoker's sexual ethnology and the question of Irish nationalism', in Román De La Campa (ed.), *Late imperial culture* (London, 1995), pp 53–71, p. 57; Chris Morash, '"Ever under some unnatural condition": Bram Stoker and the colonial fantastic' in Brian Cosgrove (ed.), *Literature and the supernatural: essays for the Maynooth bicentenary* (Dublin, 1995), pp 95–119, pp 111–12. 34 Stoker, *Personal reminiscences of Henry Irving*, ii, p. 29. 35 Ibid., p. 28. 36 Murray, *From the shadow of Dracula*, p. 160. 37 Stoker, *Personal reminiscences of Henry Irving*, p. 29. 38 Morash, 'Ever under some unnatural condition', pp 111–12.

been diluted by the Protestant creed she now professes. Norah is revealed to be a Protestant; but again, Stoker moderates between the two denominations by having her raised under the Catholic guidance of the nuns in Galway, thus turning her into a point of religious contact whose result is tolerance and mutual respect. Arthur, on the other hand, is introduced as the wealthy English tourist, but as Daly suggests,[39] he is actually reminiscent of that sense of non-belonging and isolation which was typical of the Protestant class to which Stoker belonged: he is an orphan whose parents were lost at sea, 'in a fog when crossing the Channel' (p. 5). He admits that their loss projected him into a 'blank', and that his inability to account for his origins was exploited by his cousins who treated him badly, and always make him feel like 'an "outsider"' – he is the embodiment of 'a class whose identity might well seem to have been lost somewhere in the waters between Ireland and England' (pp 5–6).[40] However, despite his troublesome childhood, Arthur grew into a handsome and generous man, and the sense of liminality that he represents is resolved through the active role he plays in the discovery of the treasures, through his recognition of their value, and through his sharing and improving their potential.

It is this very couple, representing the positive marriage of Irish enterprise and English expertise, that Stoker proposes as the worthy recipient of the national treasures uncovered, because they will not exploit them for their own interests. The chest of gold, for instance, is immediately employed for an unselfish and altruistic purpose, with Phelim Joyce affirming that '[t]ake it I will, an' gladly; but not for meself. The money was sent for Ireland's good, to help them that wanted help, an' plase God, I'll see it doesn't go ashtray now' (p. 207). That gold was offered by Revolutionary France to support Ireland's claims for independence, and the perfectly preserved skeletons of the French soldiers, who preferred to die rather than let go of the treasure, become a lesson of devotion and bravery for what this new Ireland should aspire to be. Although Phelim Joyce does not name the cause the treasure is going to support, Stoker's political bias towards Gladstone's peaceful plan for Ireland's autonomy within the Empire can easily be read between the lines of the novel. In fact, all kinds of violence are rejected, so that a direct allusion to the agrarian society of the Moonlighters is resolved in a humorous way, after the romantic Arthur is mistaken by the dull local policeman for one of the agitators:

> 'From information received, A come to talk till ye regardin' the interest ye profess to take in moonlichtin".
> 'What on earth do you mean?' I asked.
> [...] 'Why, A larn that ye're always out at night all over the country, and that ye've openly told people here that ye're interested in moonlichtin".

39 Daly, 'Irish roots', 60–1. **40** Ibid., p. 61.

[…] 'I don't know anything about moonlighting'.

'Then why do ye go out at nicht?'

'Simply to see the country at night – to look at the views – to enjoy the effects of moonlight'.

'There ye are, ye see – ye enjoy the moonlicht effect'.

'Good lord! I mean the view – the purely aesthetic effect – the chiaroscuro – the pretty pictures!'

'Oh, aye! A see now – A ken weel! Then A needn't trouble ye further'. (p. 98)

Stoker plays down the historical threat represented by the violent, agrarian Moonlighters by describing them as 'the scum of the country-side – "corner-boys" and loafers of all kinds – [who] would be only too glad to find an unexpected victim to rob' (p. 97), and by ridiculing them as nothing more than a group of local criminals.

Norah and Arthur's marriage, then, becomes indicative of a national union from which all sides will benefit, a union which is not based on the claimed superiority of the husband, or the English, over the wife, colonial Ireland, but rather on mutual respect and admiration, the consequences of a closeness which is not merely geographical, but also cultural and spiritual. The image of the snake, once again, is offered as the key for the interpretation of this closeness. If we go back to the beginning of the novel, when Arthur arrives in Co. Mayo, he learns the ancient legend of St Patrick, and how he saved Ireland by chasing away the evil snake who was at that time spreading horror and despair over the country. As the legend goes:

> wanst in ivery year there had to be brought to him a live baby; and they do say that he would wait until the moon was at the full, an' thin would be heerd one wild wail that made every sowl widin miles shuddher, an' thin there would be black silence, and clouds would come over the moon, and for three days it would never be seen agin. (p. 12)

Emblematically, the same battle between saint and hungry snake features in the legend of St George, the patron saint of England, who, like Patrick, delivered his people from the dragon of paganism in the name of Christianity. Stoker returned to this imagery in his last novel, *The lair of the white worm* (1911), which is, in fact, set in England, and which features the Christian hero Adam Salton fighting the primordial monster of the title, here metamorphosed into Lady Arabella March, the controversial New Woman.[41]

---

[41] Bram Stoker, *Dracula* and *The lair of the white worm* (London, 1986).

In *The snake's pass* the acceptance of a common ground between Catholics and Protestants, within Ireland and the Empire, drains the quaking bog of its power, revealing a fertile land underneath, and analogously resolves an unstable Irish national identity by jettisoning demeaning stereotypes and replacing them with a noble image of the Irish as an enterprising, industrious and beautiful hybrid nation. In 1844, scientist Robert Kane wrote in his *Industrial resources of Ireland* that 'our bogs may become, under the influence of an enlightened energy, sources of industry and eminently productive'.[42] Kane was trying to promote the development of Ireland's natural resources, for which he recognized the vital importance of the combination of English capital and Irish initiative.[43] And the very new form of committed and enterprising landlordism embodied by Norah and Arthur is exactly the enlightened energy that Stoker believes Ireland needed to move forward. Dick Sutherland eventually manages to 'cure' the bog, 'by both surgical and medical process' (p. 44), and the limestone uncovered is used to improve the estate, which is partly sold to those tenants 'who wished to purchase [...] on easy terms', and partly transformed into a 'fairyland' of 'exquisite gardens' and murmuring waters (pp 162, 212). This is the idyllic landscape where the Severns start their life together, and, in their words: 'There was never a cloud to shadow our sunlit way; and we felt that we were one' (p. 216).

When Bram Stoker wrote *The snake's pass*, in 1890, he was trying to create an idealistic reconciliatory scenario in response to the problematic reality which was afflicting his country. Ireland was troubled by sectarian factions, and Stoker proposed a common and noble past to unify them under the same national identity, in line with the literary tradition of his time. But his 'book of Ireland [...] dealing with Irish ways' included the point of view of the Irishman living outside Ireland, who recognized the importance of the wise marriage between an autonomous Ireland and a protective England.[44] Thus, in a response to Victorian caricatures, Norah stands for Erin, the black-haired beauty in humble clothes, whose melancholy eyes conveyed the suffering of her rebellious country. Norah, like Stoker's ideal Ireland, is brave and strong, her unrefined hands rescuing her man from the treacherous bog. But still, she recognizes her position and limits, and is willing to be educated and guided, to be worthy of her husband. The threat posed to Norah's safety is embodied by the serpentine Black Murdock, the negative stereotype of the Irish as uncivilized 'bog-trotters' or violent 'Paddys'. But while Erin's distress was usually soothed by the intervention of England, in the shape of sister Britannia or the valorous John Bull, Stoker depends instead on Paddy's positive alter ego, the handsome and honest Pat.[45] It is the peaceful and proactive Arthur

---

[42] Morash, 'Ever under some unnatural condition', p. III. [43] Murray, *From the shadow of Dracula*, p. 159.
[44] Stoker, *Personal reminiscences of Henry Irving*, ii, p. 29. [45] Sir John Tenniel, 'Two forces', *Punch*, 29 Oct. 1881; William H. Boucher, 'Ireland for the Irish! – Yes, But Which Irish?', *Judy*, 26 Oct. 1887.

who becomes Erin's worthy husband and who helps her improve her land, taking as a model the English landscapes of his childhood. In *The snake's pass*, then, Stoker establishes the basis for an intra-national and inter-national harmony, which would finally free his class from that sense of strangeness which accompanied it on both sides of the Channel. Ireland could be one nation, if willing to probe the unstable bog of stereotypes and accept her unity in a common past. Ireland could be a privileged nation in the British Empire, if both sides would recognize that they shared the same values and fought the same snakes.

The lair of the white worm; or, what became of Bram Stoker?

DARRYL JONES

Bram Stoker is an unusual case: a significant literary figure whose reputation rests entirely on one work. This, of course, is *Dracula*, published in 1897. Over the last thirty years or so, this novel has received as much analysis and attention as any work of the nineteenth century, but the rest of Stoker's work remains largely ignored and unread. While there's no doubt that *Dracula* is a major novel, capable of sustaining multiple readings in multiple contexts, it does seem to me strange that the rest of his œuvre is passed over in almost complete silence. Between 1875 and 1911, Stoker wrote twelve novels,[1] as well as numerous short stories and works of non-fiction – *Dracula* is the fifth novel. In other words, students and readers of Stoker have plenty more to go on. Bram Stoker has certainly not wanted biographers, and while a few critics, notably David Glover and William Hughes, have engaged with his writing career in the round, the general assumption, tacit or otherwise, seems to be that *Dracula* was a freak success from an otherwise very minor or even talentless novelist, and that the rest of his work is simply not worth bothering with.[2]

The subject of this essay is Stoker's last novel, *The lair of the white worm*, first published by Rider and Son in 1911. The novel has a complex publication history, to put it mildly. Although it appeared in several reprints after 1911, these were all edited and abridged versions, in which over one hundred pages of what was not anyway a particularly long novel were excised, and in some versions the title changed to *The garden of evil*. It wasn't until 2006 that the complete text was restored, with the publication of the Penguin Classics version meticulously edited by Kate Hebblethwaite. But even now, you won't find *The lair of the white worm*

---

[1] The number of novels written by Stoker is a matter of some disagreement among Stoker scholars. Some count up to thirteen, others stop at eleven. It depends on whether problematic texts like *Snowbound*, *The primrose path* and *The watter's mou'* are counted. [2] See David Glover, *Vampires, mummies and liberals: Bram Stoker and the politics of popular fiction* (Durham, NC); William Hughes, *Beyond* Dracula: *Bram Stoker's fiction in its cultural contexts* (Basingstoke and London, 2000).

in any bookstore, at least not under that title: Hebblethwaite's edition appends the novel to Stoker's posthumous 1913 collection *Dracula's guest and other weird tales*.³ It was the only way the novel could get published: she initially approached Penguin with a proposal to publish *The lair of the white worm*, but was told that only a Stoker book with 'Dracula' in the title would be commercially viable, so *White worm* found itself snuck into the volume, almost as a kind of samizdat publication. Fortunately, the critical and commercial success of the volume allowed Hebblethwaite to persuade Penguin that it *was* worth publishing other Stoker novels, and so in 2008 she edited a new version of his 1903 mummy novel *The jewel of seven stars*, appearing in a complete text for the first time since its original publication (like *White worm*, *The jewel of seven stars* had appeared in a heavily edited or even bowdlerized version until this time).⁴

Why all this doctoring and editing? Those few people who read *The lair of the white worm* all seem to agree that it is a frankly deranged novel, perpetually veering towards and occasionally diving head-first into downright incoherence, loading subplot upon subplot in a way which is simply narratively uncontainable – Jarlath Killeen is surely being polite when he calls *White worm* 'textually dishevelled'.⁵

We don't expect realism from a novel called *The lair of the white worm*, but here Stoker seems to have abandoned fundamental plausibility, or has even forgotten how to write a novel. On the very first page, the protagonist simultaneously spends the night in the Great Eastern Hotel in London and on board a ship in Southampton; major characters disappear from the narrative without trace or explanation; one major character simultaneously falls to her death and does not; characters set sail for the Isle of Man or County Cork but immediately find themselves back in England; lengthy and abstruse disquisitions interrupt the narrative, sometimes for pages on end, and are then dropped without further reference; the novel somehow takes in voodoo, mesmerism, druidism, Romano-British Christianity, an infestation of birds, electrical engineering, palaeontology, the etiquette of tiger hunting, fantasias upon evolution, mining engineering, geology, precise descriptions of weaponry and much else besides.

Faced with this apparent mess, some commentators – notably two of Stoker's biographers, Daniel Farson and Paul Murray – have chosen to read the novel as a symptom of Stoker's own insanity brought on by the last stages of syphilis (and whether or not Stoker died of syphilis remains a subject of vigorous debate for Stoker scholars),⁶ or as the product of a mind rendered incapable by the heavy use of opium, to which the older Stoker became addicted partially as a palliative for his illness.⁷ Gamely and ingeniously, Hebblethwaite has countered this dominant

---

3 Bram Stoker, *Dracula's guest and other weird stories*, ed., Kate Hebblethwaite (London, 2006).   **4** Stoker, *The jewel of seven stars*, ed. Kate Hebblethwaite (London, 2008).   **5** Jarlath Killeen, *Gothic literature, 1825–1914* (Cardiff, 2009), p. 120.   **6** See Paul Murray's view of this issue in Chapter 2 of this collection.   **7** See

view by attempting to read the novel as a literary experiment, its very form breaking down the boundaries between consciousness and fantasy:

> Although this story was written between 3 March and 12 June 1911, its hasty composition belies a text that embodies all the concerns and contradictions of Stoker's work. In thrall to the abiding power of myth and legend, yet also attuned to contemporary scientific ideas, the novel crosses borders between the logical and the illogical, the old and the new, the impulsive and the considered, whilst also being thematically engaged in the transgression of boundaries between male and female, human and animal, right and wrong. Simultaneously displaying both irrational flights of imagination and careful research, unconscious impulses and measured ideas, it is Stoker's most inaccessible yet his most revealing work. Like the man himself, *The lair of the white worm* is a complex amalgam of self-possession and passion that defies any ready definition.[8]

In order to get a sense of the novel's complexities/disorganization, it might be worth pausing here to attempt to summarize the plot of *White worm*.

The novel's action takes place across four big houses in the Peak District, on the Staffordshire–Derbyshire border. Adam Salton, the novel's hero, arrives from his native Australia to live with his great uncle at Lesser Hill, which he is to inherit. At the same time, Edgar Caswall arrives at nearby Castra Regis, the grandest of the houses. The Caswalls seem to be the victims of a family curse, with rumours of an ancestor having sold his soul to the Devil, and like Adam, Edgar returns to England from the colonies: he has spent his life in sub-Saharan Africa. Mr Salton senior's neighbour and confidant is Sir Nathaniel de Salis, a retired diplomat who hints at service in St Petersburg and Peking, and who now pursues his antiquarian interests in his ancestral home of Doom Tower. The fourth house is Diana's Grove, built on the ruins of a Romano-British Temple, which was itself built on top of an ancient Druidic Temple. Diana's Grove is the home of the sinister and seductive Lady Arabella Marsh, who is plotting to marry Edgar Caswall in order to get her hands on his vast fortune. The main plot of the novel concerns the gradual discovery that Lady Arabella is herself the human manifestation of the titular White Worm, who has lived since time immemorial in a nauseously stinking well, fathomlessly deep, over which the Druidic temple was initially built (and which is in some unexplained way connected to its rites). Meanwhile, Edgar goes mad atop his tower, obsessed with a gigantic kite shaped like a hawk, which he flies in order to keep off a mysterious bird infestation. On the novel's climactic

---

Daniel Farson, *The man who wrote* Dracula: *a biography of Bram Stoker* (London, 1975), p. 217; Paul Murray, *From the shadow of Dracula: a life of Bram Stoker* (London, 2004), pp 262, 265–6. **8** Hebblethwaite, 'Introduction', *Dracula's guest*, p. xxiii.

stormy night, both Castra Regis and Diana's Grove are destroyed by lightning, killing both Edgar and the White Worm herself, who explodes from her hole in a foul gush of blood, entrails, fat and other abject substances (there is no doubt a good article to be written on sexual terror in *The lair of the white worm*, but this one isn't it, so I shall pass over this startling episode without further comment).

II

Bram Stoker was extremely interested in folklore, and tended to research his novels quite meticulously. We know, for example, that he read as widely as he could in Eastern European folklore and history, as well as travel literature, while preparing *Dracula* – traditionally, accounts of the novel's genesis have asserted that he did much of the reading across successive summer holidays in Whitby, where the first part of the novel is set, and which he supposedly visited annually from 1890 to 1896, though new research by Christopher Frayling, published in this volume, suggests that in fact he only holidayed in Whitby once. We do, however, have Stoker's working notes for this novel, and his reading has been collected in Clive Leatherdale's anthology *The origins of Dracula* and Robert Eighteen-Bisang and Elizabeth Miller have painstakingly transcribed these notes for a recent facsimile edition.[9] In terms specifically of Irish folklore, he was very familiar with the works of the Wildes, Sir William and Speranza (as well as with the family themselves – he was a frequent visitor to their home in Merrion Square, Dublin, and his wife Florence Balcombe had, of course, been engaged to Oscar), and drew on their work for his 1891 novel *The snake's pass*, his only Irish-set novel, and one steeped in national serpent-lore. This, specifically, seems to be the passage from the Lady Wilde's *Ancient legends, mystic charms and superstitions of Ireland* (1887) which animates *The snake's pass*:

> We are told by the ancient chroniclers that serpent-worship once prevailed in Ireland, and that St Patrick hewed down the serpent idol *Crom-Cruadh* (the great worm) and cast it into the Boyne (from whence arose the legend that St Patrick banished all venomous things from the island). Now as the Irish never could have seen a serpent, none existing in Ireland, this worship must have come from the far East, where this beautiful and deadly creature is looked upon as the symbol of the Evil One, and worshipped and propi-

---

[9] See Clive Leatherdale, *The origins of* Dracula: *the background to Bram Stoker's Gothic masterpiece* (London, 1987); an excellent account of Stoker's working notes can be found in Christopher Frayling (ed.), *Vampyres: Lord Byron to Count Dracula* (London, 1992), pp 303–16. For the notes themselves see *Bram Stoker's notes for* Dracula: *a facsimile edition*, annotated and transcribed by Robert Eighteen-Bisang and Elizabeth Miller (Jefferson, NC, 2008).

tiated by votive offerings, as all things evil were in the early world, in the hope of turning away their evil hatred from man, and to induce them to shew mercy and pity [.][10]

It seems likely that Stoker drew at least in part on memories of this again in 1897 when choosing to name his great vampire Dracula, 'Son of the Dragon' (in the working notes, the earliest of which dates from March 1890, he is originally named, less resonantly, 'Count Wampyr').[11] *The lair of the white worm* clearly continues this longstanding interest, and marks on Stoker's part a very conscious engagement with specifically *British* folklore.

In the novel, Stoker draws particularly on two Northumbrian legends, 'The Laidly Worm of Spindleston Heugh', and 'The Lambton Worm'. These tales exist in many forms, and particularly as local ballads, but seems probable that Stoker's direct sources here are two of the most high-profile collections of English folktales from the 1890s, Joseph Jacobs' *English fairy tales*, which contained 'The Laidly Worm', and Edwin Sidney Hartland's *English fairy and other folk tales*, which contained 'The Lambton Worm'. In 'The Laidly [Loathly] Worm', a princess at Bamborough Castle on the Northumberland coast is transformed into a giant dragon by her new stepmother, a wicked witch-queen:

> So Lady Margaret went to bed a beauteous maiden, and rose up a Laidly Worm. And when her maidens came up to dress her in the morning they found coiled up on the bed a dreadful dragon, which uncoiled itself and came towards them. But they ran away shrieking, and the Laidly Worm crawled and crept, and crept and crawled till it reached the Heugh or rock of the Spindlestone round which it coiled itself, and there lay basking with its terrible snout in the air.[12]

So gigantic is the worm that it can coil its tail around a ship, and so rapacious is it that it drains the milk of seven cows daily. Margaret is rescued when her brother returns from his campaigns overseas and kisses the worm three times, with which it turns back into his sister (the witch-queen then transforms into a toad).

'The Laidly Worm' has clear connections with three Scottish Border ballads collected by the influential American folklorist and philologist Francis Child in his collections of *English and Scottish popular ballads* (8 vols, 1857–9). In 'Kemp Owyne' (or 'Kempion'), a wicked stepmother transforms her stepdaughter into 'The fieryest beast that ever was seen', cursed to dwell 'in Wormie's Wood' until

---

10 Lady [Jane] Wilde ('Speranza'), *Ancient legends, mystic charms and superstitions of Ireland. To which is appended a chapter on 'the ancient races of Ireland' by the late Sir William Wilde* (Boston, 1887), p. 14. **11** Frayling, *Vampyres*, pp 303–16; Eighteen-Bisang and Miller, *Notes*, pp 26–7 for 'Wampyr'. **12** Joseph Jacobs, *English fairy tales*, 3rd ed. (New York, c.1902), pp 191–2.

'Kempion, the kingis son / Come to the craig and thrice kiss thee'.[13] In 'Allison Gross', an ugly witch curses a young man who refuses her advances: 'She's turned me into an ugly worm, / And gard me toddle about the tree.'[14] The curse is lifted when the queen strokes him three times. Very similar is 'The Laily Worm and the Machrel of the Sea': a wicked stepmother turns her stepson into 'the lailly worm / That lays at the fitt of the tree', and his sister into 'The machrel of the sea', who comes to the worm each Saturday to comb and wash his hair. The worm slays seven knights until his father commands the stepmother to return the children to their original forms, before burning her to death.[15]

In 'The Lambton Worm', a fourteenth-century tale with many similarities to 'The Laidly Worm', the heir of Lambton Hall on the banks of the Wear neglects churchgoing to go fishing, and catches a repulsive worm, which he throws into a nearby well:

> The worm remained unheeded in the well till it outgrew so confined a dwelling-place. It then emerged, and betook itself by day to the river, where it lay coiled round a rock in the middle of the stream, and by night to a neighbouring hill, round whose base it would twine itself, while it continued to grow so fast that it could soon encircle the hill three times. This eminence is still called the Worm Hill. It is oval in shape, on the north side of the Wear, and about a mile and a half from old Lambton Hall.
>
> The monster now became the terror of the whole country side. It sucked the cows' milk, worried the cattle, devoured the lambs, and committed every sort of depredation on the helpless peasantry. Having laid waste the district on the north side of the river, it crossed the stream and approached Lambton Hall, where the old lord was living alone and desolate.[16]

When the heir of Lambton returns from the crusades, a local sibyl (wise woman) instructs him on how to slay the apparently indestructible worm (which has the magical power of reuniting its severed parts), on condition that, having killed the worm, he must then sacrifice the first living thing he encounters. On returning home, he first meets his son, but he sacrifices his hound instead, thus violating the agreement and causing a family curse which falls upon the Lambtons for nine generations. The Lambton family curse may underlie the curse of the Caswalls in *The lair of the white worm*: Sir Nathaniel tells Adam that locals believe that the Caswalls 'have in the past sold themselves to the Devil'.[17] When the heir of Lambton first

---

13 [Francis James Child], *English and Scottish popular ballads*, ed. Helen Child Sargent and George Lyman Kittredge (Boston and New York, 1904), pp 60–1. **14** Ibid., p. 62. **15** Ibid., pp 62–3. **16** Edwin Sidney Hartland, *English fairy and other folk tales* (London and Felling-on-Tyne, c.1890), p. 79. **17** Stoker, *The lair of the white worm* in *Dracula's guest*, p. 167.

catches the worm, under profane circumstances (he has gone fishing instead of to mass), he exclaims, 'Why, truly, I think I have caught the devil himself.'[18]

Hartland's source for 'The Lambton Worm', from whom he lifts the text verbatim, is William Henderson's *Notes on the folk-lore of the northern counties of England and the Borders* (1866) (the revised 1879 edition of Henderson's book was published under the auspices of the Folklore Society, of which Hartland was at one point president).[19] Henderson's book contains a chapter on 'Worms or Dragons', which asserts: 'Among the rich and varied Folk-Lore of the North of England, it is imposible [sic] not to remark how numerous and characteristic are the legends respecting dragons, or, as we locally call them, worms – a name taken from the Norse *Ormr*, a serpent or dragon. .... The legends of serpents and dragons rife in other parts of England are, on the whole, but meagre when compared with these Northern tales.'[20]

In making this assertion, Henderson is in part here following the lead given by Sir Walter Scott's *Minstrelsy of the Scottish Border* (1802–3). In a disquisition on dragon-lore, Scott notes that 'There are numerous traditions upon the Borders, concerning huge and destructive snakes', and relates the legend of 'the fabulous dragon, slain in Northumberland by *Sir Bevis*' – that is, the dragon-slaying Middle English romance of *Bevis of Hampton*, which is generally not Northumbrian but rather set around Arundel Castle in Sussex – and the legend of Sir John Conyers of 'The manor of Sockburne, in the bishopric of Durham ... who, as tradition says, slew, with his falchion, a monstrous creature, a dragon, a worm, or flying serpent, that devoured men, women, and children.'[21]

Henderson's main source, however, is Sir Cuthbert Sharpe's collection of County Durham ballads and stories, *The Bishoprick garland* (1834), which contains 'The Worme of Lambton'. In turn, Sharpe's source for the legend is Robert Surtees' monumental *The history and antiquities of the County Palatine of Durham* (4 vols, 1816–40), which unearths a manuscript source naming the heir: 'Johan Lambeton that slewe ye worme, was knight of Rhoodes [Rhodes] and Lord of Lambeton and Wod Apilton efter the death of fower brothers, sans esshew masle [without male issue]. His son Robert Lampton was drowned at Newebrigg.'[22] Sharpe is much more emphatic than Henderson about the unholy nature of the heir's behaviour, which leads to his catching the worm: 'The young heir of Lambton led a dissolute and evil course of life, equally regardless of the obligations of his high estate and the sacred duties of religion.'[23] Sharpe also goes into detail

---

18 Hartland, *English fairy and other folk tales*, p. 79. **19** William Henderson, *Notes on the folk-lore of the Northern Counties of England and the Borders. A new edition with many additional notes* (London, 1879). 'The Lambton Worm' is on pp 288–91. **20** Ibid., pp 281, 298. **21** Sir Walter Scott, *The poetical works of Sir Walter Scott, Bart. Vol. III. Minstrelsy of the Scottish border* (Edinburgh, 1833), pp 234–5. **22** Robert Surtees, *The history and antiquities of the County Palatine of Durham*, 2 (Wakefield, 1972), p. 171. In Surtees' version, the heir refuses to kill his father after slaying the worm, not his son. **23** [Sir Cuthbert Sharpe],

about the nature and outcome of the family curse: Sir William Lambton was killed in the English Civil War, at the Battle of Marston Moor (2 July 1644), while his heir William had already 'received his death's wound at Wakefield' in 1643, killed while commanding a troop of dragoons. Sharpe writes of the last cursed Lambton, Henry:

> The fulfilment of the curse was inherent in the ninth of descent, as above noted, and great anxiety prevailed during his life-time, amongst the hereditary depositories of the traditions of the county, to know if the curse would 'hold good to the end.' He died, in his chariot, crossing the New Bridge [across the Wear at Lambton Castle – this is also where Robert Lambton was drowned] – thus giving the last connecting link to the chain of circumstantial tradition connected with the history of the Worme of Lambton.[24]

To this, Henderson adds that 'popular tradition is clear and unanimous in maintaining that, during the period of the curse, no lord of Lambton ever died in his bed.'[25]

It's tempting to speculate that Stoker drew on these northern legends as a result of spending time in Whitby, just down the coast from Wearside, and not far from Bamborough. In order to accommodate the Druidic and Romano-British elements necessary to his narrative, as well as the vast cave-systems, he relocated the story south to the Peak District, on the Staffordshire–Derbyshire border. The novel makes much of its location at the heart of the ancient kingdom of Mercia, 'where there are traces of all the various nationalities which made up the conglomerate which became Britain.'[26] Mercia itself abounded in worm-lore, as demonstrated by still-extant place-names and geographical features such as Drakelow ('The Dragon's Mound') near Kidderminster, Drakeholes ('The Dragon's Valley') in Nottinghamshire, Wormwood Hill in Cambridgeshire, and Wormhill and Wormsley, both in Herefordshire.[27] Beyond Mercia (which means 'land of the border people') lies, the novel tells us, 'savage Wales'.[28] We know that Stoker was familiar with Wirt Sikes' 1880 collection *British goblins: Welsh folk-lore, fairy mythology, legends and traditions*, a copy of which he possessed.[29] Sikes was US Consul to Wales, based in Cardiff, from where he collected an enormous number of local folktales; his book closes with an account of 'the dragon-haunted caves and treasure-hills of Wales', and includes a story which is clearly an analogue of St

---

The Bishoprick garland, or a collection of legends, songs, ballads, &c. belonging to the County of Durham (London, 1834), p. 21. **24** Ibid., p. 30. **25** Henderson, *Notes on the folk-lore of the Northern Counties of England and the Borders*, p. 292. **26** Stoker, *Lair*, p. 161. **27** See Hebblethwaite, 'Introduction', *Dracula's guest*, pp xxxvii–xxxviii, n. 26. **28** Stoker, *Lair*, p. 171. **29** For Stoker's reading of Sikes, see Murray, *From the shadow of Dracula*, pp 174, 263. Murray suggests that traces of Sikes' book can also be found in *Dracula*.

Patrick and the serpent, as St. Samson drives out of Wales a 'pestiferous beast ... of vast size ... [which] by its deadly breath had destroyed two districts.'[30]

III

My reading so far has placed *The lair of the white worm* within a rich economy of narratives of local serpent-lore. While there's no question of the depth of Stoker's engagement with this subject, this does not address the novel's incoherence. Killeen, for one, recognizes the novel's range of interests, and from this concludes that with *The lair of the white worm*, Stoker has effectively bitten off more than he can chew:

> A[n] ... explanation for the bizarrely dissipated nature of the novel may simply be that in it Stoker attempted to synthesize and summarize the mythological, folkloric, religious and political themes which run through his other texts, and is simply not up to such a job. The novel, on this account, is extraordinarily ambitious but simply beyond the talents of the writer. In *Dracula*, Stoker managed to successfully synthesize seven years of research on Transylvania and vampire lore to produce a compelling narrative; in *The lair of the white worm*, he tries to cram a lifetime's worth of study in English and Irish folklore, myth and religious traditions into a relatively short novel, and cannot manage it.[31]

This strikes me as a reasonable conclusion. But it's worth noting that, from a critical and scholarly point of view, ambitious artistic failures can often be more rewarding than works which fully realize their aesthetic and intellectual aims (and especially so if those aims are relatively modest). In other words, *The lair of the white worm* may be a mess, but its very messiness may be what's interesting about it.

Having said that, I want to draw to a close by proposing a way in which the novel does make a kind of sense, and one which is intimately connected to Stoker's interest in snake-lore. The novel, I would propose, is at least in part the fruit of Stoker's engagement with *fin de siècle* Symbolist art, itself heavily inflected by the overlapping discourses of decadence and occultism. The Symbolist movement originated in European art in the 1880s, as a response to the dominant aesthetic and philosophical modes of naturalism and positivism. Robert Goldwater, the major historian of Symbolism, writes:

> It was a reaction against the 'sole concern with the world of phenomena' which had dominated the art of the middle years of the century and which was expressed not only in the purer realism and impressionism of what was

---

30 Wirt Sikes, *British goblins: Welsh folk-lore, fairy mythology, legends and traditions* (London, 1880), pp 394, 393. **31** Killeen, *Gothic literature*, p. 120.

9: 'They could follow the tall white shaft'

10: 'Lady Arabella was dancing in a fantastic sort of way'

then the *avant-garde*, but also in the naturalistic vision of the most traditional artists ... who produced an 'idealist' art that illustrated a theme.[32]

Symbolist *Gedankenmalerei* ('thought painting') sought to 'give pictorial shape to "the invisible world of the psyche"', and in doing so was typically characterized by aesthetic disjunction, a 'tension between work and image (with the resulting ambivalence of image and idea)'.[33]

The lair of the white worm has a clear provenance here, in the context of European Symbolism – a pointer to commentators which few, if any, have bothered to follow. When first published in 1911, the novel contained a series of illustrations by the artist and occultist Pamela Colman Smith, a well-known figure in occult circles, who had been inducted into the Hermetic Order of the Golden Dawn in 1901 by no less a personage than W.B. Yeats, the *ipsissumus* of the Order, whose work she also illustrated.[34] Stoker knew Colman Smith very well, as she was for some years the principal set-designer for Henry Irving's Lyceum Theatre, of which Stoker was the manager. I reproduce here two of these illustrations: the worm itself (fig. 9), and the snake-witch Lady Arabella (fig. 10).

Two years earlier, in 1909, Colman Smith had produced the work for which she is by far best known, the Waite-Rider Tarot Deck (sometimes known as the Waite-Smith deck), which has gone on to become the definitive Tarot. Colman Smith produced this Tarot in conjunction with the occultist and Rosicrucian A.E. Waite, a close friend of Arthur Machen and the nearest thing the Golden Dawn had to an official scholar, and it was published by the occult publisher William Rider, who also published *The lair of the white worm*.[35] A number of the heavily symbolized images from Smith's Tarot recur, sometimes explicitly, both in her illustrations to *White worm* and in the novel itself. In her illustration of 'The World' (fig. 11), a naked seductress is wreathed in serpentlike folds, very much like those which Smith paints around Lady Arabella.

'The Tower' (fig. 12) shows a tower struck and destroyed by lightning, an image on which I would suggest Stoker draws explicitly for the novel's climactic scene (in which the reference to 'a house of cards' might just be a giveaway):

> At length there came a flash so appallingly bright that in its glare nature seemed to be standing still. So long did it last that there was time to dis-

---

32 Robert Goldwater, *Symbolism* (London, 1979), p. 17. **33** Ibid., pp 9, 17, 23. **34** For the fullest and most authoritative account of Smith's life and work, on which I draw here, see Melinda Parsons, *To all believers: the art of Pamela Colman Smith* (Wilmington, DE, 1975). Smith worked on *The illustrated verses of William Butler Yeats* (New York, 1898), and was the set-designer for London and New York productions of *The Countess Cathleen*. On induction into the Golden Dawn, initiates chose Latin mottos for themselves: Smith's was *Quod tibi id allis* ('Whatever you would have done to thee'). **35** For Waite's contribution to the Golden Dawn, see Ellic Howe, *The magicians of the Golden Dawn: a documentary history of a magical order, 1887–1923* (Wellingborough, 1985), pp 252–72, and passim.

11: Colman Smith, 'The World' (1909)

12: Colman Smith, 'The Tower' (1909)

tinguish its configuration. It seemed like a mighty tree inverted, pendant from the sky. The roots overhead were articulated. The whole country within the angle of vision was lit up till it seemed to glow. Then a broad ribbon of fire seemed to drop on the tower of Castra Regis just as the thunder crashed. By the glare of the lightning, he [Adam] could see the tower shake and tremble and finally fall to pieces like a house of cards.[36]

As Bram Dijkstra demonstrates in his classic study *Idols of perversity: fantasies of feminine evil in* fin de siècle *culture*, a work which focuses heavily on Symbolist painting, the serpent-seductress was a figure to whom artists at the turn of the nineteenth century returned time and again, part of an overarching fascination with mythological female monsters (the Medusa, the Sphinx, the Siren), and with mythical narratives of female sexual congress with animals (Leda and the Swan, and others).[37] Combining Christian ideas of temptation and the Fall, pagan overtones of bacchanalian sexual excess, and a version of phallic femininity which resonated powerfully with *fin de siècle* anxieties concerning the proto-feminist 'New Woman' (anxieties which Stoker understood and appreciated, and which inform *Dracula*, as well as his 1905 novel *The man*), the serpent-woman was one of the most striking symbolic representations of the recurring trope of the *femme fatale*.

The great models for the nineteenth-century serpent-seductress were two of the canonical works of English Romanticism, Samuel Taylor Coleridge's 'Christabel' (1816) and John Keats' 'Lamia' (1820), works which were themselves frequently illustrated around the *fin de siècle*, and well into the twentieth century by *avant-garde* illustrators influenced by Symbolism and Art Nouveau. Sir George Frampton's sculpture *Lamia* (1899), for example, now on display in the Royal Academy of Arts in London, is a life-size bust in ivory and bronze, whose half-closed eyes, white visage, and bronze snake-armour confront viewers with an unknowable silence.[38] The Irish artist Norah McGuinness depicted a memorably decadent version of the serpent-woman Lady Geraldine, smiling in the foreground while, in the background, Christabel herself gets into bed.[39] The image is heavily influenced by Aubrey Beardsley and Harry Clarke. Although a generation younger, McGuinness' career offers several parallels with Smith's. Like Smith, McGuinness worked as a set-designer for performances of Yeats' plays (she worked on the first production of *Deirdre* for the Abbey in 1926). McGuinness also illus-

36 Stoker, *Lair*, p. 363. **37** Bram Dijkstra, *Idols of perversity: fantasies of feminine evil in* fin de siècle *culture* (Oxford and New York, 1986), pp 304–14, and passim. Notable works of this kind include Jean Delvile's *The idol of perversity* (1891) and Franz Von Stuck's *Sensuality* (also 1897). Hebblethwaite, who has also been reading Dijkstra, briefly raises parallels with Symbolist art: 'Introduction', *Dracula's guest*, p. xxviii. **38** For a representation and account of Frampton's Lamia, see Henk van Os, et al., *Femmes fatales, 1860–1910* (Antwerp and Groningen, 2003), pp 84–5. **39** In 2008, this illustration came up for auction in Whyte's auction house, Dublin, where it fetched a price of €5200: http://www.whytes.ie/iArtistsGallery Display.asp?Auction=20080929&Lot=122. Accessed 3 March 2013.

trated Yeats' poetry: the first edition of *The stories of Red Hanrahan and the secret rose* (1927) was illustrated by McGuinness, to whom the volume's opening (and most significant) poem, 'Sailing to Byzantium' was dedicated.[40]

Of all Irish artists influenced by Symbolism, the great stained-glass artist and illustrator Harry Clarke is the most important. When Clarke was commissioned to illustrate A.C. Swinburne's poems in 1928, one of the poems he chose was 'Satia Te Sanguine' ('Satiate Thyself With Blood') – Clarke's free rendering of the poem shows a naked serpent-woman straddling a Sebastian-like martyr, impaled upon a bed of thorns. Clarke's spine-illustration to the volume has yet another serpent-woman, suggesting that for him this was the collection's governing symbol.[41]

I would suggest, then, that *The lair of the white worm* should be read in this broader context, as Stoker's own engagement with one of the main strands of European symbolist art – a movement which has, I have tried to show, important Irish connections. This is not – far from it – to say that reading it in this light makes the novel narratively coherent. I'm not sure anything could do that. It is merely to argue that in expecting narrative coherence to be the novel's primary concern we may be making a category mistake. *The lair of the white worm* is a novel of shape and symbol rather than one of character and event; its apparent incoherence mirrors the 'tension between work and image' characteristic of Symbolism. That Stoker's last novel cannot reconcile this tension – the immediate image wins out every time over the work as a whole – is part of what makes it so intriguing.

As a coda to this essay, it's worth noting that in 1988 *White worm* probably found its ideal reader, an interpreter in tune both with the novel's deranged anti-logic and with its symbolic power. This was, of course, Ken Russell, one of the great wayward talents of British cinema, whose film of Stoker's unfilmable novel brought together a remarkably outré cast including a young Hugh Grant, *Dynasty* star and member of the Serbian royal family Catherine Oxenberg, future foul-mouthed spin doctor Peter Capaldi, and former *Z-Cars* star Stratford Johns. Presiding over the whole brilliant mess is Amanda Donohoe as Lady Arabella, giving a performance truly worthy of the novel's insanity. Those who have seen the film won't need me to tell them that she spends large amounts of time in various states of undress, whether fellating a boy scout to death, or, most notoriously, planning to sacrifice Princess Catherine Oxenberg to the snake-god by use of an enormous strap-on dildo. Officially, perhaps, Bram Stoker himself could never have approved of this film, but with hindsight it appears to me to be a fittingly excessive memorial to his last and strangest novel.

---

40 Rebecca Minch, 'McGuinness, Norah', *Dictionary of Irish biography*, http://dib.cambridge.org.elib.tcd.ie/quicksearch.do. Accessed 3 March 2013. See also Pat Donlon, 'Drawing a fine line: Irish women artists as illustrators', *Irish Arts Review Yearbook*, 18 (2002), 80–92. **41** For Clarke's illustrations of Swinburne, see A.C. Swinburne, *Selected poems* (London, 1928).

Mr Stoker's holiday

CHRISTOPHER FRAYLING

The novelist and poet John Fowles once wrote of Arthur Conan Doyle that fans of Sherlock Holmes were patronizing his contribution to literature while seeming to praise it.[1] By pretending the stories actually happened – and arguing about the exact dates of fictions as if they were history, or about factual inaccuracies in the stories; by reading the author's life into the work in unproblematic ways, as if the stories were just piles of bits of information about a more or less interesting man; by turning the stories into social phenomena with lives of their own; by speculating wildly about meanings which blurred fiction and reality – meanings which were metaphorical rather than actual, and could never be proved or disproved in the usual ways; by searching for sources and inspirations for which there was no documentary evidence – elevating gossip into gospel: all of these approaches, concluded Fowles, distracted attention from Conan Doyle's undoubted literary gifts as a great writer of dialogue, and his commendable ability to create memorable characters in a couple of lines of prose. They diminished him as a *writer*. The fans were enthusiastic, loving even – no doubt about that – but in expressing their enthusiasm, they had taken their favourite stories out of the world of literature – and of literary criticism – altogether: which, John Fowles reckoned, in the end was patronizing to the author *and* his fictions.

The same could certainly be said – with even more force, in my view – of Bram Stoker, about whose *inner* life hardly any evidence of significance seems to have survived. His professional letters – and he wrote, he said, about fifty of them a day – tended to be about the day-to-day business of the Lyceum Theatre. His autobiographical *Personal reminiscences of Henry Irving*, published in two volumes in 1906, is more about the people he met than what he saw or felt, and refers sev-

---

This essay is a revised and expanded version of a paper given at the Bram Stoker Centenary Conference, Trinity College Dublin, on 6 July 2012. I would like to thank Jarlath Killeen and Professor Darryl Jones for inviting me to the conference, and for convening it. [1] See John Fowles, *A study in scarlet*, in *New Statesman*, 26 November 1976, and his Afterword to *The hound of the Baskervilles* (London, 1974), pp 186–8.

eral times to an appointments diary which has since disappeared. Of all the many pieces of occasional journalism he wrote, not one is about himself, though they are often about the life and work of other people. His recently published Dublin journal, covering the eleven years from 1871 to 1882, tells us much more about his social life than his personal life, and what emerges is the blurred portrait of a humane and high-minded man, who went out to the theatre a lot, enjoyed his friends and a good yarn, kept in touch with Trinity College Dublin, and loved the sea. He also had an ear – already – for weird story ideas: 'Mem: boy with bottled flies'; 'the devil eels of the Wey'; and so on.² The impression he gives at times, in the *Journal*, is that it was the feeling of being strangled by red tape in the gingerbread court of the Viceroy at Dublin Castle – his day job – that helped to explain his taste for such vestigial horror stories. Even here, though, it is difficult to tell from the *Journal* whether the anecdotes and stories are his, or whether they were overheard from other people. A curious mixture of the mundane and the Gothic or catastrophic runs through his adult life. Is this saying much? Many children share the same mixture, after all.

When Bram Stoker died, on 26 April 1912, his obituaries emphasized his geniality, his capacity for friendship, his long-term business partnership with the actor Henry Irving, his associations with the powerbrokers of his day – and sometimes but not always, the eighteen books he wrote. They scarcely mentioned *Dracula* (1897) at all. Today, a hundred years later, they would mention little else. And this has much more to do with the history of film and popular culture than with the history of literature. Since the rise of the movies, *Dracula* has become, on the rebound, one of the most widely *known about* books in all world fiction, whether or not people have read it: the most-filmed character in the history of cinema, with Sherlock Holmes running second. Unlike Conan Doyle, though, the focus with Stoker has been on a single book, the only one of his to enter the cultural bloodstream, and that is *Dracula*. *Dracula*, rather than any other of his novels and short stories, has inspired the kinds of adulation – and, if we are to go with John Fowles' observations, the accidental patronizing – which have been devoted to Sherlock Holmes.

Not surprisingly, the full-length biographies of Bram Stoker – and four of them have appeared so far – all put his most famous work in the shop window, and more-or-less and in different ways interpret the man through the prism of *Dracula*:³ the first, by Harry Ludlam, was called *A biography of Dracula: the life*

---

2 For some of these weird story ideas, see ed. Elizabeth Miller and Dacre Stoker, *The lost journal of Bram Stoker* (London, 2012), pp 46–7, 66–9. **3** See Harry Ludlam, *A biography of Dracula* (London, 1962); Daniel Farson; *The man who wrote* Dracula (London, 1975); Barbara Belford, *Bram Stoker: a biography of the man who wrote* Dracula (London, 1996); and Paul Murray, *From the shadow of Dracula* (London, 2004). A fifth biographical study by Peter Haining and Peter Tremayne: *The un-dead – the legend of Bram Stoker and Dracula* (London, 1997), focuses on the writing of *Dracula* and matters arising.

story of Bram Stoker (1962) – its title elided the author and his uncharacteristic creation; the second, by the television journalist Daniel Farson, one of Stoker's great-nephews, was called *The man who wrote* Dracula*: a biography of Bram Stoker* (1975); the third was American journalist Barbara Belford's *Bram Stoker: a biography of the author of* Dracula (1996); and the most recent, and most convincing so far, is Paul Murray's *From the shadow of Dracula: a life of Bram Stoker* (2004), which carefully attempts to extricate the man from the shadows, with help from family papers. Allowing for publishers' pressure – putting the pre-sold brand on the cover – these titles raise the *expectation* of reading the man through the work, or at least providing an original answer to today's central question about Bram Stoker, though not Bram Stoker's own central question or even that of his obituarists at the time he died: how on earth this conventional, genial, ex-civil servant from Dublin came to possess such a bizarre Gothic imagination as to produce *Dracula*. It is as if a book about James Joyce were to be called *A biography of Ulysses* – or of Oscar Wilde *A biography of Ernest*. As John Fowles wrote, this would never happen to writers who had been fully accepted into literature's first team. As an aside, I used regularly to make a pilgrimage to Kenny's Bookshop on Quay Street, Galway, and spend some time admiring the first editions in the justly celebrated 'Irish literature' section. When first I visited, in the mid-1970s, neither Oscar Wilde nor Bram Stoker had yet been admitted to the pantheon of distinguished Irish writers. Their works were located elsewhere in the shop, under 'miscellaneous novels and plays'. Then in the late 1970s/early 1980s Oscar Wilde started appearing. And then in the mid-1980s, a single copy in its distinctive expressionist dust jacket, complete with silhouette wolves and bats, of the 1933 Irish-language edition of *Dracula* – translated by Seán Ó. Cuirrín – crept in.⁴ And finally, Bram Stoker's complete works were admitted to the apostolic succession, nestling next to Sheridan's. So his acceptance into *this* world of literature, into this canon, is relatively recent – paralleling the rise of 'new Gothic criticism' in universities; a fashionable concern with the politics of identity; and probably, generations of literary critics who have grown up with film versions of *Dracula*, post-Hammer Films in 1958.

And this welcome extended by the literary archive to a once-prodigal son – possibly the most prodigal of all the prodigal sons – has been accompanied by all sorts of fresh speculations about that central question: what *was* Bram Stoker so frightened of? He seems to have been a man in the shadow of history, let alone of *Dracula*; always in his mature years the regulation two steps behind his employer Henry Irving, to judge by photographs. A quadruple enigma: the man himself; his transformation from bureaucrat and man about town into writer of *Dracula* and other weirderies; the Dublin Stoker and the London Stoker; and the way in which

---

4 Bram Stoker, *Dracula* (Dublin, 1933).

his readers/viewers have subsequently treated or remade him. Even *Dracula* ends with his heroes looking at the evidence they have amassed – the letters, diaries, recordings and cuttings – and saying it all looks highly improbable: as *evidence*, strictly speaking it amounts to very little.

> We were struck with the fact, that in all the mass of material of which the record is composed, there is hardly one authentic document; nothing but a mass of type-writing... We could hardly ask anyone, even did we wish to, to accept these as proofs of so wild a story.⁵

Stoker never had the self-esteem as a professional writer to look after his posterity – to keep his important letters and papers (if there were any) and give them to an executor who would secure their place in the archive, or even to claim public ownership of his ideas. He was the polar opposite of a literary celebrity with a sense of his own greatness – such as W.B. Yeats. Within a year of his death, his widow Florence had dispersed his papers and his book collection at auction, because she needed the money.

The American critic Ludovic Flow once wrote of Bram Stoker:

> He is the master of the commonplace style in which clichés flow as if they were impelled by the same pressure as genius. I don't say this lightly. There is a semi-heroic, Everyman quality about his intense command of the mediocre – as if the commonplace had found a champion who could wear its colours with all the ceremony of greatness. When such a man, just once, is thoroughly afraid, the charade stops and what you get is *Dracula*.⁶

Whether or not we agree with this – and there's a whiff of A.N. Wilson's patrician critique of *Dracula* about it – it does pose that central question.

So what *was* he so 'thoroughly' frightened of? With the rise of the 'new Gothic criticism' since the late 1970s, suggestions have tended to follow the intellectual fashions of the day.⁷ Answers have ranged from the 'New Woman' to colonization by 'the Other' and late Imperial anxieties; from sexual identity (a tug of war between masculine and feminine) to a fear of racial degeneration and decadence – plus concerns about the decline of religion and the rise of materialism; from repressed pain about the trial of Oscar Wilde – actually, the dates don't work – to

---

5 See Bram Stoker, *Dracula* (Penguin Classics edition, 2003), p. 402. The words are Jonathan Harker's, in a valedictory note. **6** Cited in Christopher Frayling, *Vampyres – Lord Byron to Count Dracula* (London, 1991), p. 79. **7** For interesting surveys of the critical afterlife of *Dracula*, especially since the 1960s, see Robert Mighall, 'Vampires and Victorians' in *A geography of Victorian Gothic fiction* (Oxford, 1999), pp 236–49) and 'Sex, history and the vampire', *Bram Stoker: history, psychoanalysis and the Gothic*, ed. William Hughes and Andrew Smith (Basingstoke, 1998), pp 62–77; and – more sympathetically as well as extensively – William Hughes, *Bram Stoker's* Dracula: *a reader's guide to essential criticism* (Basingstoke, 2008).

a transposition of the Jack the Ripper murders in Whitechapel (the dates do work, and Stoker himself mentioned this as an inspiration); from his wife Florence's frigidity and her gynaecological problems to his own death from tertiary syphilis (for none of which is there a shred of real, sustainable evidence); from a love–hate relationship with Henry Irving to inspiration from any number of celebrities of late-Victorian times, up to and including Benjamin Disraeli, Alfred Lord Tennyson and Sir Richard Burton. If Stoker happens to mention their teeth, they immediately become prime candidates for the 'original' of *Dracula*.

As early as 1958, Maurice Richardson wrote a Freudian analysis of ghost stories – partly tongue-in-cheek, it seems – in which he referred to *Dracula* as 'a kind of incestuous, necrophilious, oral-anal-sadistic all-in wrestling match. And this is what gives the story its force.'[8] Well, it would, wouldn't it? Richardson was writing at around the time of the first Hammer Films *Dracula* – with Christopher Lee (1958; dir. Terence Fisher) – which foregrounded in seaside postcard colour the sexual relationship between vampire and victim, accompanied by orgasmic music on the soundtrack in case audiences did not get the point. Before then, no literary critic – so far as I know – had even noticed this theme in the novel.[9] Since then, critics have often assumed that Bram Stoker thought about little else: *Dracula* as big daddy; repressed sexual desires; civilization and its discontents; sex from the neck up; sex and blood. He certainly had sex on his mind – but he had other things on his mind as well. And one of the fascinating features of this is that if he did have sex on his mind it was sex without any mention of it. Some of these post-Freudian perspectives are – in R.F. Foster's phrase – 'vulnerable if pressed'. Paul Murray, in his biography, is rightly impatient with them.

As the proprietors of Kenny's bookshop astutely noticed, since the mid-to-late 1980s – and increasing academic interest in diaspora, roots, identity and Irish cultural studies – it has become fashionable to reclaim *Dracula* as in some sense an Irish novel, just as the work of other prodigal sons and daughters such as Francis Bacon, Eileen Gray and indeed Oscar Wilde has been brought back into the fold: to be more precise, to make sense of *Dracula* in Irish terms.[10] So Bram Stoker's fears – embodied in his best-known book – have been interpreted as about the decline and fall of feudalism in Ireland; about a besieged Protestant elite post-1870s dramatizing its fears; about an absentee Anglo-Irish landlord who has run out of useable land – and who carries his soil with him; lower down the social

---

8 See Maurice Richardson, 'The psychoanalysis of ghost stories', Frayling, *Vampyres*, pp 418–22. **9** For an elaboration of this argument, see Christopher Frayling, 'Hammer's Dracula' in *It came from the 1950s!*, ed. Darryl Jones, Elizabeth McCarthy and Bernice Murphy (Basingstoke, 2011), pp 108–34. **10** See, for example, Joseph Valente, *Dracula's crypt: Bram Stoker, Irishness and the question of blood* (Champagne, IL, 2002); Bruce Stewart, 'Bram Stoker's *Dracula* – possessed by the spirit of the nation?', *That Other World*, ed. Bruce Stewart (Gerrards Cross, 1998), vol. 2, pp 65–83; Hughes, *Bram Stoker's* Dracula, pp 103–22; and R.F. Foster, *Paddy and Mr Punch* (London, 1995), pp 220–7.

scale, about a gombeen man, preying on the peasantry; about a coffin-ship (literally); about Charles Stewart Parnell as the Count; about Stoker's distant forebear Manus 'the Magnificent' O'Donnell, a warrior clan leader who rebelled against King Henry VIII; about memories of Bram Stoker's Sligo-born mother telling him folk-tales as a sickly child – or memories of tales he heard on his travels around Ireland as Inspector of Petty Sessions in his late twenties – or memories of Lady Wilde's salon. And – more plausibly perhaps – about a form of Protestant Irish Gothic – in dialogue with Maturin and Le Fanu – simultaneously repulsed by and envious of Catholic magic, complete with crumbling big houses and castles, eccentric aristocrats who stay up all night; ancestry, guilt and the occult.

Predictably, some of the more reductive of these 'explanations' have recently themselves been revised: *was* Bram Stoker Anglo-Irish in any significant sense – he certainly was not a landed ascendancy grandee; he was a middle-class Protestant Dublin civil servant. How can Dracula have been an absentee landlord, a gombeen man *and* arrive in England in a coffin-ship, all at the same time? Has the theme of insecurity and guilt been overplayed? And if so, why? Would studies of Bernard Shaw, or Wilde, or Joyce so emphatically feel they had to assert their subjects' Irishness: I think not, because their work is more confidently within the literary canon, because the Irishness of their work almost goes without saying. There is evidently more going on in Bram Stoker studies than questions of national identity… And what about Irish *Catholic* contributions to the Gothic? And isn't it somewhat irritating to read, over and over again, how smart *we* are and how benighted the late-Victorians were? Have some of these insights been *too* reductive – dealing as they do with a culture that was 'a very complex intellectual and cultural phenomenon'. Was *Dracula* about magic at all – or rather about typewriters, phonographs, high-speed trains, advanced weaponry, cameras and blood transfusions – a kind of late-Victorian techno-fiction, where the tech does not always function: Stoker's fiction is full of fascination with modern technology. And are many such perspectives – if not most of them – 'vulnerable if pressed' or a bit over-ingenious. Or, to put it more strongly, as John Fowles did about Arthur Conan Doyle, are they in the end metaphorical rather than actual, and thus improvable in the normal way. The thing is: there is no real *evidence* for any of them. All we really know for sure is that in the only novel Bram Stoker *set* in Ireland – the West Coast, by the sea – *The snake's pass*, published as a book in November 1890, he showed very little serious interest in the Irish countryside, its folk-tales or its politics – and that although he seems at one stage in his life, over in England, to have favoured Home Rule within the British Empire (he once called himself a 'philosophical Home Ruler' and enjoyed the odd exchange with William Gladstone about Irish politics), this was not by any means at the heart of his interest. At least not at a conscious level. It may have been, or it may not.

We do not really know. What we do know is that *Dracula* as myth seems to contain legions.

So I was thinking – taking my cue from John Fowles, believing as I do that Bram Stoker is too important an author to be patronized, and as an alternative to much of this unfounded speculation, fun though it may be, I was thinking 'is there any aspect of his life for which there *is* a lot of significant evidence, where one *can* take Bram Stoker's word for things at face value, where we can begin to piece together the outer and (maybe) the inner person?'

And then I read an article by psychobiographer Joseph S. Bierman writing in 1998, about the section of *Dracula* which is set in Whitby. It argues that the Whitby section of the novel is a walking through of childhood insecurities, where the empty graves of the Whitby churchyard and the port's enclosed harbour reflect an enclosed space or *claustrum*, the interior of the mother's body, an orally regressive safe haven from anxieties, especially sexual anxieties. Whitby, therefore, represents a regression to a childhood fantasy of the prenatal state as a place of safety. 'The intrusion into the *claustrum* that causes the anxiety is the fantasized father's penis ...'

> The town of Whitby thus presented four potential claustral spaces to a receptive Stoker. There were the empty tombs with 'lies' on their stones. There was the twin-piered mouth to the port that could offer safety, at least at first, to ships like the Russian *Dmitry*. There was the Whitby Abbey of Sir Walter Scott's story about a fatal enclosure after a sexual transgression, and there was the Nuremberg-like architecture evocative of the Iron Virgin and her inside.[11]

Quite apart from the astonishing suggestion that Whitby harbour is in any way intended to be a place of *safety* in the novel – the Whitby episode, and the thinking behind it, happen to be the best-documented three-to-four weeks in the whole of Bram Stoker's life. Among his working papers, there is more on Whitby, much more, than on anything else. We have his extensive notes on what he saw and heard in Whitby, his extracts in handwriting and typescript from what he was reading, the evidence of a local newspaper, a contemporary diarist and local records and a great deal of visual material as well.[12] And then we have the corre-

---

[11] See Joseph S. Bierman, 'A crucial stage in the writing of *Dracula*' in *Bram Stoker: history, psychoanalysis and the Gothic*, ed. William Hughes and Andrew Smith (Basingstoke, 1998), pp 151–72. The quotation is from p. 171. See also Hughes, *Bram Stoker's* Dracula, pp 28–34. [12] For Bram Stoker's 'foundation notes and data' on Whitby, see *Bram Stoker's notes for* Dracula, annotated and transcribed by Robert Eighteen-Bisang and Elizabeth Miller (Jefferson, NC, 2008), pp 138–71 – hereafter referred to as Eighteen-Bisang and Miller. I first studied these manuscripts and typescript notes, held in the Rosenbach Museum and Library, Philadelphia, in the early 1980s – while preparing my *Vampyres*. The 2008 transcriptions by Eighteen-Bisang and Miller are by far the most accurate available, and helpfully include all the originals

sponding section of the novel, in the three chapters 6, 7 and 8 – three chapters out of twenty-seven – mainly consisting of Mina Murray's journal for 24 July to 18 August, plus a cutting from *The Dailygraph*, the captain's log of the cargo ship *Demeter* and a couple of short letters. So I decided to take a really close and detailed look at Mr Stoker's holiday – sticking as closely as possible to the primary evidence, as a form of radical empiricism, post-post-modernism, to see where a strictly forensic approach might take us.

Bram Stoker and family went on holiday to Whitby, the Yorkshire seaport and fishing town, for most of August 1890. There is no evidence that he had ever visited the town before, and none that he ever visited again. The photographs of Frank Meadow Sutcliffe give a neo-romantic impression of what Whitby looked like at the time: Sutcliffe had opened a second shop, on the West Cliff near the Crescent, 'for the sale of studies of fisherfolk and views', in July 1890, the month before the Stokers arrived. Postcards dating from the early 1890s have also survived, giving a tourist glimpse of the town – paralleling Mina's in the novel. The weekly *Whitby Gazette* noted that Mr, Mrs and Master Stoker from London were there on the 8, 15 and 22 August – and that Mr was there by himself on the 1st August. Actually, as we'll see, Bram arrived at least three days before this, at the end of July. He was 42 years old, Florence Stoker 31 and Noel was 10½ – though most of the biographers say he was 'about seven' for some reason, and learned to swim at that age in Whitby. They stayed at No. 6 Royal Crescent (not No. 7 and not East Crescent as two of the biographies confidently assert), a large house set back from the town's West Cliff which accommodated several other visitors in the summer season – mainly from the Midlands and the North of England. At its most full, the house accommodated twelve people including the Stokers – plus the landlady Mrs Emma Veazey (a widow aged 46) and her 21-year-old daughter Emma, *not* a landlord named 'William Harker'. The other paying guests tended to have companions or nurses with them, and the husbands were mainly from the professions.

Let us examine first of all what Stoker's biographers (the full-length ones) have made of this holiday.[13]

Harry Ludlam devotes one-and-a-half paragraphs to it – this being before Stoker's working notes were rediscovered in Philadelphia. Of the novel, he asks 'why Whitby? Because it was a wonderful place to set a story, and because Bram

in facsimile. My thanks to local historian David Pybus and his team, for sharing the results of their detailed research with me. Elizabeth Miller, in her Dracula – *sense and nonsense* (Westcliff-on-Sea, Essex, 2000) examines some of the errors made by commentators and critics writing about the Whitby section, on pp 52–3, 68, 90–105 and 170–2. Clive Leatherdale's annotated edition of *Dracula unearthed* (Westcliff-on-Sea, Essex, 1998) contains useful and usually reliable notes to the Whitby section, on pp 115–13, 128–66. **13** See Ludlam, *A biography*, p. 104; Farson, *The man*, pp 148–51; Belford, *Bram Stoker*, pp 220–7; and Murray, *From the shadow*, pp 166, 175–7. Haining and Tremayne, *The un-dead*, describe Stoker's stay in Whitby on pp 135–44.

knew it well – he had been there with Irving.' Then a long quote from *Dracula*, in which Mina describes 'the houses of the old town' and the Abbey. And that is all. In fact, Bram had *not* been there with Irving before 1890 and he did *not* know it well. Daniel Farson devotes a chapter of three-and-a-half pages to Whitby – entitled 'Count Dracula Makes His Entrance' – in which he speculates that a photograph by Frank Meadow Sutcliffe of a great ship beached at Tate Hill Sands in 1885 may well have given Stoker the idea for the shipwreck of the *Demeter*; says that he cannot locate the exact graveyard inscriptions mentioned in the novel; writes about *Moby-Dick* (1851); mentions that Bram may have stayed at 7, East Crescent and describes Henry Irving staying at the Hotel Metropole after the publication of *Dracula*. In fact, there is no evidence that Bram Stoker ever saw that particular photograph, he stayed at Royal Crescent – the files of the *Whitby Gazette* were available – and the Irving reference is not relevant. The inscriptions *are* indeed in the graveyard, but they are extremely difficult to decipher – thanks to erosion, salt in the wind and the passage of time. I had to make rubbings of 'Tulley' and 'Swales'. Barbara Bedford, who did know about Stoker's manuscript and typescript notes and made full use of them, starts her five pages on Whitby by stating as fact that 'Stoker's three weeks there in 1890 with Florence and Noel made the creative genesis of *Dracula*, the first time he made notes on a supernatural tale about an undead man.' Actually, his first notes on what would become *Dracula* – with the name 'Count Wampyr' added to them – dated from five months earlier, on 8 March 1890 as we'll see. She then describes Bram going for walks and bellowing at the sea; Noel and Florence going to the theatre and circus performances at the Spa while Bram was busy doing his research; Bram pulling some books from the shelf of Whitby Library as well as reading the *Whitby Gazette*, meeting a coastguard 'at the lighthouse', seeing the Sutcliffe photographs, watching the bats flying from St Mary's churchyard tower and spectating at the Grand Fête – a procession of boats – on the River Esk, which apparently gave him the idea for the Captain's funeral in the novel. For none of these is there a shred of actual evidence. Yes, we know that Bram Stoker did bellow at the sea, but that was said of him a few years later at Cruden Bay on the Aberdeen coast of Scotland. We also know that readers had to order books from the library rather than pulling them from the open shelves. They had to know author and title, which is interesting in Stoker's case. We know that he met a coastguard, but the lighthouse is poetic licence (it was at the Coastguard Station on West Cliff). As are the bats. There is no evidence that he read the *Whitby Gazette*, though he may have done. The second-ever 'Grand Water Fête' did indeed take place on the Esk on 15 August 1890 – the wind blew so strongly the wrong way that all the decorated boats had to be towed by a steam-yacht – but we do not know if the Stokers were watching it. Paul Murray devotes a page and a half to Whitby, in which he correctly observes that the holiday of 1890 was 'of crucial importance to the early development of *Dracula*'. He adds that 'Various addresses have been mooted as the place where Stoker and his family spent that fateful vacation in the summer of 1890, but there is no doubt that they lodged close to the scenery in *Dracula* which Stoker described with extraordinary fidelity.' This is curious, because we know exactly where they stayed. Murray goes on usefully to compare Stoker's notes with the novel as published, and is particularly persuasive on the ways he used the tombstone inscriptions from the clifftop churchyard. He refers to the notes as diary entries, which strictly speaking they were not, and writes of the books Stoker consulted in 'Whitby public library'. It was not, in fact, a public library – it was a private subscription library, and Stoker visited *two* separate libraries while he was in Whitby. He also has – again – Noel aged 'about seven' learning to swim at Whitby, apparently a piece of family folklore. But those things said, Murray's account is by far the most carefully researched so far.

So, what do we know *for sure* about Bram Stoker and family in Whitby? Well, as a starting-point we know that in Stoker's earliest notes for the novel – dated 8 March 1890 – the arrival of the Count on English soil was referred to as 'Dover Custom House' and that the Count would have two servants waiting for him in England – a deaf mute woman and a silent man; six days later, on 14 March, the chapter introducing the Count's arrival in England was to be called 'the auctioneer'.[14] And, some considerable time later, Stoker added in the margin 'Whitby – argument uncanny things', 'Whitby – the storm – ship arrives' and 'Whitby. Lucy walks in sleep – bloody', and developed these incidents, presumably after his summer holiday of 1890.[15] He also referred to a derelict ship running into the harbour, with no-one on board, bodies washed up on the shore and a hold full of clay.[16] These last two details he did not pick up at Whitby (there were no bodies, 'the crew landed safely' and the ship in question was 'light ballasted with silver sand') and they raise the possibility, no more than that, that he had the general idea of a phantom ship, courtesy perhaps of the *Flying Dutchman* (1843), *before* he went there.

At an early stage, too, Lucy Westenra was to find a strange brooch on the shore and pin it on – 'wound in throat and brooch covered in blood. I must have pricked myself in my sleep…' At first, 'Prick of brooch theory accepted' – including by a doctor who examines her – but when Lucy begins to have pains in her teeth, her friends begin to have doubts about this diagnosis. The 'brooch' idea lasted for the next two years, at least until February 1892; then it was dumped.[17]

On the manuscript of *Dracula*, though not in the published text, Mina Murray arrives in Whitby by train at 4.35 p.m. 'ten minutes late'.[18] Stoker would also have travelled the six-hour journey from London – the 10.25 a.m. from King's

---

[14] See Eighteen-Bisang and Miller, pp 19, 29. [15] Ibid., p. 29. [16] Ibid., p. 49. [17] Ibid., pp 50–3. [18] See Leslie S. Klinger, ed., *The new annotated* Dracula (New York, 2008), p. 118. On the manuscript of *Dracula*, see Bruce Francis (ed.), *The Book Sail – 16th anniversary catalogue* (Orange County, CA, 1984), n.p.

Cross to York via Leeds; then change at York to travel via Malton and Pickering to Whitby. According to the summer timetable, he would have arrived on the 10.25 at 4.20 – so Mina was almost correct about the delay. Then he would have taken a horse-drawn carriage from Dock End Station to No. 6 Royal Crescent and checked in. We do not know the exact date of this, but on 30 July Stoker was talking with three old fishermen on the cliffside of the churchyard – the other side of the bay from his guesthouse on West Cliff – about a whaling ship that was lost thanks to the stubbornness of its captain. Also about 'legend of bells at sea' when a ship goes down, and 'white lady in Abbey window', the ghost of St Hilda its founder.[19] 'Them things be all wore out', says one of the fishermen – the origin of Mr Swales' scornful attitude in the novel to local legends about the resurrection of the physical body. 'Them things be all wore out.' On the 8 August, by which time Florence and Noel had joined Bram and settled in, the family went to Broad Ings Farm, just out of town between Whitby and Robin Hood's Bay, to have tea and cakes with the writer and novelist Violet Hunt, daughter of the woman who was the first to translate Grimm's *Fairy Tales* into English.[20] According to her diary, Violet found Stoker 'a dear, and Mrs is so pretty and kind. Noel came and played in the low haystack at Broad Ings.' Stoker was 'a nice healthy stalwart Irishman, as sweethearted and gentlemanly as it is possible to be' and he remained in her London circle or salon of literary friends, after summer 1890. In the novel, Mina and Lucy have a 'capital severe tea' at Robin Hood's Bay, overlooking 'the seaweed-covered rocks of the strand'; Mina writes 'I believe we should have shocked the New Woman with our appetites. Men are more tolerant, bless them.' They then walk home to Whitby. As an aside, it has been pointed out that when Dracula sinks his teeth into Lucy, as a result of such a tea he would probably have swallowed a mouthful of cholesterol. On to three days later, the evening of 11 August, and Bram is by himself – this time talking with the coastguard William Leach Petherick, born in Devon, who was stationed in Whitby from 1886–93.[21] Petherick tells him of various wrecks including 'A Russian schooner 120 tons from the Black Sea [which] ran in with all sails ... slewed round against pier ... light ballasted with silver sand'. This seems to have been the first Stoker had heard of this particular story. He was evidently very struck by it, because he wrote further notes on the details and then asked someone – at the Coastguard Station on West Cliff – probably Petherick himself – to transcribe the logbook entry for the night of 24 October 1885, including all the details of times, wind directions, rigging and so on. 'Crew landed safe by their own resources.'[22] It turned out from the log that there had in fact been *two* ships in distress that night: the *Mary and Agnes* (British) and

---

19 Eighteen-Bisang and Miller, pp 151–3. **20** See Belford, *Bram Stoker*, p. 226, based on Violet Hunt's diary entry for 8 August 1890. **21** Eighteen-Bisang and Miller, p. 155. **22** Ibid., pp 138–41, and pp 133–7. For Frank Meadow Sutcliffe's photograph of 'The Dmitry of Narva', see the Sutcliffe Gallery, Whitby, catalogue No. 76, reference 3–88.

the *Dmitry* (Russian, out of Narva). The extract from the log was written on an official form headed 'On Her Majesty's Service' – which the coastguard was not supposed to do: it was misuse of government property! Stoker took his own detailed notes, introducing the extract from the log, on the back of a page – one of many – detailing wind direction and speed, eleven meticulous notes all taken from a *Fishery barometer manual* of 1887. One reason he was so attracted to the reminiscence may well have been that among his earliest thoughts for *Dracula* was a visit by Jonathan Harker to Wagner's *The flying Dutchman* at the Munich Opera. And as we have seen, he *may* have had the idea of a phantom ship pre-Whitby. On the same day he spoke to Petherick, 11 August, he wrote this:

> Grey day – sun high over Kettleness – all grey – green grass – grey earthy rock – sand points jutting out all grey – grey clouds, tinged with sunburst grey sea tumbling in over flats with roar muffled in sea mist drifting inland – horizon lost in grey mist – all vastness – clouds piled up and 'brool' [low roar] over the sea – like a presage – dark figures on beach here and there – men like trees walking – fishing boat, going and coming through mist.[23]

When he scribbled this down, he must have been sitting or standing near the so-called 'suicide's seat' on the cliff edge of St Mary's churchyard – Mina's and Lucy's favourite seat in the novel. Evidently the weather was not exactly suitable for buckets and spades on the beach, but it was good enough for a walk. It is also interesting that one of the very first entries in Stoker's *Lost journal*, written at Greystones on the coast on 3 August 1871, nineteen years before, was very similar:

> A grey sky, broken by dark patches of cloud that make even the grey look bright. A low line of light along the horizon in the East. A dark grey sea luminous towards the horizon just before moonrise... The fishermen dragging their nets in silence.[24]

All those 'greys' – with no synonym coming into Stoker's mind. His vocabulary, it has to be said, was never particularly varied, on the spot or in retrospect.

Two days later, on 13 August, at 6.30 p.m., he drew a couple of quick ink sketches of the shoreline and cliff from Sandsend – 'green and grey' – from above Upgang – 'blue black clouds'[25] – and on the 18 August he wrote on the back of the 'Grey day – sun high over Kettleness' note:

> Whitby Cliff 9 p.m.
> Lights scattered town and West Cliff and up river Esk – black line of roof on left – near Abbey House – sheep and lambs bleating – clatter of

[23] Eighteen-Bisang and Miller, pp 156–7. [24] Millerand Stoker, *The lost journal*, p. 17. [25] Eighteen-Bisang and Miller, pp 160–3.

donkey's hoofs up paved road; Band on pier harsh [or loud] waltz. Salvation Army in street off Quay neither hearing each other we hearing both.[26]

This 'we' is the only reference to the rest of his family in all Bram Stoker's notes at Whitby: they were together that evening at 9 p.m. The family would be staying until the following week. According to the *Gazette*, the band on the pier's repertoire included *Come back to Erin* (1866) and Tennyson's *Come into the garden, Maud / For the black-bat night has flown* (1855): they also played on Scotch Head, as well as the pier. There is an almost-contemporary painting by regional artist Lionel Townsend – now in York Museum and Art Gallery – called *Dancing on the Pier at Whitby*, first exhibited in 1905, which gives a colourful impression of the atmosphere that evening from eye level. Then, on the 19 August Bram Stoker signed the register at the Whitby Museum, Subscription Library and Warm Bathing Establishment on the Quay (now Pier Road), opposite the Fishmarket, and paid his 'special subscription rate for visitors'. The top floor housed the Museum – the top right-hand window housed the Library of the Literary and Philosophical Society, the middle floor housed the Subscription Library and the bottom floor housed the Baths, offering its customers both salt and fresh water.[27] This *wasn't* a public library, as most of the biographies state. Stoker used *both* libraries in the course of the day. In the Museum, he read F.K. Robinson's *A glossary of words used in the neighbourhood of Whitby* (published fourteen years before), carefully wrote down 164 of those words and their Standard English equivalents, over four pages, and was later to use an astonishing 64 of them in *Dracula* – mainly put into the mouth of the old salt Mr Swales – crossing them out on his notes as he went along.[28] He was later, in London, to make a similar list of words and meanings from the book *Magyarland*, but only used two of them – meaning 'Satan' and 'Hell' – repeatedly overheard by Jonathan Harker in Bistritz.[29] In the Subscription Library, he read diplomat William Wilkinson's book *An account of the principalities of Wallachia and Moldavia* (1820), took copious notes on it and subsequently typed them up or had them typed up.[30] He even noted the shelf mark 'Whitby Library 0.1097'. By far the most important transcription was of the footnote on page 19, the first of the notes he took on the book:

DRACULA in Wallachian language means DEVIL. Wallachians were accustomed to give it as a surname to any person who rendered himself conspicuous by courage, cruel actions or cunning.

26 Ibid., pp 158–9. **27** Frank Meadow Sutcliffe photographed the exterior of the Museum and Subscription Library at around this time – see Sutcliffe Gallery, Whitby, reference 20–8. **28** Eighteen-Bisang and Miller, pp 142–9. **29** Ibid., pp 201–5. **30** Ibid., pp 245–51.

This, and the related passages of text on pages 18 and 19 was the only reference to the historical Dracula in all of Stoker's notes, and it gave Stoker the name – though he did not decide to call the book *Dracula* until the last minute, just before publication in 1897, seven years later. Before summer 1890 – not on the earliest notes but evidently before Whitby – the villain was called, more prosaically, 'Count Wampyr'. Bram Stoker may also have consulted, if he had time that day, *Curious myths of the Middle Ages* by Sabine Baring Gould (1888 edition) and *On the track of the crescent* by Major E.C. Johnson (1885), both of which were in the catalogue of the Subscription Library and both of which he mentioned or transcribed in his notes.[31] The Johnson book contains several comparisons between the local inhabitants of Transylvania and 'Paddy' in rural Ireland – but Stoker did not take any notes on them and we do not even know if he read those passages. The books in the Whitby libraries were not on the open shelves. Readers had to order them from the librarian – so Stoker must have known from the catalogue entry that a book on Wallachia and Moldavia would be of interest to him, which strongly suggests that he had decided to shift the location of the story from Styria in South Eastern Austria (where Le Fanu had located *Carmilla* (1871–2), Stoker's original choice) to further East – *before* he arrived in Whitby. Or – less likely – *because* he read the title of that particular book in the catalogue. It *may* be significant here that Arminius Vámbéry – Hungarian professor of oriental languages – visited the Lyceum Theatre on 30 April 1890 – that is, between the writing of Stoker's notes about Austrian Styria on 14 March and Stoker's visit to Whitby. Maybe. Whatever the inspiration, the change of locale happened earlier than scholars have suggested up to now.

Two days later, on 21 August, Stoker made another ink drawing, from above, on the East Cliff again – the most important one as it was to prove – of Tate Hill Pier, and of a ship about to run aground next to it. On the back of this, he wrote:

> When ship ran in to Collier's Hope, big dog jumped off and ran over pier – up Kiln Yard and church steps and into churchyard. Local dog found ripped open and graves torn up. Ship had all sails set and ran over waves. Ground in corner of pier – sand heap.[32]

This memo on the back of the drawing *looks* as though it is dated 15 October 1890 – that is, well after the Stokers had returned to London; but on closer inspection of the manuscript it could well be 15 *August* – which may be why it is on the same sheet as the subsequent drawing of the pier. If so, it was written on the same day as the 'Grand Water Fête', of which there is no mention. Also among the notes are two photographs of the ruins of thirteenth-century Whitby Abbey, and

---

31 Ibid., p. 173 *(Myths)*, pp 221–33 *(Crescent)*. **32** Ibid., pp 164–5 and 168–9.

ten typescript pages of meticulously transcribed inscriptions from the tombstones in 'Whitby Churchyard on Cliff – (Note M.M. means Master Mariner)': 87 names with epitaphs, plus 4 in more detail, 91 in total.[33] 91 out of the 1530 legible inscriptions. We do not know exactly when Stoker originally made these notes, but he must have wondered around the graveyard with a notebook in his hand – maybe on one of the days when he spoke to the fishermen or coastguard, or when he made his sketches. In the churchyard, he found the name Swales – as in 'Ann Swales 6th February 1795, aged 100'. The headstone was located across the path from the south transept of St Mary's Church:

SWALES
In memory of Thomas Swales who died July 5th 1786 aged 91 years
also Ann his wife who died 6th February 1795 aged 100 years.
Our heavy loads and weary days are past.
We hope our Souls in Heaven will dwell at last.

Bram Stoker simply wrote down a cryptic note about Ann Swales. He used five other names from the graveyard in the novel, though in all but one case he subtly altered the spellings of the real names for his fiction. He seems to have been particularly intrigued by the number of gravestones marked 'drowned at sea' or 'lost at sea' or 'perished with all the crew' – because it meant that the graves were empty: of the 91 names he noted down, 86 were of empty graves. Maybe they were considered as suitable sanctuaries for Count Dracula at one point: in the end, Stoker opted for the unhallowed rather than unoccupied grave of a suicide. His original handwritten notes have not survived, but his typescript transcriptions have. They seem to have been typed, and annotated, by someone else – perhaps a secretary at the Lyceum Theatre. St Mary's churchyard had been closed to new burials in 1837 – 53 years earlier – when the new Whitby cemetery had been opened on the South East outskirts of town, though one or two new family headstones were installed by special dispensation up until the 1850s. In the novel, the Captain's burial takes place in St Mary's when in fact it should have happened at the more prosaic new cemetery, and it certainly would not have involved a cortège of boats, on the river, watched by large crowds. There were no recorded funerals of sea captains or master mariners while the Stokers were staying in Whitby – a timely reminder that Bram Stoker was writing a *novel* not a travel guide or a piece of journalism. He was using his imagination rather than a camera. He may possibly have been inspired, for the funeral arrangements, by the 'Grand Water Fête' on the 15 August. Or he may not. The notes do not say.

[33] Ibid., pp 194–7 (photographs) and pp 252–71 (tombstones). Thanks to Margaret Grundy, of St Mary's Parish Church Whitby, for help with transcriptions and locations – and for the Parish Church *Gravestone catalogue*, 1994.

Then, some time after 22 August, the family took the long train journey back to King's Cross via York and home to 17 St Leonard's Terrace, Chelsea. And the story of *Dracula* switched to London too. One literary excitement that autumn was that *The snake's pass* – his first novel – was published on 18 November 1890 by 'Bram Stoker MA' as he then liked to style himself, which some of his Trinity friends found a tad pompous. It had already been serialized in *The People* in 1889.

At some stage before February 1892 – we cannot be more precise – Bram Stoker made some embellishments to his Whitby notes, revisited his earlier book outline, juggled with the dates of Mina's visit on an all-purpose calendar – would her first journal entry be on 17 or 24 July?[34] – and generally proceeded to turn his scribbles and typescripts into the cosmic events surrounding the arrival of Count Dracula in England, as part of the longest, most ambitious piece of writing he had ever undertaken, including his tome on the *Duties of clerks of petty sessions* (1879). He wrote in hotels on tour with the Henry Irving Company – to judge by the different headed notepapers – on summer holidays along the Buchan coast of Scotland – he never revisited Whitby for a holiday as far as we know – probably in the round Reading Room of the British Museum, for which he had a (mislaid) reader's ticket – and at home in Chelsea. Irving allowed him no time for such pursuits in the normal run of things: staff development does not seem to have been his strongest suit. The 'documentary' or 'epistolary' style of the novel – perhaps inspired by Wilkie Collins' best-selling *The woman in white* (1859–60) – matched the fragmented way in which the book was assembled over several years: a collection of diary and journal entries, letters, press cuttings, transcribed phonograph recordings – the documents in the case, from all points of view except one, that of the Count himself. Stoker was cutting and pasting his final draft right up to the proof stage in 1897, seven years after Whitby.

His lists of gravestone inscriptions and reading of the *Glossary* became in the novel the conversations between Lucy, Mina and Mr Swales; the schooner *Dmitry* became the *Demeter* – which carries the Count into Whitby harbour – and Mina's description on 6th August of the gloomy atmosphere which heralds the appearance of the vampire almost exactly matches her creator's. This time, the prose is more 'ornate', though not perhaps ornate enough for some tastes:

> To-day is a grey day, and the sun as I write is hidden in thick clouds, high over Kettleness. Everything is grey – except the green grass, which seems like emerald amongst it; grey earthy rock; grey clouds, tinged with the sunburst at the far edge, hang over the grey sea, into which the sand-points

---

[34] For the all-purpose printed calendar, with Stoker's many manuscript entries, see for the Whitby dates Eighteen-Bisang and Miller, pp 100–5. In the novel, Mina writes to Lucy on 9 May saying that she is longing to be with her 'by the sea', without specifying the location. Stoker was not at first sure exactly which date in July Mina should arrive – and in the end opted for a date close to his own experience.

stretch like grey fingers... The horizon is lost in a grey mist. All is vastness; the clouds are piled up like giant rocks, and there is a 'brool' over the sea that sounds like some presage of doom. Dark figures are on the beach here and there, sometimes half-shrouded in the mist, and seem 'men like trees walking'. The fishing boats are racing for home, and rise and dip in the ground swell as they sweep into the harbour, bending to the scuppers. Here comes old Mr Swales ... he wants to talk.[35]

Incidentally, Stoker's reference to 'men like trees walking', written on 11 August 1890 and published some seven years later, is not – as might be expected – a reference to Birnam Wood moving to Dunsinane in the last Act of *Macbeth*, but a quotation from the Gospel of St Mark, Chapter 8, when the healed blind man looks up and says, 'I see men as trees, walking'. A rather different kind of miracle. Stoker knew his St Mark, even when he was on holiday, and it came into his mind when he saw figures on the beach. When Mr Swales does talk, he makes extensive and improbable use of the Glossary which Stoker had so carefully annotated. For example, when Mina asks him about the legends of bells at sea, and of the White Lady in a Shroud who is said to appear in one of the windows of the Abbey, which she has just heard about, he replies:

'I wouldn't fash masel' about them, miss. Them things be all wore out [the exact words used by one of Stoker's fishermen] ... They be all very well for comers and trippers, an' the like, but not for a nice young lady like you ... I must gang ageeanwards home now, miss ... it takes me time to crammle aboon the grees [climb those steps], for there be many of 'em; an', miss, I lack belly-timber sairly by the clock [I'm very hungry].'[36]

This *can*, perhaps, be read aloud in the style of *Finnegans wake*, but that would surely be giving the passage the benefit of the doubt!

And one of Bram Stoker's preferred research bases – the 'suicide's seat' on the cliff edge of the churchyard – was turned into the location for the very first sighting of the Count on British soil. For, as Mina Murray writes:

... there, on our favourite seat, the silver light of the moon struck a half-reclining figure, snowy white [Lucy Westenra]. The coming of the cloud was too quick for me to see much, for shadow shut down on light almost immediately; but it seemed to me as though something dark stood behind the seat where the white figure shone, and bent over it. What it was, whether man or beast, I could not tell ... There was undoubtedly

[35] Bram Stoker, *Dracula*, ed. Maurice Hindle, intro. Christopher Frayling (London, 2003), p. 82. [36] Ibid., pp 72–3.

something, long and black, bending over the half-reclining white figure. I called in fright, 'Lucy! Lucy!' and something raised a head, and from where I was I could see a white face and red, gleaming eyes.[37]

From the same vantage-point, Mina also notes that:

> The band on the pier is playing a harsh waltz and further along the quay there is a Salvation Army meeting in a back street. Neither of the bands hears the other, but up here I hear and see them both.[38]

'I' rather than 'we' this time... otherwise almost identical.

He also wrote Lucy's sleepwalking scene, based on his knowledge – or memory – of the geography of old Whitby. The only way to cross the river Esk from the West Cliff to the East Cliff was across the swing bridge – which was still known as the 'drawbridge' even though it had ceased to be a drawbridge in 1833. When the Stokers visited, a new purpose-built tourist view and seat had recently been installed on the West Cliff near their accommodation – as had the 199 steep steps up the East Cliff to the Abbey. Bram Stoker recalled all this, or referred to some now-lost notes which he had with him in London. He even remembered the chime of the clock from the domed top of the town hall: the church clock was installed after his visit.

What, in the end, do these documents – this unique assembly of primary materials about three to four weeks in Bram Stoker's life – tell us about the man and his work?

- that he returned home to London with a name for his vampire, a title for his book (though he did not know that yet), a new itinerary for the Count's arrival in England – no longer via Dover; a change of Eastern European location from Styria to Transylvania; much background on Lucy Westenra being vampirized by the Count – plus a wealth of dialect and local colour.
- that he was a very meticulous man: all those minute details of inscriptions and glossaries, wind velocities and times of day – with a tendency to be literal rather than literary about them in his first impressions.
- that he was well practised in keeping records – from his experiences in the Petty Sessions office at Dublin Castle, and from his duties as manager of the Lyceum Theatre and of Irving's tours. He claimed to be a graduate in Pure Mathematics, with a keen eye and a passion for recording what he saw; he clearly liked facts and numbers.

37 Ibid., p. 101. 38 Ibid., p. 77.

- that he spent a great deal of time away from his wife and son – when he was on holiday – just as he did during the working year in his demanding job, with its unusually long hours, at the Lyceum: Mr Stoker was researching, while Florence and Noel presumably played together. Or maybe not. A cartoon for *Punch* drawn by the illustrator and novelist George du Maurier (11 September 1886) entitled 'A Filial Reproof' depicts Mr and Mrs Stoker sitting in wicker-chairs at a weekend garden party. An eager Noel is standing behind his mother, who is paying no attention to him. The caption says: 'Mamma to Noel, who is inclined to be talkative, "Hush, Noel! Haven't I told you often that little Boys should be *Seen* and not *Heard*?"' To which Noel replies, 'Yes, Mamma! But you don't look at me!' Bram leans forward, as preoccupied with his thoughts as his wife appears to be. There is a tennis racquet on the ground at his feet.[39] Du Maurier was in fact also in Whitby in summer 1890, though there is no evidence so far that his visit coincided exactly with the Stokers'. He once referred to Florence as 'one of the three most beautiful women in London'. Only one of Stoker's notes written in Whitby refers to 'we': he spent time on six days – possibly plus his long visit to the graveyard – away from the rest of the family.
- that he wrote his notes and memos on the run: he needed to write for money whenever he could, to sustain his Chelsea lifestyle and augment what must have been a modest salary at the Lyceum.
- that he enjoyed the company of the local fishermen – as he had in his Dublin *Lost journal* and was indeed to do, in Scotland, in his 1902 novel *The mystery of the sea* – but, by today's standards, he adopted a slightly patronizing late-Victorian attitude to folklore and legend, as he had also revealed in *The snake's pass*.
- that he enjoyed writing dialogue phonetically – to modern readers, perhaps the most embarrassing aspect of this section of the novel, as of *The snake's pass*, *The watter's mou* (1895) and several other novels by Stoker. In a passage on the manuscript of *Dracula* – cut before publication – he wrote this, in the voice of a reporter from the *Dailygraph*:

  The method of her [the schooner's] arrival is thus graphically given in the words of a bystander – merely reduced into conversational phrase for the benefit of those to whom the Yorkshire dialect is not familiar. 'She ran in as soft as a seal flappin' under an ice-floe'.[40]

- that he climbed the 199 recently installed steps to the churchyard on the East Cliff several times – and was drawn to the view of the harbour and the

39 See Belford, *Bram Stoker*, p. 227 and Haining and Tremayne, *The un-dead*, p. 136.   **40** See Klinger, *The new annotated* Dracula, p. 142.

bay ahead of him, with the ruins of Whitby Abbey behind him, sitting on the suicide's seat by the cliff edge.
- that he loved the sea and ships and the crews who worked on them – as he noted in his Dublin *Lost journal*, *The snake's pass* and in the revealing confessional letter he wrote to Walt Whitman in February 1872 and sent four years later in February 1876, where he cited the line 'the weather-beaten vessels entering new ports'. In the letter, he recalled reading Whitman's *Selected poems*, for the first time, while sitting on the beach one summer's day, possibly at Greystones.[41] Elsewhere, though, Stoker said it was under a tree in a park in Dublin, so we cannot be sure.
- that he was intrigued by all those empty tombs, and must have spent a very long time deciphering and transcribing them; in the end, the fictional Count finds sanctuary in a suicide's grave which should not by rights have been in the churchyard at all.
- that the story of the ship *Dmitri* really appealed to him – as a suitably dramatic entrance to England for his Count, *Flying-Dutchman*-style – so much so that he included it even though it confused the novel's plot which he had already outlined before travelling to Whitby: why does Count Dracula engineer a situation where the ship runs aground? Why does he draw so much attention to his arrival, when a quiet entry into the harbour would have been so much more sensible? And why does he kill – or cause to die – the entire ship's crew of eight men? Seven sailors vanish, one kills himself, and the Captain dies lashed to the wheel with a crucifix and beads. The Custom House in Dover would have been more plausible as a device. But it did make for a great, melodramatic entrance.
- that he was fascinated by deeds of masculine physical prowess – like that captain of the whaling ship who 'knocked them down one by one as they came to implore him [to slacken sail]'.
- that he was also fascinated by the intricacies of technologies and crafts – the rigging, the equipment on ships, barometers, marine engineering.
- that he had almost certainly decided to set his novel in Wallachia or Transylvania – or somewhere east of Styria – *before* he arrived in Whitby: he knew roughly what he was after, when he ordered that Wilkinson book – otherwise, why did he order a book, while on holiday, with the unprepossessing title *An account of the principalities of Wallachia and Moldavia*, by the late consul at Bucharest, unless he already had a strong interest in the subject. The book was also exceptionally dull to read, full of conventional Balkanizing and the careful clichés of a retired diplomat.
- that he *could* have taken notes about rural Ireland and its folklore from

---

41 Stoker, *Dracula* (2003), p. 409, with commentary pp 403–11.

- that the only references to identity in the notes were at the level of colourful dialect, the seafaring culture and local folklore – which were there to be gently debunked: local identity as difference from the norm.
- that the clichés of the Gothic tended to come into his mind when he caught sight of apparently spooky prospects – all those 'grey days' and 'grey clouds', 'grey seas' and 'grey mists'. He had internalized the clichés through his reading. His writing style had not moved on much since his diary entry of summer 1871.
- related to this, that he did not have a wide vocabulary – either on the spot or in the novel. There is an immediacy about his descriptions, though – the result of writing them down as they happened – which can sometimes be evocative.
- that a reference to the New Testament was in the front of his mind, when he looked at the distant view: an example, perhaps, of what R.F. Foster has called his 'religious sensibility'.[42]
- that in creating his fiction, Stoker found it a struggle to cut loose from the material reality of the world around him – and to differentiate characters/their perceptions: Mina writes her *Journal* exactly as if she was Bram Stoker taking his notes – so his voice becomes the same as that of a young middle-class English girl; it is also the same as the Captain of the *Demeter*, and in a different way as Mr Swales.
- that Stoker's gathering of material as a tourist on summer holiday was matched in the novel by Mina Murray's description – also as a tourist, as Catherine Spooner has pointed out:[43] the landscape, the antiquities, the architecture, the historical anecdotes; the local folklore and legends. So Bram Stoker positions the reader as the tourist *he* was when he was writing. Mr Swales makes the distinction, in *Dracula*, as we've seen, between vulgar, credulous trippers – who swallow local legends whole – and nice, middle-class, well-educated ladies like Mina, who is expected to have more cultured interest. This was a clever move on Stoker's part, flattering the reader – but still Mina, like her creator, was in some ways drawn to both. It is interesting that when in 1901 Bram Stoker abridged *Dracula* for the Constable paperback version – cutting a total of 25,000 words out of the novel – he removed several of Mina's descriptions of Whitby: out went the White Lady of the Abbey, the 199 steps, the references to *Marmion* by

[42] See R.F. Foster, *Paddy*, pp 220, 226–7. [43] Catherine Spooner: unpublished paper on 'literary tourism' delivered at the Bram Stoker Centenary Conference, University of Hull, on Thursday 12 April 2012, entitled 'Swishing about and spookiness – Whitby and Gothic Literary Tourism from Bram Stoker's *Dracula* to Paul Magrs' *Never the bride*'.

Walter Scott (1808) and *The rime of the Ancient Mariner* by Coleridge (1798), the tea at Robin Hood's Bay, and the comparison with the architecture of Nuremberg.
- that the strange mixture in *Dracula* of *Diary of a nobody* and Gothic nightmares was already present in the notes – as if a horror story was being written by Mr Pooter: the mundane and the catastrophic, the ordinary and the uncanny, which runs through the *Lost Journal* as well.

Which brings us back to that critical comment about the 'semi-heroic, Everyman quality' of Bram Stoker's imagination and literary output with which I began. It is precisely *because* of this quality in *Dracula*, I would argue, that it has become the most celebrated novel, the world over, to have emerged from late-Victorian society: a crucible of yesterday's attitudes and assumptions, full of workaday descriptions and dark fantasies when the author allowed his imagination off the leash – and a haunting quality when they meet – an ordinariness rather than a literary-ness: all of which has fitted well with mass culture, inspired great films, enabled generations of scholars to feel superior, and mattered a great deal to millions of people who have projected their own meanings and desires into the story – through print, stage and screen – and have identified with Stoker's journey. If this kind of longevity and of critical debate, if the move from literature to popular myth, are forms of greatness – and I believe they are – then *Dracula* has something in it of greatness. And if Bram Stoker still remains – even after research in microscopic detail – in some ways the least-known author of the best-known book in the world, well at least someone should put a commemorative plaque on the wall of what used to be Whitby Subscription Library on the Quay: 'Count Dracula was named here, summer 1890'. That would be saying a great deal.

Index

Adams, Quincey P., 98
Age, The, 128
Aladdin, 54
Anderson, Hans Christian, 51
   Wonderful stories for children, 51
Arabian nights, 51
Ardille, Richard, 37–8
Arnold, Matthew, 151
   On the study of Celtic literature, 151
Athenaeum, 19–20
Austen, Jane, 24, 42
   Northanger Abbey, 42

Bacon, Francis, 183
Baldick, Chris, 26
Ballard, J.G., 31
   Crash, 31
Baring, Evelyn (Lord Cromer), 96
Baring-Gould, Sabine, 192
   Curious myths, 192
Baron, Prof. Denis, 65
Beardsley, Aubrey, 60, 177
Beckett, Samuel, 36
Belford, Barbara, 57, 58, 60, 61, 62–3, 64, 88, 181, 187
   Bram Stoker, 181
Bell's Life in London, 127
Bevis of Hampton, 169
Bierman, Joseph, 115–16, 185
Blake, George, 156
Blake, Matilda, 156
Bluebeard, 53–4
Bookman, 20
Breuer, Josef, 47
   Studies on hysteria, 47
Browne, Dr James, 63–4, 66, 67, 68, 72
Burdon-Sanderson, Sir John, 114
'Burial of the rats, The', 133–4, 137–8, 139, 141
'Buried treasures', 75
Burton, Sir Richard, 183
Butt, Isaac, 88, 157

Caine, Hall, 16, 71–2
Capaldi, Peter, 178
Carpenter, William B., 114
Carroll, Lewis, 48
Carroll, Noel, 24
Cassell's family doctor, 127–8
Charcot, Jean-Martin, 115
Child, Francis, 167–8
   English and Scottish popular ballads, 167–8
Churchill, Jennie (née Jerome), 100
Churchill, Winston, 100
Cinderella, 54
Clarke, Harry, 177–8
Clover, Carol, 25
Clutterbuck, Henry, 40
Cockburn, W.V., 121–2, 123–4, 125
Cody, William ('Buffalo Bill'), 99, 104, 111
Coleridge, Samuel Taylor, 177, 200
   'Christabel', 177
   'Rime of the ancient mariner', 200
Collins, Wilkie, 194
   Woman in white, 194
'Coming of Abel Behenna, The', 138–9, 143
Coquelin, Benoit-Constant, 84
Corkery, Daniel, 152
Craft, Christopher, 23
Creed, Barbara, 25
Crews, Frederick, 27, 28
Cronenberg, David, 31
   Crash, 31
Cruise, Tom, 20
'Crystal cup, The', 74–5
Churchill, Lord Randolph, 100
Cyrano de Bergerac, 84

Daly, Nicholas, 25–6, 159
Darwin, Charles, 53
   Origin of species, 53
Davitt, Michael, 158
Day, William Patrick, 25

De Palma, Brian, 25
  Dressed to kill, 25
Dean, Bradley, 96
Dickens, Charles, 77
Dickens, Henry, 77
Dijkstra, Bram, 177
  Idols of perversity, 177
Dillon, John, 157–8
Disraeli, Benjamin, 183
Dobbs, Noel, 57, 59, 73
Donohoe, Amanda, 178
Dowden, Edward, 79, 82
Doyle, Arthur Conan, 16, 37, 85, 179, 180, 184
  Waterloo, 85
Dracula, 15–24, 26, 29–30, 32, 33, 34–6, 37, 40, 41, 42, 49, 53, 54–5, 56, 57, 58, 60, 62, 73, 74, 76, 77, 79, 81, 84, 86, 87, 97, 98–9, 100, 102, 104, 106, 107, 110, 112, 113, 114–15, 116, 117, 125, 127, 1`29, 130, 132, 133, 134, 136, 138, 139, 141, 142, 144, 145–6, 147, 150, 163, 164, 166, 167, 171, 177, 180, 181–200
Dracula's guest and other weird tales, 17, 164
'Dracula's guest', 133, 134–5, 136–7, 139
'Dream of red hands, A', 141
Drury Lane, 54
Du Maurier, George, 197
'Dualatists, The', 143
Dublin Evening Mail, 37–8, 74, 79
Dublin Evening News, 45
Duties of clerks of petty sessions, The, 32, 89, 98, 194

Eagleton, Terry, 15, 35
Edgeworth, Maria, 148
Edwards, Ruth Dudley, 23–4
Eighteen-Bisang, Robert, 17–18, 98, 166
Ellmann, Richard, 65
Elrod, P.N., 99
  Quincey Morris, vampire, 99
Eltis, Sos, 131
Encyclopædia Britannica, 66, 67, 68, 70, 153

Famous imposters, 49
Farson, Daniel, 44, 50, 57, 59, 64, 65, 68, 69, 70, 88, 164, 181, 187
  The man who wrote Dracula, 181
'Fate of Fenella, The', 142
Ferrier, David, 114
Fife Herald, 128
Fisher, Terence, 183
  Dracula, 183
Fitzgerald, William, 122
Flow, Ludovic, 182

Ford, John, 113
  The searchers, 113
Foster, R.F., 42, 63, 147–8, 183, 199
Fournier, Alfred, 70–1
Fowles, John, 179, 180, 181, 181, 185
Frampton, Sir George, 177
  Lamia, 177
Frankfurt, Harry, 24
Frawley, Oona, 148, 154
  Irish pastoral, 154
Frayling, Christopher, 26, 166
Freud, Sigmund, 19, 24, 25, 26–8, 34, 47, 48, 57
  Studies on hysteria, 47
Friedkin, William, 30
  French connection, 30
Fromm, Erich, 35
Fulci, Lucio, 25
  House by the cemetery, 25

Gaiety, 79
Gibbons, Luke, 87, 154–5
  Gaelic Gothic, 87
Gibson, Matthew, 97
Gillam, T. Bernhard, 124
'Gipsy prophecy, A', 135, 138, 142, 143
Gladstone, William Ewart, 29, 88–9, 148, 158, 159, 184
Glimpse of America, A, 97–8
Glover, David, 63, 89, 163
Gogol, Nikolai, 200
  Diary of a nobody, 200
Goldwater, Robert, 171, 174
Gowers, W.R., 67, 70
Graetz, F. Fritz, 123–5
Grahame, Kenneth, 36
  The wind in the willows, 31
Gramaldi, Joseph, 54
Grant, Hugh, 178
Graves, Alfred Perceval, 157
Gray, Eileen, 183
'Great white fair, The', 95
Gregory, Lady Augusta, 147, 148
Grimm, Jacob, 51, 189
  German popular stories, 51
Grimm, Wilhelm, 51, 189
  German popular stories, 51

Haggard, H. Rider, 96
Haggis, Paul, 31
  Crash, 31
Haining, Peter, 57, 64–5, 88
  The undead, 64–5
Hamlet, 18–19, 76, 80, 82, 84

INDEX 203

Harland and Wolff, 34, 95–6
Harlequin Dr Faustus, 53
Harmon, Robert, 31
　The hitcher, 31
Harper's Weekly, 124
Hartland, Edwin Sidney, 167, 168–9
　English fairy and other folk tales, 167
Haslam, Richard, 26–7
Hearn, Lafcadio, 56
Hebblethwaite, Kate, 17, 131, 134, 163, 164–5
Henderson, William, 169, 170
　Notes on the folk-lore, 169
Hibernian tales, 51
Hickey, Aidan, 36
Hitchcock, Alfred, 25
　Psycho, 25
　Spellbound, 25
Hoffmann, Heinrich, 52–3
　Slovenly Peter, 52–3
Holland, John Philip, 33
Holroyd, Michael, 77
Holt, Ian, 16
Dracula: the un-dead, 16
Hopkins, Lisa, 90, 100
Houghton, Don, 44
House that Jack built, The, 54
Hughes, William, 17, 18, 87–8, 163
Humbert, General Jean Joseph, 156
Hunt, Violet, 189

Irish Times, 154
Irving, Henry, 15, 19, 56, 58, 61, 62, 74, 77, 79, 80–1, 82–3, 84, 85, 86, 88, 103, 104, 116, 147, 157, 174, 179, 181, 194

Jack the Giant killer, 54
Jackson, Rosemary, 25
Jacobs, Joseph, 167
　English fairy tales, 167
James, E.L., 20–2
　Fifty shades of grey, 20–2
James, Louis, 131
Jewel of seven stars, The, 16, 17, 55, 96, 164
Johns, Stratford, 178
Johnson, Alan, 100, 112
Johnson, Major E.C., 192
　On the track, 192
Johnson, Sir George, 66
　The pathology, 66
Jones, Ernest, 25
Jong, Erica, 21
　Fear of flying, 21
Joyce, James, 36, 63, 181, 184

Finnegans wake, 195
Ulysses, 63, 181
'Judge's house, The', 134, 135–6, 138, 141, 144
Judy, 151–3

Kane, Robert, 161
　Industrial resources, 161
Keats, John, 177
　'Lamia', 177
Keegan, Aileen, 45–6
Keegan, Gerald, 45–6
Kendrick, Charles, 124–6
Kilgour, Maggie, 25
Killeen, Jarlath, 87, 164, 171
King of the castle, 54
King, Stephen, 25
King, William, 155
　'Of the bogs', 155
Koch, Robert, 117
Kostova, Elizabeth, 16
　The historian, 16

Labour World, 158
Lady Athlyne, 17, 29–34, 87, 89, 91–4, 95, 96, 99–100
Lady of the shroud, 17, 33, 34–5, 97, 102, 146
Lair of the white worm, 16, 17, 96–7, 130, 132, 136, 139, 141, 142–3, 160, 163–78
Landis, John, 30
　The blues brothers, 30
Lane, Edwin, 51
　Arabian nights, 51
Langella, Frank, 20
Lawrence, D.H., 32
Lady Chatterley's lover, 32
Le Fanu, Joseph Sheridan, 55, 184, 192
　Carmilla, 192
　'The child that went with the fairies', 55
Le Prince de Beaumont, Jeanne-Marie, 51
　'Beauty and the beast', 51
Leatherdale, Clive, 17, 50, 88, 166
　Origin of Dracula, 166
Lee, Christopher, 20, 183
Legends of the fairies, 51
Lewis, Matthew, 42
　The monk, 42
Liman, Doug, 30
　Bourne identity, 30
Liszt, Franz, 84
Little Bopeep, 54
Lombroso, Cesare, 114, 115
London Medical Gazette, 40
London Society, 75

London Times, 15
Lorraine, Claude, 134
Lost journal of Bram Stoker, 18, 73–81, 88, 116, 156, 179, 190, 197, 198, 199, 200
Loveday, H.J., 84
Ludlam, Harry, 57, 63–4, 69, 88, 117, 180–1, 186–7
   A biography of Dracula, 186–7
Lugosi, Bela, 20
Lyceum Theatre, 57, 62, 64, 81, 82, 83, 84, 85, 86, 88, 89, 96, 97, 116, 157, 158, 174, 179, 192, 193, 196
Lyons, Prof. J.B., 65–6, 69

Macbeth, 81, 85, 195
Machen, Arthur, 174
'Man from Shorrox, The', 87, 90–1
Man, The, 49–50, 96, 139, 146, 177
Manchester Guardian, 19
Marinetti, Filippo Tommaso, 30
Matheson, Richard, 31
   'Duel', 31
Mathew, Fr Theobald, 43
Matthews, P.J., 34
Maturin, Charles Robert, 42, 184
   Melmoth the wanderer, 42
Maunder, Andrew, 69
   Bram Stoker, 69
Mayer, M.L., 84
Mayo Constitution, 39
McCormack, Bridget, 156–7
   Perceptions of St Patrick, 156–7
McGuinness, Norah, 177–8
McLean's monthly sheet of caricatures, 122
Meyer, Stephanie, 23
   Twilight, 23
Meyers, Jonathan Rhys, 20
Mighall, Robert, 26
Mill, John Stuart, 140
Miller, Elizabeth, 17–18, 19, 36, 68–9, 88, 98, 166
   Bram Stoker's Dracula, 68–9,
   Lost journal, 88
Miller, Joaquin, 103
   Life amongst the Madocs, 103
Milton, John, 15
Miss Betty, 142
Moby-Dick, 187
Morash, Christopher, 63
Moretti, Franco, 98
Murnau, F.W., 20
   Nosferatu, 20
Murphy, Siobhán, 65–6

Murray, Paul, 18, 23, 26, 74, 87, 88, 89, 93–4, 147, 164, 181, 183, 187–8
   From the shadow, 87, 181
Mystery of the sea, The, 17, 97, 100, 132, 197

'Necessity for political honesty, The', 101–2, 158
Needham, Hal, 30
   Cannonball run, 30
   Smokey and the Bandit, 30
New York Times, 15
Nordau, Max, 114, 115
Norris, David, 23

Ó Cuirrín, Séan, 181
O'Brien, William, 158
   When we were boys, 158
O'Grady, Standish, 147, 148, 157
Order of the Golden Dawn, 174
Oriel, Dr J.D., 65
Othello, 108
Owens, Gary, 95
Owenson, Sydney (Lady Morgan), 148
Oxenberg, Catherine, 178

Pabst, Georg Wilhelm, 25
   Secrets of a soul, 25
Pall Mall Gazette, 20, 90
Parnell, Charles Stewart, 151, 184
People, 148, 194
Perrault, Charles, 51, 52
   Tales of Mother Goose, 51
Personal reminiscences of Henry Irving, 15, 81–2, 83, 86, 88, 179
Pitt, Brad, 20
Plunkett, Horace, 34
Poe, Edgar Allan, 42, 43, 76
   Tales of mystery and imagination, 42, 76
Pomfret, J.E., 154
   Struggle for land, 154
Postman, Neil, 30
Powell, Michael, 25
   Peeping Tom, 25
Primrose path, The, 75, 78, 87, 89–90
Puck, 123
Punch, 151–2, 197
Puss in boots, 54

Queen's (Theatre), 79–80

Radcliffe, Ann, 42
   The Italian, 42
   Mysteries of Udolpho, 42
'Red stockade, The', 101

Reed. John, 133
Richardson, Maurice, 21, 57, 183
Rider, William, 174
Robinson, F.K., 79, 191
   Whitby glossary, 79, 191, 194
Romeo and Juliet, 83
Roosevelt, Theodore, 85, 103
Roxburgh, Richard, 20
Royal fairy tales, 51
Russell, Ken, 178
Ruthner, Clemens, 36

Sadler Wells, 53, 54
Schneider, Steven J., 25
Schumacher, Joel, 21
   Lost boys, 21
Scott, Sir Walter, 84, 169, 185, 199–200
   Bride of Lammermoor, 84
   Marmion, 199–200
   Minstrelsy of the Scottish borders, 169
'Secret of the growing gold, The', 141, 142, 144
Sedgwick, Eve Kosofsky, 24
Senf, Carol, 17, 104, 112–13
Seymour, Frank, 80
Seymour, Robert, 122–4
Shamrock, 75, 89
Sharpe, Sir Cuthbert, 169–70
   The bishoprick's garland, 169–70
Shaw, George Bernard, 60, 184
Shepard, Leslie, 68, 96
Sheridan, Richard Brinsley, 79, 181
   The rivals, 79, 80
   School for scandal, 79
Shoulder of Shasta, The, 17, 98, 99, 103–13, 142
Shrek, Max, 20
Shuttle, Penelope, 59
Shuttle, Peter, 59
   Wise wound, 59
Shyamalan, M. Night, 25
   Sixth sense, 25
Sikes, Wirt, 170–1
   British goblins, 170–1
Simmons, James R., 98
Sitting Bull, 111
Smith, Andrew, 25, 89, 97
Smith, Mary, 51
Smith, Pamela Colman, 174–7
Snake's pass, The, 17, 32, 75, 89, 90, 91, 102, 145, 147–62, 166, 184, 194, 197, 198
Snow, Dr John, 120, 129
Snowbound, 98, 99
Spencer-Churchill, Charles Richard John, 101

Spielberg, Steven, 31
   Duel, 31
'Squaw, The', 100, 134, 135, 138, 143–4
Steele, J.C., 128
   Dictionary of domestic medicine, 128
Sterne, Laurence, 48
   Tristram Shandy, 48
Stewart, Bruce, 155
Stoker, Abraham (Snr), 39, 41, 46, 50, 51, 53, 54, 62, 62, 74, 79, 89, 90
Stoker, Ann, 57, 59
Stoker, Charlotte, 39, 41–4, 46, 50–1, 52, 55, 88, 90, 117–24, 127, 129
Stoker, Dacre, 16, 22, 88
   Dracula: the un-dead, 16, 22
Stoker, Enid, 50
Stoker, Florence (neé Balcombe), 60, 69, 70–2, 76, 83, 88, 96, 166, 182, 183, 186–9, 197
Stoker, George, 83, 90, 115, 127
Stoker, Margaret, 90
Stoker, Matilda, 39
Stoker, Noel, 57, 64, 70, 73, 81–2, 116, 186–9, 197
Stoker, Richard, 46, 90, 115, 127
Stoker, Thomas, 44, 46, 90
Stoker, William Thornley, 39, 62, 63, 88, 90, 115, 127
Surtee, Robert, 169
   History and antiquities, 169
Sutcliffe, Frank Meadow, 186–7
Swinburne, A.C., 178
   'Satia Te Sanguine', 178

Tarantino, Quentin, 30
   Death proof, 30
Taylor, Edgar, 51
Taylor, Jenny Bourne, 132
Tennyson, Alfred, 183, 191
Terry, Ellen, 58, 60, 77, 83, 84
Theatre Royal, 53, 79, 80, 82
Thompson, Sir William, 90
Thomson, Spencer, 128
   Dictionary of domestic medicine, 128
Todhunter, John, 115, 157
Tone, Theobald Wolfe, 156
Townsend, Lionel, 191
Tremayne, Peter, 57, 64, 88
   The undead, 64–5
Trinity College Dublin, 17, 36, 74, 79, 82, 88, 89, 96, 115, 157, 180
Twain, Mark, 104

Under the sunset, 75, 55, 88, 90, 114–30, 132, 133, 141, 145

Valente, Joseph, 147
Vámbéry, Arminius, 192
Vanderbilt, Consuelo, 101
Victoria (Theatre), 80
Vlad the Impaler, 35–6

Wagner, Richard 190
   Flying Dutchman, 188, 190, 198
Waite, A.E., 174
Walpole, Horace, 24
Castle of Otranto, 24
Ward, Genevieve, 60, 82
Warren, Louis S., 100
Watter's mou', The, 17, 141, 197
'Way of peace, The', 89
Wayne, John, 113
Weininger, otto, 31
Weldon, Fay, 59
West, Samuel, 66
   Granular kidney, 66
Whitby Gazette, 186, 187, 191
Whitman, Walt, 74, 82, 198
   Selected poems, 198

Wiene, Robert, 25
   Cabinet of Dr Caligari, 25
Wilde, Jane Francesca, 49, 88, 166–7, 184
   Ancient legends, 166–7
Wilde, Oscar, 19, 49, 60, 65, 166, 181, 182, 183, 184
   Importance of being earnest, 109, 181
Wilde, Sir William, 88, 92, 115, 157
Wilkinson, William, 191–2, 198
   An account, 191–2, 198
Williams, Anne, 25
Wills, Christopher, 128
Wilson, A.N., 182
Wilson, James, 131
Wilson, Woodrow, 102
Wood, Robin, 25
'World's greatest shipbuilding yard, The', 95–6

Yates, Peter, 30
   Bullitt, 30
Yeats, W.B., 147, 148, 174, 177–8, 182
   Deirdre, 177
   Stories of Red Hanrahan, 178

Z-Cars, 178